HUMAN RIGHTS AND HUMANITARIAN NORMS
AS CUSTOMARY LAW

Human Rights and Humanitarian Norms as Customary Law

THEODOR MERON

CLARENDON PRESS · OXFORD
1989

Oxford University Press, Walton Street, Oxford OX2 6DP
Oxford New York Toronto
Delhi Bombay Calcutta Madras Karachi
Petaling Jaya Singapore Hong Kong Tokyo
Nairobi Dar es Salaam Cape Town
Melbourne Auckland
and associated companies in
Berlin Ibadan

Oxford is a trade mark of Oxford University Press

Published in the United States
by Oxford University Press, New York

British Library Cataloguing in Publication Data
Meron, Theodor, 1930–
Human rights and humanitarian norms as customary law.
1. Human rights. International legal aspects
I. Title
341.4'81
ISBN 0-19-825239-0

Library of Congress Cataloging in Publication Data
Meron, Theodor, 1930–
Human rights and humanitarian norms as customary law / Theodor
Meron. Includes index.
1. Human rights. 2. War victims—Legal status, laws, etc.
3. Customary law, International. I. Title.
K3240.4.M484   1989   341.4'81—dc20   89-9227
ISBN 0-19-825239-0

Set by Oxford Text System
Printed in Great Britain by
Courier International Ltd.
Tiptree, Essex

For Monique

Preface

I wish to express my gratitude to the Filomen D'Agostino and Max E. Greenberg Research Fund of New York University Law School for its generous support of this study; to All Souls College of Oxford University for its Visiting Fellowship which proved to be extremely useful for the completion of the manuscript; to my colleagues Professors Thomas Buergenthal, Luigi Condorelli, Yoram Dinstein, Herbert Reis, Oscar Schachter, and Marina Spinedi, and to Ms Donna Sullivan, for reading parts of the manuscript and for their invaluable suggestions; to my research assistants Daniel Smith, Lemuel M. Srolovic, and William Walker for their important help; and to my secretary Madelon Blavatnik, for her infinite patience in typing and retyping the manuscripts.

I also express my appreciation to the American Journal of International Law, in which a part of the material contained in Chapter I of this book has previously appeared.

T.M.

All Souls College, Oxford
February 1989

Table of Contents

Abbreviations

AJIL	American Journal of International Law
ASIL	American Society of International Law
CSCE	Conference on Security and Co-operation in Europe
ECOSOC	Economic and Social Council
ESC	Economic and Social Council
ESCOR	Economic and Social Council Official Records
GAOR	General Assembly Official Records
IACHR	Inter-American Commission on Human Rights
ICJ	International Court of Justice
ICRC	International Committee of the Red Cross
ILC	International Law Commission
ILM	International Legal Materials
ILO	International Labour Organisation
NGO	Non-governmental organization
OAS	Organisation of American States
OEA	Organizacion de los Estados Americanos
TIAS	Treaties and Other International Acts Series
TS	Treaty Series
UNTS	United Nations Treaty Series

Introduction

There has been a rapid growth in the number and scope of international human rights instruments, in the establishment of judicial and non-judicial supervisory organs and procedures designed to secure respect for human rights, in the scholarly literature on human rights and humanitarian norms (i.e. rights and norms protecting human dignity in situations of peace or international or non-international armed conflicts), and in the interest shown by decision-makers, the media, and the public at large in the international protection of such rights. Nevertheless, inadequate attention has been paid to the place of human rights and humanitarian norms in the discipline of international law. The purpose of this book is to attempt to bridge that gap by clarifying the status of international human rights and humanitarian norms in public international law, and by examining the sources, evidence, and process of the creation of such rights. The first principal area of inquiry concerns the relationship of human rights and humanitarian norms with customary law, including the examination of the role of treaties in the development of customary human rights and humanitarian norms. The second area concerns the relationship of human rights and humanitarian norms with the law of state responsibility. I will examine how the contemporary human rights and humanitarian law meshes with the general principles of international law and particularly with the principles governing the international responsibility of states for acts and omissions of their officials and organs. By coupling human rights and humanitarian norms with the corpus of law governing state responsibility, the latter is mobilized to serve the former and to advance its effectiveness.

I shall address only such aspects of customary law, including state responsibility, as are significant for the effectiveness of human rights and humanitarian norms and important for assessing their place and role in public international law. I do not intend this study as a treatise either on customary law or on state responsibility, on both of which there is already abundant literature.

I

Humanitarian Instruments as Customary Law

I. THE IMPORTANCE OF A NORM'S CUSTOMARY CHARACTER

General practice of states which is accepted and observed as law, i.e. from a sense of legal obligation, builds norms of customary international law. Article 38(1)(b) of the Statute of the International Court of Justice describes international custom 'as evidence of a general practice accepted as law'. Because general practice demonstrates custom and not vice versa, § 102(2) of the Restatement Third, of the Foreign Relations Law of the United States of 1987, provides, more accurately, that customary international law 'results from a general and consistent practice of states which is followed by them from a sense of legal obligation'. In the highly codified humanitarian law context, the primary and the most obvious significance of a norm's customary character is that the norm binds states that are not parties to the instrument in which that norm is restated. It is, of course, not the treaty norm, but the customary norm with identical content, that binds such states. Additionally, because instruments of international humanitarian law do not address all of the relevant rules, the identification of the applicable customary rules is also important for states parties. As the following discussion of the Geneva Conventions of August 12, 1949 for the Protection of Victims of War[1] will demonstrate, this question has significance beyond these results.

At first glance, an inquiry into the customary character of the

---

[1] Convention for the Amelioration of the Condition of the Wounded and Sick in Armed Forces in the Field (Geneva Convention No. I), Aug. 12, 1949, 6 UST 3114, TIAS No. 3362, 75 UNTS 31; Convention for the Amelioration of the Condition of Wounded, Sick, and Shipwrecked Members of Armed Forces at Sea (Geneva Convention No. II), Aug. 12, 1949, 6 UST 3217, TIAS No. 3363, 75 UNTS 85; Convention Relative to the Treatment of Prisoners of War (Geneva Convention No. III), Aug. 12, 1949, 6 UST 3316, TIAS No. 3364, 75 UNTS 135; Convention Relative to the Protection of Civilian Persons in Time of War (Geneva Convention No. IV), Aug. 12, 1949, 6 UST 3516, TIAS No. 3365, 75 UNTS 287.

Geneva Conventions might appear academic. After all, the question arises infrequently given the universal acceptance of the Conventions as treaties (they are binding on even more states than the Charter of the United Nations).[2] That the matter may have a lasting practical importance, however, was recently brought home by the consideration of the problem by the International Court of Justice (ICJ) in the merits phase of *Military and Paramilitary Activities in and against Nicaragua*.[3] The Court's discussion of the relationship between treaty and custom further highlighted the question. The Court stated that

even if two norms belonging to two sources of international law appear identical in content, and even if the States in question are bound by these rules both on the level of treaty-law and on that of customary international law, these norms retain a separate existence.[4]

In the numerous countries where customary law is treated as the law of the land but an act of the legislature is required to transform treaties into internal law, the question assumes importance if no

[2] In Feb. 1988, 165 states were parties to the Geneva Conventions. International Committee of the Red Cross, Dissemination No. 9, Aug. 1988. There are 159 states members of the United Nations. Multilateral Treaties Deposited with the Secretary-General: Status as at 31 December 1987, at 3–6, UN Doc. ST/LEG/SER.E/6 (1988).

[3] *Military and Paramilitary Activities in and against Nicaragua (Nicar. v. US)* Merits, 1986 ICJ Rep. 14 (Judgment of 27 June).

Art. 38(1)(b) of the Statute of the International Court of Justice refers to 'international custom, as evidence of a general practice accepted as law'. An important statement of the constitutive elements of custom, general practice, and *opinio juris* is contained in the *Columbian–Peruvian Asylum Case*: 'The Party which relies on a [regional] custom . . . must prove that this custom is established in such a manner that it has become binding on the other Party. The Colombian Government must prove that the rule invoked by it is in accordance with a constant and uniform usage practised by the States in question, and that this usage is the expression of a right appertaining to the State granting asylum and a duty incumbent on the territorial State. This follows from Article 38 of the Statute of the Court. . . .' 1950 ICJ Rep. 266, 276 (Judgment of 20 Nov.).

In the *North Sea Continental Shelf Cases (FRG/Den.; FRG/Neth.)*, the Court emphasized that '[n]ot only must the acts concerned amount to a settled practice, but they must also be such, or be carried out in such a way, as to be evidence of a belief that this practice is rendered obligatory by the existence of a rule of law requiring it. The need for such a belief, i.e., the existence of a subjective element, is implicit in the very notion of the *opinio juris sive necessitatis*.' 1969 ICJ Rep. 3, 44 (Judgment of 20 Feb.). In the *Nicaragua* case, ICJ stated that '[t]he Court must satisfy itself that the existence of the rule in the *opinio juris* of States is confirmed by practice'. 1986 ICJ Rep. at 98.

[4] 1986 ICJ Rep. at 95.

Humanitarian Norms 5

such law has been enacted.[5] Certainly, the failure to enact the necessary legislation cannot affect the international obligations of these countries to implement the Geneva Conventions. Invoking a

[5] In the United States, the Geneva Conventions are, of course, the supreme law of the land. US Const. Art. VI, cl. 2. The US government is of the opinion that these Conventions 'were not intended to create private rights of action, and the provisions of the Conventions are generally deemed to be non-self-executing in the context of judicial proceedings. *See, e.g., Handel v. Artukovic*, 601 F. Supp. 1421, 1425 (C.D. Cal. 1985); *Tel-Oren v. Libyan Arab Republic*, 726 F. 2d 774, 809 (D.C. Cir. 1984), *cert. denied*, 470 U.S. 1003 (1985). . . . However, the provisions of the Hague and Geneva Conventions can generally be implemented by the armed forces.' Affidavit of Kerri L. Martin, *United States* v. *Shakur*, 82 Cr. 312, Exhibit A, at 18 (SDNY, 23 Mar. 1988). It may be noted that the Geneva Conventions contain provisions requiring implementation through municipal law.

In the Federal Republic of Germany, the fact that many provisions of the Geneva Conventions embody customary law gives them a preferential place in the hierarchy of national laws. A recent study thus observes: 'Article 25 of the Basic Law provides that the general rules of public international law shall be directly applicable internally and take precedence over all Acts. Consequently, as far as the provisions of the four Geneva Conventions constitute rules, which are "general rules of public international law" within the meaning of this constitutional provision, i.e. as far as they are part of the universally applicable customary international law, under national law in the Federal Republic of Germany they take priority over all ordinary Acts. Today a considerable part of the provisions of the four Geneva Conventions and the Protocols additional thereto must be considered part of customary international law. This does not apply, however, to each single provision.' International Society for Military Law and the Law of War, German National Section, Reports for Presentation to the XIth International Congress (Edinburgh, Sept. 1988) at 4 (1988).

For a discussion of legislation implementing the Geneva Conventions, see Bothe, *The Role of National Law in the Implementation of International Humanitarian Law*, in Studies and Essays on International Humanitarian Law and Red Cross Principles in Honour of Jean Pictet 301, 305-6 (C. Swinarski ed. 1984). Many states parties to the Geneva Conventions have not adopted such legislation. Levasseur and Merle, *L'Etat des législations internes au regard des obligations contenues dans les conventions internationales de droit humanitaire*, in Droit humanitaire et conflits armés 219, 225, 228, 249 (Université Libre de Bruxelles, 1976).

Only 49 governments answered an ICRC inquiry about legislative action taken to repress violations of the Geneva Conventions. This group included some governments that reported having taken no such action, e.g. Indonesia, Iraq, Lebanon, South Africa, and Syria. International Committee of the Red Cross, Respect of the Geneva Conventions: Measures Taken to Repress Violations (Reports submitted by the International Committee of the Red Cross to the XXth and XXIth International Conferences of the Red Cross) (1971); Twenty-Fifth International Conference of the Red Cross, Respect for International Humanitarian Law: National Measures to Implement the Geneva Conventions and their Additional Protocols in Peacetime 4 (Doc. CI/2.4/2, 1986). See also ibid. at 13. For recent efforts to encourage states to fulfil their obligation to adopt the national legislation necessary for the effective application of the Geneva Conventions and, as the case may be, of the Additional Protocols, see Resolution V of the Twenty-Fifth International Conference of the Red Cross (1980), reprinted in Int'l Rev. Red Cross, No. 263, Mar.-Apr. 1988, at 127. See also ibid. at 121-40.

certain norm as customary rather than conventional in such situations may be crucial for ensuring protection of the individuals concerned, however.

The transformation of the norms of the Geneva Conventions into customary law may have certain additional effects beyond its consequences for the internal law of some countries. One such effect, already reflected in common Article 63/62/142/158 concerning denunciation of the Geneva Conventions, as pointed out by the *Nicaragua* Court,[6] is that parties could not terminate their customary law obligations by withdrawal. Common Article 63/62/142/158 provides that the denunciation of one of the Conventions:

shall in no way impair the obligations which the Parties to the conflict shall remain bound to fulfil by virtue of the principles of the law of nations, as they result from the usages established among civilized peoples, from the laws of humanity and the dictates of the public conscience.

This principle is also reflected in Article 43 of the Vienna Convention on the Law of Treaties, which states that the denunciation of a treaty 'shall not in any way impair the duty of any State to fulfil any obligation embodied in the treaty to which it would be subject under international law independently of the treaty'.

The existence of a denunciation clause in a treaty should not weaken a claim that some of its provisions are declaratory of customary law. Similarly, the absence of comment in a denunciation clause upon the effects of the denunciation on customary law (e.g. Article 99 of Additional Protocol I, Article 25 of Additional

The Israeli Supreme Court has refused to review the acts of the military government on the West Bank in light of Geneva Convention No. IV on the ground that the law of the Convention is conventional rather than declaratory of customary law and has not been transformed into the law of the land by legislation. See Cohen, *Justice for Occupied Territory? The Israeli High Court of Justice Paradigm*, 24 Colum. J. Transnat'l L. 471, 484-9 (1986); Roberts, *What Is a Military Occupation?*, 55 Brit. YB Int'l L. 249, 283 (1984).

For views suggesting that some provisions of Convention No. IV are declaratory of customary law, see dissenting opinion of Justice H. Cohn in *Kawasme* v. *Minister of Defence*, 35(1) Piskei Din 617, summarized in 11 Isr. YB Hum. Rts. 349, 352-4 (1981); Dinstein, *Expulsion of Mayors from Judea*, 8 Tel Aviv U. L. Rev. 158 (Hebrew, 1981); Meron, *West Bank and Gaza: Human Rights and Humanitarian Law in the Period of Transition*, 9 Isr. YB Hum. Rts. 106, 111-12 (1979). For further discussion of Geneva Convention No. IV and the territories occupied by Israel, see below n. 131 and text accompanying nn. 147-9. See also below n. 167 and Meron, *Applicability of Multilateral Conventions to Occupied Territories*, 72 AJIL 542, 543, 548-50 (1978).

[6] 1086 ICJ Rep. at 113-14. See also below n. 76 and accompanying text.

Protocol II, and Article 14 of the Convention on the Prevention and Punishment of the Crime of Genocide) does not constitute good evidence that the treaty rules are solely conventional. Such clauses may have been drafted for a variety of reasons (e.g. past practice, implementation, or settlement of disputes) which are wholly unrelated to the question of whether or not the treaty is declaratory of customary law. The effects of the denunciation must still be assessed in light of the general international law reflected in Article 43 of the Vienna Convention. Nevertheless, as suggested by the ICJ in the *Nicaragua* case, the explicit reference to customary law in the Geneva Conventions' common Article on denunciation strengthens the Conventions' claim to embody customary law.

The distinction between a customary and a conventional rule is particularly important in disputes beween two states in which one of them exercises the right, under Article 60 of the Vienna Convention on the Law of Treaties, to terminate or suspend the operation of a treaty on the ground that the other party has violated an essential provision of that treaty. It should, however, be noted that Article 60(5) of the Vienna Convention establishes a rule of *lex specialis* for provisions relating to the protection of the human person contained in treaties of a humanitarian character, even where such provisions have not matured into customary law. In the *Nicaragua* case, the Court asserted that 'if the two rules in question also exist as rules of customary international law, the failure of the one State to apply the one rule does not justify the other State in declining to apply the other rule'.[7] Because subject to certain conditions state A may respond to a violation of a customary rule by state B through a proportional violation of another customary rule, this comment by the Court is, perhaps, overbroad. Of course, a conventional rule which parallels a customary rule may be subject to different treatment as regards organs competent to verify their implementation.[8]

Another effect of this distinction is that reservations to the Conventions cannot affect the obligations of the parties under provisions reflecting customary law to which they would be subject independently of the Conventions.[9] This question, to be addressed

[7] 1986 ICJ Rep. 95 (Judgment of 27 June).

[8] Ibid.

[9] See generally Imbert, *Reservations and Human Rights Conventions*, 6 Hum. Rts. Rev. 28 (1981). On reservations made by parties to the Geneva Conventions, see Pilloud, *Reservations to the Geneva Conventions of 1949* (pt. 1), Int'l Rev. Red

further in Section II, below, is particularly relevant to humanitarian and human rights conventions since reservations to these instruments are frequently made. Many of these reservations reflect conflicts between the instruments and the internal law of the reserving states.

Finally, turning from the question of application to that of interpretation, if treated as customary law, the norms expressed in the Conventions might be subject to a process of interpretation different from that which applies to treaties. This possibility was suggested by the *Nicaragua* Judgment, where the Court stated that '[r]ules which are identical in treaty law and in customary international law are also distinguishable by reference to the methods of interpretation and application.'[10] While it is obvious that the Vienna Convention's rules of treaty interpretation do not apply to customary norms outside of the treaty context, the Court's cryptic reference to interpretation (the Court elaborated somewhat only on the difference in application) leaves many questions unanswered.

Those who doubt the significance of determining the question might point out that treaties, such as the Geneva Conventions, which virtually the entire international community has accepted through formal and solemn acts, have as strong a legal claim to observance as customary law. After all, customary law rests largely on the practice of a limited number of states. They might also argue that a treaty which embodies strongly felt humanitarian ideals has a moral as well as a legal claim to observance. In such circumstances, transposing the treaty's norms into customary law will not necessarily add to its moral claim.

Nevertheless, consensus that the Geneva Conventions are declaratory of customary international law would strengthen the moral claim of the international community for their observance by emphasizing their humanitarian underpinnings and deep roots in tradition and community values. Such consensus might also represent a step in a process that begins with the crystallization of

---

Cross, No. 180, Mar. 1976, at 107 (Pilloud observes that customary law must be applied to determine the validity and 'extent' of the reservations made, ibid. at 108), and (pt. 2), Int'l Rev. Red Cross, No. 181, Apr. 1976, at 163.

[10] 1986 ICJ Rep. 95 (Judgment of 27 June). A case for a particular interpretation of conventional rules (e.g. Arts. 87 and 100 of Geneva Convention No. III) is strengthened by its concordance with 'commonly accepted international law'. *Public Prosecutor* v. *Koi*, [1968] 1 All ER 419, 425 (PC).

a contractual norm into a principle of customary law and culminates in its elevation to *jus cogens* status.[11] The development of the hierarchical concept of *jus cogens* reflects the quest of the international community for a normative order in which higher rights are invoked as particularly compelling moral and legal barriers to derogations from and violations of human rights. To be sure, the Geneva Conventions already contain some norms that can be regarded as *jus cogens*.[12]

This discussion of the relationship between the Geneva Conventions and customary law may also be instructive as regards other multilateral conventions with fewer parties than the Geneva Conventions, such as the two 1977 Additional Protocols, in situations where there has been little significant practice by non-parties.

Obviously, the invocation of a norm as both conventional and customary adds at least rhetorical strength to the moral claim for its observance. Thus, to underline the gravity of certain violations, the ICJ observed in the Iranian *Hostages* case that the obligations in question were not 'merely contractual . . . but also obligations under general international law'.[13]

In the *Nicaragua* case, the question under discussion arose in an unusual context: the multilateral treaty reservation of the United States appeared to preclude the ICJ from applying the Geneva Conventions as treaties. Consequently, the status of the Conventions as declaratory of customary law presented a crucial issue. In its treatment of this issue, the Court refrained from mentioning the two Additional Protocols of 1977 and from considering the manner in which the Protocols confirm, supplement, or modify provisions of the Conventions themselves. The extent to which the Protocols are declaratory of customary law has begun to attract scholarly attention. This important and difficult question will be addressed in Section VI, below.

[11] See T. Meron, Human Rights Law-Making in the United Nations: A Critique of Instruments and Process 194 (1986). A norm of *jus cogens* can also mature through other processes. *Jus cogens* is discussed further in Chapter III, Section VIII.

[12] The International Law Commission (ILC) has observed that 'some of [the rules of humanitarian law] are, in the opinion of the Commission, rules which impose obligations of *jus cogens*. . . .' Report of the International Law Commission on the Work of its Thirty-Second Session, 35 UN GAOR Supp. (No. 10) at 98, UN Doc. A/35/10 (1980).

[13] *United States Diplomatic and Consular Staff in Tehran (US v. Iran)*, 1980 ICJ Rep. 3, 31 (Judgment of 24 May).

I shall begin by considering some aspects of the question of reservations to humanitarian and human rights instruments and then consider certain aspects of the *Nicaragua* Judgment that implicate humanitarian law. It must be remembered that while protecting the rights of states and governing their duties, humanitarian law also contains a prominent human rights component.[14] Although humanitarian considerations are a powerful motivating force behind the law of armed conflict, these considerations blend with others, such as economic advantage, to create a counterforce to military necessity. Because humanitarian instruments state some reciprocal (state to state) obligations and many humanitarian/human rights protections, the disentangling of custom and treaty may require the use of different types of evidence and different burdens of proof for each of these two components of humanitarian instruments. I shall focus primarily on those humanitarian law rules which concern protection of victims of armed conflict ('law of Geneva'), rather than those that regulate combat ('law of the Hague'). I will next discuss the process through which customary law can develop alongside conventional law, with reference to the Geneva Conventions. Finally, I shall address the customary law character of the Additional Protocols.

II. RESERVATIONS TO HUMANITARIAN AND HUMAN RIGHTS INSTRUMENTS AND CUSTOMARY LAW

The advisory opinion of the ICJ on *Reservations to the Convention on Genocide* enunciated the principal statement of contemporary

---

[14] See Meron, *On the Inadequate Reach of Humanitarian and Human Rights Law and the Need for a New Instrument*, 77 AJIL 589, 593 (1983) (hereinafter cited as *Inadequate Reach*). On the relationship between human rights law and humanitarian law, see also T. Meron, Human Rights in Internal Strife: Their International Protection 3–70 (1987). On humanitarian norms and reciprocity, see ibid. at 10–14. See also Partsch, *Human Rights and Humanitarian Law*, [Instalment] 8 Encyclopedia of Public International Law 292 (R. Bernhardt ed. 1985); Kunz, *The Laws of War*, 50 AJIL 313, 316 (1956).

Human rights are stated largely in human rights instruments adopted by the United Nations and their specialized agencies. See also Henkin, *Human Rights*, above 8 Encyclopedia at 268. Humanitarian rights are articulated largely in the Geneva Conventions and the Additional Protocols and in other instruments applicable in armed conflicts. Both human and humanitarian rights comprise conventional as well as customary law and 'contain rules for the treatment and protection of human beings based on considerations of humanity'. Partsch, above. Although human rights apply primarily in times of peace and humanitarian norms primarily in times of armed conflict, there is a growing overlap in their applicability

international law on reservations.[15] This opinion concerned the Convention on the Prevention and Punishment of the Crime of Genocide[16] which is now widely and correctly regarded as declaratory of customary law.[17] The Court pointed out that the General Assembly of the United Nations, together with the states which adopted the Convention, intended to obtain the widest possible participation of states in the Convention without sacrificing its object. The Court concluded that

[t]he object and [purely humanitarian and civilizing] purpose of the Convention thus limit both the freedom of making reservations and that of objecting to them. It follows that it is the compatibility of a reservation with the object and purpose of the Convention that must furnish the criterion for the attitude of a State in making the reservation on accession as well as for the appraisal by a State in objecting to the reservation.[18]

The Court emphasized that the crime of genocide shocked the conscience of mankind and was contrary to moral law and to the spirit and aims of the United Nations. Moreover, the Court explained, 'the principles underlying the [Genocide] Convention are . . . recognized by civilized nations as binding on States even without any conventional obligation'.[19] Although the Court did not explicitly address the question of reservations to customary law, it thus, at least implicitly, recognized two points. First, the principles underlying the Convention are declaratory of customary law. Second, states have the right to make reservations to the treaty rules stated in the Convention, if those reservations are not incompatible with the purpose and object of the Convention. The Court emphasized that the contracting parties did not intend to

ratione materiae. There is also a very large convergence and parallelism between norms originating in human rights instruments and those originating in humanitarian instruments. While both human rights instruments and humanitarian instruments contain not only provisions regulating relations between the government and the governed, but also provisions governing relations between states by laying down their mutual rights and duties, such latter provisions are much more central to humanitarian instruments.

[15] 1951 ICJ Rep. 15 (Advisory Opinion of 28 May).
[16] Opened for signature 9 Dec. 1948, 78 UNTS 277.
[17] Restatement of the Law Third, Restatement of the Foreign Relations Law of the United States § 702(a) and comment *d* and Reporters' note 3 (1987). The prohibition of genocide may be regarded as a peremptory norm. Ibid. Reporters' note 4.
[18] Ibid. at 24.
[19] Ibid. at 23.

sacrifice the object and purpose of the Convention in order to secure as many participants as possible. Nor did they intend to exclude from the participation in the Convention states making minor reservations.

The Court's opinion does not address the question whether reservations to conventional rules which are identical to customary rules are in general possible. But in the specific case of the Genocide Convention, the Court appears to suggest that because the principles of the Convention, which correspond to customary law, determine its humanitarian and civilizing objects, such reservations would be contrary to these objects and thus inadmissible.

For treaties which do not provide different guidelines for reservations by prohibiting or permitting specific reservations, Article 19 of the Vienna Convention on the Law of Treaties[20] requires that a reservation be compatible with the object and purpose of the treaty. The concept of compatibility is related to the treaty itself, not to customary law. Thus, every reservation which is not specifically permitted or prohibited must be assessed in light of its compatibility with the object and purpose of the treaty to which it is addressed. Whether the concordance of a reservation with customary law is a relevant consideration to the determination of its compatibility with the objects or purposes of a treaty depends on the treaty itself. The yardstick for assessing the admissibility of reservations is thus to be found within the treaty (by reference to the treaty's object and purpose) and not dehors the treaty, by reference to customary law. However, because even within the treaty itself it is difficult to find an objective standard for assessing the compatibility of a reservation with the treaty's purposes and objects, every state may normally judge for itself whether a reservation is compatible or not.

Ideally, a reservation to a substantive provision of a clearly codificatory treaty, like the Vienna Convention on the Law of Treaties, should be considered by the parties to that Convention as incompatible with the objects or purposes of the Convention. In reality, even such reservations have been accepted by most parties to the Vienna Convention without raising the question

---

[20] Vienna Convention on the Law of Treaties, opened for signature 23 May 1969, Art. 19, 1155 UNTS 331, reprinted in 63 AJIL 875 (1969), 8 ILM 679 (1969).

of compatibility.[21] The connection between compatibility and customary law status is thus not useful for assessing the admissibility of reservations.

In the *North Sea Continental Shelf Cases*[22] however, the ICJ appeared to depart from the position taken in its advisory opinion on *Genocide*. There, the Court states that treaty clauses permitting reservations to specified provisions of the treaty normally imply that such provisions are not declaratory of existing or emergent rules of customary law.[23] The Court suggests that there is a general expectation that reservations to conventional provisions which are declaratory of general or customary law will not be admitted because such rules must have equal force for all members of the international community.[24]

Dissenting, Judge Morelli emphasized that 'the power to make reservations affects only the contractual obligation flowing from the convention,' adding that '[i]t goes without saying that a reservation has nothing to do with the customary rule as such. If that rule exists, it exists also for the State which formulated the reservation, in the same way as it exists for those States which have

---

[21] *See* e.g. the reservation made by the Syrian Arab Republic to Art. 62(2)(a) of the Vienna Convention on the Law of Treaties. Multilateral Treaties Deposited with the Secretary-General: Status as at 31 December 1987 at 770, UN Doc. ST/LEG/SER.E/6 (1988); I. Sinclair, The Vienna Convention on the Law of Treaties 65–6 (2nd edn. 1984).

[22] *North Sea Continental Shelf Cases (FRG/Den.; FRG/Neth.)*, 1969 ICJ Rep. 3 (Judgment of 20 Feb.).

[23] The Court stated that: 'speaking generally, it is a characteristic of purely conventional rules and obligations that, in regard to them, some faculty of making unilateral reservations may, within certain limits, be admitted;—whereas this cannot be so in the case of general or customary law rules and obligations which, by their very nature, must have equal force for all members of the international community, and cannot therefore be the subject of any right of unilateral exclusion exercisable at will by any one of them in its own favour. Consequently, it is to be expected that when, for whatever reason, rules or obligations of this order are embodied, or are intended to be reflected in certain provisions of a convention, such provisions will figure amongst those in respect of which a right of unilateral reservation is not conferred, or is excluded. This expectation is, in principle, fulfilled by Article 12 of the Geneva Continental Shelf Convention, which permits reservations to be made to all the articles of the Convention "other than to Articles 1 to 3 inclusive"—these three Articles being the ones which, it is clear, were then regarded as reflecting, or as crystallizing, received or at least emergent rules of customary international law relative to the continental shelf. . . .' Ibid. at 38–9. For a critique of the ICJ's position, see Akehurst, *Custom as a Source of International Law*, 47 Brit. YB Int'l L. 1, 48 (1974–5).

[24] 1969 ICJ Rep. 39.

not ratified.'[25] It appears that, for Judge Morelli, no inference as to whether a treaty rule embodies a customary norm can be drawn from those treaty provisions which concern admissibility of reservations.

The Court acknowledged that the Convention's reservations clause did not exclude reservations to certain other provisions of the Convention which related to matters 'that lie within the field of received customary law'. However, the Court explained, '[t]hese matters . . . all relate to or are consequential upon principles or rules of general maritime law, very considerably ante-dating the Convention, and . . . only incidental to continental shelf rights as such.'[26] The Convention mentioned these matters 'simply to ensure that they were not prejudiced by the exercise of continental shelf rights as provided for in the Convention'.[27] Be that as it may, the reservations clause of the 1958 Geneva Convention on the Continental Shelf (Article 12) undeniably had the effect of permitting reservations to provisions reflecting customary law.[28]

The Court's discussion of the relationship between the admissibility of reservations to certain treaty provisions and their customary law content gives rise to the question whether the effect of such reservations (except those concerning *jus cogens* rules) upon the relationship between the reserving state and the state accepting the reservation is not similar to that produced by a treaty establishing a conventional rule which displaces *inter partes* a rule of customary law.[29]

---

[25] Ibid. at 198 (Morelli J. dissenting).

[26] Ibid. at 39.

[27] Ibid. Professor Bowett supports the approach of the ICJ (above n. 23): 'A Party cannot, under the guise of a reservation to an article to which reservations are permitted, seek to find acceptance for a legal proposition which is at variance with, or even concerned with, rules of law based upon some quite different treaty or even rules of customary international law.' Bowett, *Reservations to Non-Restricted Multilateral Treaties*, 48 Brit. YB Int'l L. 67, 73 (1976–7). Shelton criticizes the ICJ for its advisory opinion on the Genocide Convention: '[I]t would seem illogical to allow substantive reservations as the conventional principles are derived from an equally authoritative legal source already binding upon the state in question.' Shelton, *State Practice on Reservations to Human Rights Treaties*, 1 Can. Hum. Rts. YB 205, 208–9 (1983).

[28] Baxter, *Treaties and Custom*, 129 Recueil des cours 27, 48 (1970–I). For the text of the Geneva Convention on the Continental Shelf, done at Geneva 29 Apr. 1958, see 499 UNTS 311.

[29] See L. Henkin, R. Pugh, O. Schachter, and H. Smit, International Law: Cases and Materials 86–7 (2nd edn. 1987). Coccia argues cogently that 'States can modify by agreement customary norms between themselves, unless they are norms of *jus*

Of course, a single state is not permitted to derogate from any
rule of international law, peremptory or not, unless the state can
establish a justification precluding wrongfulness, such as *force
majeure*, state of necessity, or self-defence.[30] But as regards
customary rules which are *jus dispositivum* several states acting
strictly in their mutual relations may substitute a rule of conventional
law for a rule of customary law. Articles 20-1 of the Vienna
Convention on the Law of Treaties, opened for signature on 23
May 1969 shortly after the Court's judgment of 20 February 1969,
create, as between the reserving state and the accepting state, a
separate set of conventional relations displacing, to the extent of
the reservation, conflicting rules of customary law. It follows that
reservations to those customary norms, including humanitarian and
human rights norms which are not *jus cogens* are made effective
by their acceptance under the provisions of the Vienna Convention
which govern the acceptance of such reservations.

The difference between the judgment in the *Genocide* case and
the Vienna Convention, and the judgment in the *North Sea
Continental Shelf Cases*, may, however, be more apparent than real.
At the time of the latter judgment, the Court was, of course,
familiar with the work of the International Law Commission on
law of treaties and the developments taking place at the Vienna
Conference which had begun in 1968. Focusing on reservations to
codifying conventions, the Court intended perhaps to enunciate the
principle that some reservations could be inadmissible because of
incompatibility with the codifying object and purpose of the
convention. Indeed, such reservations may even give rise to questions
pertaining to the good faith of the reserving state. But reservations
merely seeking to adapt a codifying convention to a particular
situation, or reservations to conventional provisions which are only
partly declaratory of customary law, would not necessarily be
excluded as incompatible with the object and purpose of the treaty.
Most reservations would not present the question of compatibility
in such clear-cut terms, however, and would, in practice, be

cogens. Accordingly, it is possible for States, through an accepted reservation, to
modify *inter se* a customary norm not of peremptory character.' Coccia, *Reservations
to Multilateral Treaties on Human Rights*, 15 Cal. W. Int'l LJ 1, 31 (1985).
The Inter-American Court of Human Rights established that reservations to
non-derogable rights are incompatible with the object and purpose of the American
Convention on Human Rights. T. Meron, above n. 11, at 194.
[30] Meron, *On a Hierarchy of International Human Rights*, 80 AJIL 1, 20 (1986).

regulated through acceptance of and objection to reservations in accordance with the Vienna Convention.

A state sometimes enters a reservation to one provision of a treaty because it disagrees with the statement of the law contained therein. Judge Baxter observed, with regard to the Geneva Convention on the High Seas,[31] that 'reservations markedly diminish the declaratory force of the articles to which they relate, but they hardly deny the evidentiary force of either these articles or the articles not yet the subject of reservations.'[32] Unquestionably, reservations may adversely affect the claims to customary law status of those norms which they address. In assessing this effect, the number and the depth of the reservations actually made must be considered. In practice, those provisions of human rights treaties which clash with national laws and prevailing religious, social, economic, and cultural values are particularly likely to be the subject of reservations. To be sure, under the *Genocide* test, every state must be guided by the principle of compatibility when deciding whether to make a reservation or whether to object to a reservation made by another state. Because different considerations motivate states in making such assessments, there is an obvious danger that reservations will result in far-reaching modifications of customary law. This danger is heightened by the reluctance of most states to object even to far-reaching reservations to human rights treaties. The system of *laissez-faire* which typifies the Vienna Convention's provisions on reservations, characterized by the absence of a third-party organ authorized to rule on the compatibility of reservations, establishes the reserving states, and other parties to human rights treaties acting *ut singuli*, as the final arbiters of compatibility. This system has failed to curb excessive reservations[33]

[31] Done at Geneva 29 Apr. 1958, 450 UNTS 11.

[32] Baxter, above n. 28, at 51.

[33] For an example of an excessive reservation, see the 'general reservation' of Egypt to the fundamental Art. 2 of the Convention on the Elimination of All Forms of Discrimination Against Women, adopted 18 Dec. 1979, GA Res. 34/180, 34 UN GAOR Supp. (No. 46) at 193, UN Doc. A/34/46 (1979): 'Egypt is willing to comply with the content of this article, provided that such compliance does not run counter to the Islamic Sharia.' Multilateral Treaties, above n. 21, at 163. See also the reservations by Bangladesh, ibid. at 161, and objection by Sweden, ibid. at 171. Such reservations prompted the Committee on the Elimination of Discrimination against Women to request 'the United Nations system as a whole, in particular the specialized agencies . . . and the Commission on the Status of Women, to promote or undertake studies on the status of women under Islamic laws and customs and in particular on the status and equality of women in the

and to shield the integrity of human rights treaties. Dissatisfaction with this situation has triggered proposals to recognize the power of supervisory organs established under human rights treaties to rule on the compatibility of reservations made to such treaties.[34]

The Inter-American Court of Human Rights, in its advisory opinion on the *Effect of Reservations on the Entry into Force of the American Convention on Human Rights (Arts. 74 and 75)*,[35] further confirmed that human rights treaties are subject to the criterion of compatibility of reservations with the object and purpose of such treaties. In that opinion, the Court considered whether a state which ratifies or adheres to the American Convention on Human Rights[36] with one or more reservations is deemed to have become a party to the American Convention on Human Rights from the date of the deposit of its instrument of ratification, or upon the termination of the period stated in Article 20[37] of the Vienna

family on issues such as marriage, divorce, custody and property rights and their participation in public life of the society. . . .' Decision 4, UN Doc. E/1987/L.20 (1987). This request has not been accepted by the Economic and Social Council in its spring 1987 session. See also UN Doc. CEDAW/C/L.3/Add.28 (1988).

For the extensive and far-reaching reservations to the International Covenant on Civil and Political Rights proposed by the Carter administration to the US Senate, see Message from the President of the United States Transmitting Four Treaties Pertaining to Human Rights, Acting Secretary of State Warren Christopher, Letter of Submittal, S. Exec. Docs. C, D, E, and FF at XI–XV, 95th Cong., 2d Sess. (1978), reprinted in [1978] Digest of U.S. Practice in International Law at 450–7 (M. Nash ed. 1980), discussed in Schachter, *The Obligation of the Parties to Give Effect to the Covenant on Civil and Political Rights*, 73 AJIL 462 (1979).

[34] Shelton, above n. 27, at 231.

[35] Advisory Opinion OC-2/82 of 24 Sept. 1982, Inter-American Court of Human Rights, Ser. A, Judgments and Opinions, No. 2.

[36] For the official text of the American Convention on Human Rights, see Organization of American States, Basic Documents Pertaining to Human Rights in the Inter-American System 25, OEA/Ser.L.V/II.71 Doc. 6, rev. 1, 23 Sept. 1987 (1988).

[37] Art. 20 of the Vienna Convention reads as follows: '1. A reservation expressly authorized by a treaty does not require any subsequent acceptance by the other contracting States unless the treaty so provides.

2. When it appears from the limited number of the negotiating States and the object and purpose of a treaty that the application of the treaty in its entirety between all the parties is an essential condition of the consent of each one to be bound by the treaty, a reservation requires acceptance by all the parties.

3. When a treaty is a constituent instrument of an international organization and unless it otherwise provides, a reservation requires the acceptance of the competent organ of that organization.

4. In cases not falling under the preceding paragraphs and unless the treaty otherwise provides: (a) acceptance by another contracting State of a reservation constitutes the reserving State a party to the treaty in relation to that other State if or when the treaty is in force for those States; (b) an objection by another

Convention on the Law of Treaties. The reservations clause of the American Convention, Article 75, provides that the convention 'shall be subject to reservations only in conformity with the provisions of the Vienna Convention on the Law of Treaties . . .'. The Inter-American Court therefore had to decide whether Article 75 of the American Convention refers to Article 20(4) of the Vienna Convention, which makes the entry into force of a ratification dependent upon the acceptance of a reservation by another state party, or to Article 20(1) of the Vienna Convention, which does not require acceptance by any other state party.

In choosing the latter alternative, the Inter-American Court confirmed that the compatibility criterion must be applied, holding that 'the reference in Article 75 to the Vienna Convention makes sense only if it is understood as an express authorization designed to enable States to make whatever reservations they deem appropriate, provided the reservations are not incompatible with the object and purpose of the treaty.'[38] This conclusion in effect confirms that the principle of reciprocity does not necessarily apply across the board to human rights treaties. In so concluding, the Court was guided by the character of such treaties and by their purposes and objects. The Court emphasized that human rights treaties

are not multilateral treaties of the traditional type concluded to accomplish the reciprocal exchange of rights for the mutual benefit of the contracting States. Their object and purpose is the protection of the basic rights of individual human beings, irrespective of their nationality, both against the State of their nationality and all other contracting States. In concluding these human rights treaties, the States can be deemed to submit themselves to a legal order within which they, for the common good, assume various obligations, not in relation to other States, but towards all individuals within their jurisdiction.[39]

contracting State to a reservation does not preclude the entry into force of the treaty as between the objecting and reserving States unless a contrary intention is definitely expressed by the objecting State; (c) an act expressing a State's consent to be bound by the treaty and containing a reservation is effective as soon as at least one other contracting State has accepted the reservation.

5. For the purposes of paragraphs 2 and 4 and unless the treaty otherwise provides, a reservation is considered to have been accepted by a State if it shall have raised no objection to the reservation by the end of a period of twelve months after it was notified of the reservation or by the date on which it expressed its consent to be bound by the treaty, whichever is later.'

[38] Advisory Opinion, above n. 35, at para. 35.
[39] Ibid. at para. 29. See also T. Meron, above n. 11, at 146-9.

The Inter-American Court invoked Article 60(5) of the Vienna Convention, which concerns humanitarian treaties, and concluded that

the [American] Convention must be seen for what in reality it is: a multilateral legal instrument or framework enabling States to make binding unilateral commitments not to violate the human rights of individuals within their jurisdiction.

A treaty which attaches such great importance to the protection of the individual that it makes the right of individual petition mandatory as of the moment of ratification, can hardly be deemed to have intended to delay the treaty's entry into force until at least one other State is prepared to accept the reserving State as a party. Given the institutional and normative framework of the Convention, no useful purpose would be served by such a delay.[40]

One year later, the Inter-American Court further refined its position on reservations to human rights treaties by addressing a question central to many of those treaties: whether reservations to the non-derogable provisions of the Convention are permissible. The Court stated that

the first question which arises when interpreting a reservation is whether it is compatible with the object and purpose of the treaty. Article 27 of the Convention allows the States Parties to suspend, in time of war, public danger, or other emergency that threatens their independence or security, the obligations they assumed by ratifying the Convention, provided that in doing so they do not suspend or derogate from certain basic or essential rights, among them the right to life. . . . It would follow therefrom that a reservation which was designed to enable a State to suspend any of the non-derogable fundamental rights must be deemed to be incompatible with the object and purpose of the Convention and, consequently, not permitted by it. The situation would be different if the reservation sought merely to restrict certain aspects of a non-derogable right without depriving the right as a whole of its basic purpose. [Such a reservation would not be] incompatible with the object and purpose of the Convention.[41]

Judge Buergenthal of the Inter-American Court commented that this decision, in establishing that a reservation purporting to suspend a non-derogable fundamental right was incompatible with

---

[40] Advisory Opinion, above n. 35, at paras. 33–4.
[41] *Restrictions to the Death Penalty (Arts. 4(2) and 4(4) American Convention on Human Rights)*, Advisory Opinion OC-3/83 of 8 Sept. 1983, Inter-American Court of Human Rights, Ser. A, Judgments and Opinions, No. 3, at 83–4.

the object and purpose of the Convention, constituted 'the first unambiguous international judicial articulation of a principle basic to the application of human rights treaties, that non-derogability and incompatibility are linked'.[42] Obviously, if a non-derogable norm constitutes a *jus cogens* norm, no reservations to it are permitted, for, as Sinclair has observed, 'if States cannot enter into a treaty contrary to a norm of *jus cogens*, it seems only logical that they should not be permitted to make reservations to those treaty provisions which embody norms of *jus cogens*.'[43]

There remains for discussion the ICJ's statement in the *North Sea Continental Shelf Cases* that the normal inference from treaty clauses permitting reservations to specified treaty provisions is that such provisions are not declaratory of previously existing or emergent rules of law.[44] Baxter agrees that a negative inference about the non-declaratory nature of the provisions to which reservations are permitted may be justified in the case of treaties that make a distinction between those provisions to which reservations may be made and those to which reservation are not allowed. This inference is not warranted if a treaty expressly or tacitly permits reservations to all of its provisions, however.[45] An examination of reservations clauses in several human rights treaties casts doubt on the Court's premiss.[46]

For example, the Convention on the Prevention and Punishment of the Crime of Genocide,[47] which embodies customary law, contains no provisions on reservations. I have already discussed the meaning of the Court's opinion allowing reservations compatible with the object and purpose of this Convention. Article 9 of the Supplementary Convention on the Abolition of Slavery, the Slave Trade, and Institutions and Practices Similar to Slavery[48] (slavery and slave-trade are, of course, prohibited by customary international

---

[42] Buergenthal, *The Advisory Practice of the Inter-American Human Rights Court*, 79 AJIL 1, 25 (1985).

It may be noted, however, that only two states have objected to a reservation by Trinidad and Tobago 'not to apply in full the provision of paragraph 2 of Article 4 of the [Political] Covenant. . . .' Multilateral Treaties, above n. 2, at 135, 137, 138.

[43] I. Sinclair, above n. 21, at 212.

[44] See above text accompanying n. 24.

[45] Baxter, above n. 28, at 49–50.

[46] See above text accompanying n. 24.

[47] 78 UNTS 277.

[48] Done 7 Sept. 1956, 266 UNTS 3, 18 UST 3201, TIAS No. 6418.

law[49]) does not permit any reservations. Neither the International Covenant on Civil and Political Rights,[50] which embodies some rules of customary law and some rules of conventional law, nor the International Covenant on Economic, Social and Cultural Rights[51] contains any provisions on reservations. Article 9 of the Convention against Discrimination in Education[52] does not permit any reservations.

The even more important *in pari materia* International Convention on the Elimination of All Forms of Racial Discrimination,[53] whose principal provisions are declaratory of customary international law,[54] offers a striking contrast. Article 20 of that instrument rather freely allows reservations which are compatible with the object and purpose of the Convention or which are not inhibitive of the operation of any of the bodies established by the Convention. The operation of those bodies is obviously based in conventional, not customary, obligations. Article 20(2) requires objections by two-thirds of the states parties to determine that a reservation is 'incompatible or inhibitive', making it unlikely that even far-reaching reservations to the fundamental principles of the Convention would be rejected by the required majority. It is thus virtually impossible to draw any inference about the customary *vel non* character of a provision of this Convention from the acceptance of a reservation. The procedure established in Article 20(2) is not necessarily exclusive, however. In the absence of a decision under Article 20(2), the ICJ acting under Article 22 of the Convention could perhaps determine that a particular reservation is inherently incompatible with the purpose and object of the Convention.

Does the Committee on the Elimination of Racial Discrimination have authority to rule on the incompatibility or the inhibitive nature of a reservation? Inglés has argued that '[i]n the absence of a

49 Restatement, above n. 17, § 702(b), comment *e* and Reporters' note 4.
50 Adopted 16 Dec. 1966, 999 UNTS 171. For the attempts of the Human Rights Committee to question some reservations made to the Covenant, see Shelton, above n. 27, at 230–1.
51 Adopted 16 Dec. 1966, 993 UNTS 3.
52 Adopted 14 Dec. 1960, 429 UNTS 93 (a UNESCO convention).
53 Adopted 21 Dec. 1965, 660 UNTS 195.
54 T. Meron, above n. 11, at 1. States parties have not made reservations to the basic customary norms reflected in the Convention, but have made reservations limiting the obligations of Art. 4 by the extent to which they may be fulfilled with due regard to freedoms of expression, assembly, and association. Ibid. at 31 and n. 90. See also below Chapter II nn. 11 and 98 and accompanying text.

definitive judicial ruling [by the ICJ under Article 22 of the Convention] on the admissibility of the reservation in question, the State party concerned might be asked [by the Committee on the Elimination of Racial Discrimination] to withdraw its reservations.'[55] If such a request suggests the authority to exceed merely hortatory comment, however, the request would apparently go beyond the Committee's powers under the Convention.[56]

The Convention on the Elimination of All Forms of Discrimination against Women,[57] which has been afforded less recognition as an embodiment of customary principles[58] than has the Convention against Racial Discrimination, prohibits reservations incompatible with the object and purpose of the Convention in its Article 28. Article 28 provides neither for specific criteria of incompatibility nor for a process by which incompatibility may be determined. Decisions concerning the compatibility of reservations are left, in the first instance, to the reserving state and to the accepting or objecting states. Article 29 of the Convention, which provides for arbitration or, failing agreement on the organization of the arbitration, for referral to the ICJ, would be applicable if a dispute regarding the interpretation of Article 28 arose. In any event, it is clear that the functions of the Committee on the Elimination of Discrimination against Women 'do not appear to include a determination of the incompatibility of reservations, although reservations undoubtedly affect the application of the Convention and the Committee might have to comment thereon in its reports in this context'.[59]

The Convention relating to the Status of Refugees,[60] in Article 42, authorizes reservations with the exception of a number of

[55] J. Inglés, Study on the Implementation of Article 4 of the International Convention on the Elimination of All Forms of Racial Discrimination, UN Doc. A/CONF.119/10, para. 224 (1983).

[56] Thus, the UN Secretariat has advised the Committee that even a unanimous decision by the Committee that a reservation is unacceptable would have no binding effect, and that the Committee was obliged to take into account the reservations made by states parties. Ibid. para. 206.

[57] GA Res. 34/180, 34 UN GAOR Supp. (No. 46) at 193, UN Doc. A/34/46 (1979).

[58] T. Meron, above n. 11, at 54.

[59] See the legal opinion of the Treaty Section of the Office of Legal Affairs of the United Nations Secretariat, 39 UN GAOR 2 Supp. (No. 45) (Ann. III) at 55–6, UN Doc. A/39/45 (1984), discussed in T. Meron, above n. 11, at 80. See also above nn. 33–4 and accompanying text.

[60] Done at Geneva 28 July 1951, 189 UNTS 137.

specified provisions. While some of the provisions to which reservations may not be made may well reflect customary law (e.g. the principle of non-discrimination stated in Article 3, or the prohibition of refoulement[61] in Article 33), other provisions are merely conventional (e.g. Article 38 on the settlement of disputes, and the articles containing the final clauses of the Convention). In contrast, Article VII of the Protocol relating to the Status of Refugees[62] allows reservations to be made to Article IV on the settlement of disputes. The Convention against Torture and Other Cruel, Inhuman or Degrading Treatment or Punishment[63] in Article 28 expressly permits reservations to Article 20 (pertaining to certain powers of the Committee against Torture). Article 30 of the Convention allows reservations to the settlement of disputes provisions. Reservations to other provisions of the Convention are thus implicitly prohibited. While the basic prohibition of torture stated in the Convention clearly reflects customary and even *jus cogens* norms, other provisions to which reservations appear to be prohibited are clearly conventional. Article 19 concerning the reporting obligations of states parties is one such provision.

Article 75 of the American Convention on Human Rights[64] states that the Convention shall be subject to reservations only in conformity with the provisions of the Vienna Convention on the Law of Treaties.[65] As previously noted, the Inter-American Court of Human Rights interpreted this provision as incorporating the principle that reservations must be compatible with the purpose and object of the Convention. The (European) Convention for the Protection of Human Rights and Fundamental Freedoms,[66] in Article 64, prohibits reservations 'of a general character' while allowing 'a reservation in respect of any particular provision of the

---

[61] Concerning the customary law character of the principle of non-refoulement, see Martin, *Non-Refoulement of Refugees: United States Compliance with International Obligations*, 23 Harv. Int'l LJ 357, 365 (1983); G. Goodwin-Gill, The Refugee in International Law 97-8 (1983). See also below Chapter II n. 48 and accompanying text. But see Hailbronner, *Non-Refoulement and "Humanitarian" Refugees: Customary International Law or Wishful Legal Thinking?*, 26 Va. J. Int'l L. 857, 866-7 (1986).

[62] Done 31 Jan. 1967, 606 UNTS 267.

[63] Opened for signature 10 Dec. 1984, GA Res. 39/46, 39 UN GAOR Supp. (No. 51) at 197, UN Doc. A/39/51 (1985).

[64] Above n. 36.

[65] Above n. 20.

[66] Done 4 Nov. 1950, 213 UNTS 221.

Convention to the extent that any law then in force in its territory is not in conformity with the provision'. These regional conventions do not make any distinctions on the basis of the customary law character of their provisions. Similarly, the Geneva Conventions,[67] their Additional Protocols, and the African Charter on Human and Peoples' Rights[68] do not contain any reservations clauses. The permissibility of reservations thus may not provide a reliable basis for distinguishing between customary and conventional provisions.

This review of just a few of the principal human rights instruments demonstrates that although reservations clauses have some probative value, they do not constitute a reliable general guide for identifying those provisions of a treaty which embody norms of customary law. Many different factors may impel law-making conferences to allow or to prohibit reservations to particular provisions of a human rights treaty. Often such conferences find it difficult to obtain a consensus on which provisions of a convention are declaratory of customary law. In some cases, the customary or the fundamental nature of a principle stated in a particular provision of a treaty may constitute the rationale for the prohibition of reservations to that provision. Reservations clauses of this type may and, indeed, should be considered as an important factor in assessing whether that provision is customary or not. This is particularly true of cases in which the formulation of the reservations clause was preceded by a discussion by the diplomatic conference of the customary law character of the relevant norms of the convention. In other cases, clauses allowing or prohibiting specified reservations may be unrelated to the customary law nature of the provisions implicated. A careful examination *in concreto* is necessary before any inference with regard to the customary *vel non* character of a treaty provision may be drawn from the reservations clauses.

A survey of the actual practice of states with regard to reservations to human rights treaties does not facilitate such an examination. In making reservations, states act to safeguard their political[69] and legal interests (e.g. to avoid conflicts with national laws), and are generally not concerned with the customary law content of the

---

[67] State practice and scholarly authority recognize that reservations to the Geneva Conventions are, in principle, permissible, subject to the Vienna Convention on the Law of Treaties. See Pilloud, above n. 9.

[68] Reprinted in 21 ILM 58 (1982).

[69] Coccia, above n. 29, at 35. Shelton emphasizes that objections to reservations to human rights treaties are rare. Above n. 27, at 228.

provision to which a reservation is made. A recent survey demonstrates that objections to reservations are often utilized as political tools and as opportunities to make unilateral statements.[70] Characteristically, states do not object to reservations made by other states. When objections are made, the objecting states occasionally assert that reservations are incompatible with a treaty, but only exceptionally that a reservation creates a possible conflict with international law.[71] Neither the practice of such human rights organs as the Human Rights Committee, which was established under Article 28 of the International Covenant on Civil and Political Rights,[72] nor that of the European Commission and Court of Human Rights[73] helps identify those treaty provisions to which reservations are made that constitute customary law.

III. THE *NICARAGUA* JUDGMENT

Because of the exceptional character of the US multilateral treaty reservation, the circumstances leading to the invocation of the

[70] Coccia, above n. 29, at 35.

[71] Ibid. at 33. For examples of objections asserting incompatibility with a treaty, see the objections by the Federal Republic of Germany to the reservations by Egypt to the Convention on the Elimination of All Forms of Discrimination Against Women, and the objections by Mexico to the reservations by Mauritius to that Convention. Multilateral Treaties, above n. 21, at 170.

For an objection referring to a conflict between the 'general reservation' made by Australia to Arts. 2 and 50 of the Political Covenant (which was withdrawn in 1984, ibid. at 149) and international law, see the following objection by the Netherlands: 'The reservation . . . is acceptable to the Kingdom on the understanding that it will in no way impair Australia's basic obligation under international law, as laid down in article 2, paragraph 1, to respect and to ensure to all individuals within its territory and subject to its jurisdiction the rights recognized in the International Covenant on Civil and Political Rights'. Ibid. at 138. The statement by the government of the Netherlands seemingly reflects its belief that Art. 2(1) of the Political Covenant embodies a customary law obligation.

[72] Concerning the consideration of reservations by the Human Rights Committee, see Ghandhi, *The Human Rights Committee and the Right of Individual Communication*, 57 Brit. YB Int'l L. 201, 229–32 (1986). Imbert explains that the absence of a reservations clause in the Political Covenant is rooted in the wish of the majority of the negotiators to abide by ILC's proposed rules on reservations to treaties. Above n. 9, at 42–3 and n. 70.

[73] Under Art. 64 of the European Convention reservations may only be made to any particular provision of the Convention to the extent that any law then in force in the reserving state does not conform to that provision. General reservations are expressly prohibited. In considering reservations to the European Convention, the Commission and the Court have focused on whether particular reservations conform to Art. 64, but not on whether they derogate from customary law. See J. Kelly, The European Convention on Human Rights and States Parties: International

Geneva Conventions as customary law in the *Nicaragua* case are unlikely to recur in future cases before the ICJ. The Court's method is none the less of general interest in determining the relationship between custom and treaty. That method may also create some perplexity.

Although both Nicaragua and the United States are parties to the Geneva Conventions, Nicaragua refrained from invoking them in the proceedings, perhaps because of its reluctance either to acknowledge that the conflict constitutes an internal armed conflict, or to have its own acts measured by the yardstick of norms contained in common Article 3.[74] The Court itself, however, alluded to the relevance of the US multilateral treaty reservation to the Geneva Conventions. Because the conduct of the United States could, in the Court's view, be judged according to fundamental principles of humanitarian law, the Court explained that it was not necessary for it to take a position on the significance of that reservation. In fact, the Court took the US reservation into account by applying certain provisions of the Geneva Conventions as customary rather than contractual obligations.

Control of Restrictions and Limitations 2–3, Council of Europe Doc. H/Coll.(80) 3 (1980); J. Frowein and W. Peukert, Europäische MenschenRechtsKonvention 486–95 (1985); 5 Digest of Strasbourg Case-Law Relating to the European Convention on Human Rights 617–23 (1985).

[74] See generally the following reports by Americas Watch Committee, Violations of the Laws of War by Both Sides in Nicaragua 1981–1985 (1985); Violations of the Laws of War by Both Sides in Nicaragua 1981–1985, First Supplement (June 1985); Human Rights in Nicaragua 1985–1986 (1986).

Common Art. 3 reads as follows: 'In the case of armed conflict not of an international character occurring in the territory of one of the High Contracting Parties, each Party to the conflict shall be bound to apply, as a minimum, the following provisions:

(1) Persons taking no active part in the hostilities, including members of armed forces who have laid down their arms and those placed *hors de combat* by sickness, wounds, detention, or any other cause, shall in all circumstances be treated humanely, without any adverse distinction founded on race, colour, religion or faith, sex, birth or wealth, or any other similar criteria.

To this end, the following acts are and shall remain prohibited at any time and in any place whatsoever with respect to the above-mentioned persons: (a) violence to life and person, in particular murder of all kinds, mutilation, cruel treatment and torture; (b) taking of hostages; (c) outrages upon personal dignity, in particular humiliating and degrading treatment; (d) the passing of sentences and the carrying out of executions without previous judgment pronounced by a regularly constituted court, affording all the judicial guarantees which are recognized as indispensable by civilized peoples.

(2) The wounded and sick shall be collected and cared for.
. . . .'

The Court began its analysis with the general and unchallengeable assessment that the Geneva Conventions represent 'in some respects a development, and in other respects no more than the expression,' of fundamental principles of humanitarian law.[75] In support of the proposition that certain provisions are declaratory of customary law, the Court mentioned as significant the common Article on denunciation,[76] which emphasizes that, by denouncing the Conventions, no state can derogate from its obligations under international law and the laws of humanity.

The pitfalls of disentangling customary from conventional norms appeared, however, as soon as the Court moved beyond this general proposition. The Court focused on two common articles of the Geneva Conventions as embodiments of general principles of humanitarian law or customary law, Articles 1 and 3. Article 1, one of the shortest provisions in the Conventions, provides that '[t]he High Contracting Parties undertake to respect and to ensure respect for the present Convention in all circumstances.' The Court concluded:

[T]here is an obligation on the United States Government, in the terms of Article 1 of the Geneva Conventions, to 'respect' the Conventions and even 'to ensure respect' for them 'in all circumstances', since such an obligation does not derive only from the Conventions themselves, but from the general principles of humanitarian law to which the Conventions merely give specific expression. The United States is thus under an obligation not to encourage persons or groups engaged in the conflict in Nicaragua to act in violation of the provisions of Article 3 common to the four 1949 Conventions. . . .[77]

Does Article 1 give expression to a general principle of humanitarian law? To the extent that Article 3 states principles of

[75] 1986 ICJ Rep. at 113.

[76] Pictet observes that a state that denounces one of the Geneva Conventions 'would nevertheless remain bound by the principles contained in it insofar as they are the expression of . . . customary international law'. *Commentary* on Geneva Convention No. I, below n. 79, at 413. Art. 43 of the Vienna Convention on the Law of Treaties provides that denunciation of a treaty 'shall not in any way impair the duty of any State to fulfil any obligation embodied in the treaty to which it would be subject under international law independently of the treaty'. See also above n. 6 and accompanying text.

[77] 1986 ICJ Rep. at 114. Elsewhere in its judgment the Court stated, in the same vein, 'that general principles of humanitarian law include a particular prohibition [to refrain from encouraging persons or groups to commit violations of Art. 3], accepted by States, and extending to activities which occur in the context of armed conflicts, whether international in character or not'. Ibid at 129.

customary law, the United States obviously has the duty to respect them, both directly and vicariously, even in the absence of the explicit obligation ('to respect') stated in Article 1. It is less clear whether there is an obligation deriving from the general principles of international law not to 'encourage' violations by others (i.e. 'to ensure respect') of the principles in Article 3.[78]

The Court's ambiguous statement seems to suggest that when the Geneva Conventions were adopted, Article 1, as well as Article 3, was declaratory of humanitarian principles. By the latter, the Court meant, in this context, customary law. There is no evidence, however, that at that time the negotiating states believed that they were codifying an existing principle of law. They appear to have chosen the words 'and to ensure respect' deliberately 'to emphasize and strengthen the *responsibility of the Contracting Parties*'.[79] Moreover, the language 'and to ensure respect' was not used in earlier Geneva Conventions.[80] The repetition of such prior usage

---

[78] A recent study argues that 'the complicity norm [stating the responsibility of one state for aiding another state to violate international law] has been acepted as customary law', Quigley, *Complicity in International Law: A new Direction in the Law of State Responsibility*, 57 Brit. YB Int'l L. 77 (1986), but that '[c]omplicity does not include moral encouragement or incitement by a State to another State to engage in an internationally wrongful act . . .'. Ibid. at 80.

[79] Commentary on the Geneva Conventions of 12 August 1949: Geneva Convention for the Amelioration of the Condition of the Wounded and Sick in Armed Forces in the Field 26 (J. Pictet ed. 1952) (emphasis added). The *Commentary* adds that 'in the event of a Power failing to fulfil its obligations, the other Contracting Parties . . . may, and should, endeavour to bring it back to an attitude of respect for the Convention.' Ibid.

The 1958 *Commentary* on Geneva Convention No. IV went further, adding that '[t]he proper working of the system of protection provided by the Convention demands in fact that the Contracting Parties should not be content merely to apply its provisions themselves, but should do everything in their power to ensure that the humanitarian principles underlying the Conventions are applied universally.' Commentary on the Geneva Conventions of 12 August 1949: Geneva Convention Relative to the Protection of Civilian Persons in Time of War 16 (O. Uhler and H. Coursier eds. 1958). The 1958 *Commentary* states that the words 'in all circumstances' (common Art. 1) do not cover the case of civil war and apply to international armed conflicts only. Ibid. See also *Commentary* on Geneva Convention No. I, above at 27.

[80] Thus, the (Geneva) Convention Relative to the Treatment of Prisoners of War, opened for signature 27 July 1929, 47 Stat. 2021, TS No. 846, provided only (Art. 82) that '[t]he provisions of the present Convention must be respected by the High Contracting Parties under all circumstances.' For an excellent discussion of Art. 82, see Condorelli and Boisson de Chazournes, *Quelques Remarques à propos de l'obligation des Etats de "respecter et faire respecter" le droit international humanitaire "en toutes circonstances"*, in Swinarski (ed.), above n. 5, 17, at 18–19. The obligation 'to ensure respect' is reiterated in Art. 1(1) of the Protocol

would have strengthened the claim that the phrase is declaratory of international law.[81] Although this was not the case here, the language 'to ensure respect' was a conventional precursor to the *erga omnes* principle enunciated by the Court in *Barcelona Traction*,[82] to which we shall return.

The contemporaneous understanding of the drafters is not necessarily dispositive of the issue; however, subsequent developments may be relevant. Since 1949 certain third states and the International Committee of the Red Cross (ICRC) have made a practice of issuing appeals to certain governments to respect the Geneva Conventions. Moreover, the ICRC and other international bodies have addressed general appeals to all states to ensure respect for the Conventions. Despite the salutary efforts of the ICRC to stimulate greater resort to this practice, it does not appear to be uniform.[83] Because of the confidential character of some of the appeals, the frequency with which appeals are made is often difficult to ascertain. This confidentiality also suggests that an insistence on extensive evidence of practice may be unwise. A recent, post-*Nicaragua* report of the UN Secretary-General to the Security Council contains an important invocation of Article 1.[84] There, the Secretary-General focused on common Article 1 discussing the duty

Additional to the Geneva Conventions at 12 August 1949, and Relating to the Protection of Victims of International Armed Conflicts (Protocol I), opened for signature 12 Dec. 1977, 16 ILM 1391 (1977), but not in the Protocol Additional to the Geneva Conventions of 12 August 1949, and Relating to the Protection of Victims of Non-International Armed Conflicts (Protocol II), opened for signature 12 Dec. 1977, 16 ILM 1442 (1977).

[81] Baxter has observed that '[t]he passage of humanitarian treaties into customary international law might . . . be justified on the ground that each new wave of such treaties builds upon the past conventions, so that each detailed rule of the Geneva Conventions for the Protection of War Victims is nothing more than an implementation of a more general standard already laid down in an earlier convention, such as the Regulations annexed to Convention No. IV of The Hague.' Baxter, *Multilateral Treaties as Evidence of Customary International Law*, 41 Brit. YB Int'l L. 275, 286 (1965-6).

[82] *Barcelona Traction, Light and Power Co., Ltd.* (*Belg.* v. *Spain*) (New Application), 1970 ICJ Rep. 3, 32 (Judgment of 5 Feb.).

[83] Condorelli and Boisson de Chazournes, above n. 80, at 27. For a discussion of practice, see ibid. at 26–9. For an example of invocation of Art. 1 by the ICRC, see Sandoz, *Appel du C.I.C.R. dans le cadre du conflit entre L'Irak et L'Iran*, 29 Annuaire français de droit international 161 (1983). More recent practice involving Art. 1 is discussed in Cassese, *Remarks on the Present Legal Regulation of Crimes of States*, in 3 International Law at the Time of its Codification: Essays in Honour of Roberto Ago 49, 57–61 (1987).

[84] UN Doc. S/19443 (21 Jan. 1988).

of Israel to apply Geneva Convention No. IV in the occupied territories.[85]

While almost all states are parties to the Geneva Conventions, the practice of states parties may merely indicate that certain states are complying with their treaty obligation 'to ensure respect' for the Conventions. As the ICJ observed in the *North Sea Continental Shelf Cases*, little support for the customary law nature of the norms implicated may be found in the conduct of parties that are 'acting actually or potentially in the application of [a] Convention'.[86] How state practice may be referred to apart from the Geneva Conventions is not obvious, given the universal acceptance of the Geneva Conventions as treaties. This difficulty will be considered in Section V below.

The reach of the duty 'to ensure respect' is not entirely clear. In addition to the obligation of the state to ensure that all of its organs observe the conventions, does it include not only the duty not to encourage third states to commit violations but also the duty actively to discourage them from such violations? Notwithstanding the Court's rather conclusory assessment of Article 1 as customary law, the Court's opinion that the United States may not encourage persons or groups engaged in the Nicaraguan conflict to act in violation of common Article 3 is indisputably correct as

---

[85] The Secretary-General stated: 'I recommend that the Security Council should consider making a solemn appeal to all the High Contracting Parties to the Fourth Geneva Convention that have diplomatic relations with Israel, drawing their attention to their obligation under article 1 of the Convention to ". . . ensure respect for the present Convention in all circumstances" and urging them to use all the means at their disposal to persuade the Government of Israel to change its position as regards the applicability of the Convention.' Ibid. at 10.

[86] *North Sea Continental Shelf Cases*, 1969 ICJ Rep. at 43. Baxter has observed that the Court 'quite properly looked exclusively to the conduct of non-parties in attempting to determine whether the treaty, in its law-creating aspect, was binding on all nations'. Baxter, above n. 28, at 64. See also Bos, *The Identification of Custom in International Law*, 25 Ger. YB Int'l L. 9, 27–8 (1982).

On treaties and custom, see A. D'Amato, The Concept of Custom in International Law 103–8, 160–4 (1971); H. Thirlway, International Customary Law and Codification 80–94 (1972); Akehurst, above n. 23, at 1; Sohn, *The Law of the Sea: Customary International Law Developments*, 34 Am. U. L. Rev. 271 (1985). For a reply to Sohn, see Charney, *International Agreements and the Development of Customary International Law*, 61 Wash. L. Rev. 971 (1986). See also Sohn, *Unratified Treaties as a Source of Customary International Law*, in Realism in Law-Making: Essays on International Law in Honor of Willem Riphagen 231 (A. Bos and H. Siblesz eds. 1986); Sohn, *"Generally Accepted" International Rules*, 61 Wash. L. Rev. 1073 (1986). On customary human rights and treaties, see A. D'Amato, International Law: Process and Prospect 123–47 (1987).

a matter of conventional obligations. The principles of good faith and of *pacta sunt servanda*,[87] which have deep historical and jurisprudential roots in international law, impose on the United States not only a duty to perform its own obligations as a party to the Conventions (*viz.* the duty 'to respect' in the language of Article 1), but also a duty not to encourage others to violate common Article 3. Beyond this negative duty, the fundamental obligation implies that each state must exert efforts to ensure that no violations of the applicable provisions of humanitarian law (i.e. 'to ensure respect') are committted, at the very least by third parties controlled by that state.

The duty not to encourage violations finds strong additional support in the *erga omnes* character of the humanitarian norms implicated. Undeniably, the Geneva Conventions, and especially common Article 3, state a great number of basic rights of the human person. Some of these (e.g. the prohibitions of murder, mutilation, and torture, mentioned in Article 3(1)(a)) have attained the status of *jus cogens*.[88] Whether such rights are peremptory or not, under *Barcelona Traction*, 'all States can be held to have a legal interest in their protection; they are obligations *erga omnes*.'[89] The *Barcelona* Court appeared to suggest that this is true both of norms accepted into the corpus of general international law and of those incorporated into instruments of a universal or quasi-universal character. The Geneva Conventions, of course, fall into the latter category. The *erga omnes* character of many of the norms in these Conventions implies that even states that are not specially affected have not only the right to make appropriate representations urging states allegedly involved in violating those norms to respect the norms concerned, but also a duty not to encourage others to violate the norms. Perhaps even a duty to discourage others from such violations may be implied. In so far as the norms concerned have the character of norms *erga omnes*, the words 'to ensure respect'

[87] See Art. 26 of the Vienna Convention on the Law of Treaties, above n. 20.
[88] See Meron, above n. 30, at 15. Although Condorelli and Boisson de Chazournes, above n. 80, at 33, appear to suggest that the whole of humanitarian law constitutes *jus cogens*, it is widely recognized that the Geneva Conventions are subject to reservations. See generally Pilloud, above n. 9. *Jus cogens* norms are discussed in Chapter III, Section VIII, below.
[89] 1970 ICJ Rep. at 32.

in common Article 1 may indeed reflect a principle of customary law.[90]

In considering common Article 3, which according to both its language and its legislative history applies to non-international armed conflicts but not to international armed conflicts, the Court briefly referred to the problem of how the Nicaraguan conflict should be characterized. The Court determined that the conflict between the contras and the government of Nicaragua was an armed conflict not of an international character. The acts of the contras against that government were therefore governed by the law applicable to non-international conflicts,[91] but 'the actions of the United States in and against Nicaragua fall under the legal rules relating to international conflicts.'[92] The Court went on to state that

Article 3 . . . defines certain rules to be applied in the armed conflicts of a non-international character. . . . [I]n the event of international armed conflicts, these rules also constitute a minimum yardstick, in addition to the more elaborate rules which are also to apply to international conflicts . . . they . . . reflect what the Court in 1949 called 'elementary considerations of humanity' (*Corfu Channel* . . .) . . ..

[90] See Abi-Saab, *The "General Principles" of Humanitarian Law According to the International Court of Justice*, Int'l Rev. Red Cross, No. 259, July–Aug. 1987, at 367, 374. Judge Schwebel, while questioning whether the delict of 'encouragement' exists in customary law, agreed that such encouragement may constitute a violation of the treaty obligation to 'ensure respect' for the Geneva Conventions. 1986 ICJ Rep. at 388–9 (Schwebel J. dissenting). His observations on customary law find support in the *Commentary* adopted by the ILC in 1978 on Art. 27 of its draft articles on state responsibility (part one). The ILC stated that '[i]n the international legal order . . . it is more than doubtful that mere incitement by a State of another State to commit a wrongful act is in itself an internationally wrongful act.' Report of the International Law Commission on the Work of its Thirtieth Session, 33 UN GAOR Supp. (No. 10) at 187, 244, UN Doc. A/33/10 (1978). It is less clear, however, whether the ILC intended to address humanitarian norms. See also Quigley, above n. 78.

[91] 1986 ICJ Rep. at 114.

[92] Ibid. on the characterization of conflicts in international humanitarian law, see Meron, *Inadequate Reach*, above n. 14, at 603; Schindler, *International Humanitarian Law and Internationalized Internal Armed Conflicts*, Int'l Rev. Red Cross, No. 230, Sept.–Oct. 1982, at 255, 258–61; Schindler, *The Different Types of Armed Conflicts According to the Geneva Conventions and Protocols*, 163 Recueil des cours 117 (1979–II); Baxter, *Jus in Bello Interno: The Present and Future Law*, in Law and Civil War in the Modern World 518, 523–4 (J. Moore ed. 1974); Gasser, *Internationalized Non-International Armed Conflicts: Case Studies of Afghanistan, Kampuchea, and Lebanon*, 33 Am. U. L. Rev. 145 (1983); Reisman and Silk, *Which Law Applies to the Afghan Conflict?*, 82 AJIL 459 (1988).

Because the minimum rules applicable to international and to non-international conflicts are identical, there is no need to address the question whether those actions must be looked at in the context of the rules which operate for the one or for the other category of conflict. The relevant principles are to be looked for in the provisions of Article 3 of each of the four Conventions of 12 August 1949, the text of which, identical in each Convention, expressly refers to conflicts not having an international character.[93]

The Court thus concluded that the core norms governing non-international armed conflicts were substantially the same as those applicable to international armed conflicts. Article 3, perceived as the 'minimum common denominator', therefore provided a rationale for not deciding whether those actions must be evaluated by the yardstick applicable to international or to non-international conflicts. This approach generates a number of questions.

Was the catalogue of protections set forth in common Article 3 ever meant to constitute the minimum core of protections applicable in international armed conflicts?[94] While Article 3 may well express the quintessence of humanitarian rules found in other substantive provisions of the Geneva Conventions that govern international armed conflicts, it is not certain that the rules of Article 3 and of these other provisions correspond perfectly, or that all of the norms stated in the latter provisions have necessarily attained the character of customary rules of international law. It is undoubtedly true, however, that the logic of the law requires that certain basic humanitarian principles (as well as an essential and non-derogable core of human rights) should be applicable in all situations involving violence of high intensity. In this sense, the Court's approach was entirely correct.

Article 3 has no antecedents in earlier Geneva Conventions and was clearly viewed in 1949 as marking a 'new step' in the

[93] 1986 ICJ Rep. at 114. For a view emphasizing the customary law character of common Art. 3, see Cassese, *The Geneva Protocols of 1977 on the Humanitarian Law of Armed Conflict and Customary International Law*, 3 UCLA Pac. Basin LJ 55, 68 (1984).

It may be regretted that the Geneva Conventions' definition of 'grave breaches' (Art. 50/51/130/147) does not cover violations of common Art. 3.

[94] Judge Baxter has aptly argued that the core of humanitarian law should be the same for all types of large-scale politically motivated violence. Cited in T. Meron, Human Rights in Internal Strife, above n. 14, at 138. The ICRC *Commentary* on Geneva Convention No. I emphasizes, however, that Art. 3 applies to non-international conflicts only. Above n. 79, at 48.

development of humanitarian law.[95] The ICRC *Commentary* on Geneva Convention No. I states that Article 3 demands respect for rules 'already recognized as essential in all civilized countries, and enacted in the municipal law of the States in question, long before the Convention was signed'.[96] True, some of the provisions of Article 3 are rooted in national legal systems. These, perhaps, might have been construed by the Court as 'general principles of law recognized by civilized nations', within the meaning of Article 38(1)(c) of its Statute. It is less clear, however, whether norms accepted by states in their national legal systems for normal situations apply equally to internal armed conflicts. Thus, an important study of Protocol II explains the deletion of a reference to the law of nations in the version of the Martens clause appearing in that Protocol as a reflection of some hesitancy about the extent to which customary international law applies to internal conflicts:

This [deletion of a reference to the law of nations] is justified by the fact that the attempt to establish rules for a non-international conflict only goes back to 1949 and that the application of common Art. 3 in the practice of States has not developed in such a way that one could speak of 'established custom' regarding non-international conflicts.[97]

I believe that the norms stated in Article 3(1)(a)–(c)[98] are of such an elementary, ethical character, and echo so many provisions in other humanitarian and human rights treaties, that they must be regarded as embodying minimum standards of customary law also applicable to non-international armed conflicts. This is also true for the obligation to treat humanely persons who are *hors de combat*, which is rooted in Hague Regulations 23(c)–(d), which undoubtedly reflect customary law, and in the customary obligation contained in the law of human rights to treat with humanity all persons deprived of their liberty. I consider at least the core due process principle stated in Article 3(1)(d)[99] (discussed further

---

[95] *Commentary* on Geneva Convention No. I, above n. 79, at 38, 41.

[96] Ibid. at 50. See also ibid. at 60.

[97] M. Bothe, K. Partsch, and W. Solf, New Rules for Victims of Armed Conflicts 620 (1982). See also below n. 127.

[98] For the text of Art. 3, see above n. 74.

[99] The *Commentary* on Convention No. IV, above n. 79, at 616, traces the roots of common Art. 3(1)(d) to Hague Regulation 30, which provides that a spy shall not be punished without previous trial. The *Commentary* further suggests that, although Art. 3 applies only to non-international armed conflicts, it 'contains rules of absolutely general application [confirmed by the due process provisions of] Article 5 and Articles 64–76'. See Convention Respecting the Laws and Customs

in Chapter II, Section I, below), to embody customary law, notwithstanding a recent authoritative enumeration of customary human rights which does not list due process of law.[100]

The norms specified in Article 3 have an indisputably humanitarian character, but elementary considerations of humanity may not necessarily have attained the status of already crystallized customary law. Elementary considerations of humanity reflect basic community values whether already crystallized as binding norms of international law or not. Professor Brownlie has observed that '[c]onsiderations of humanity may depend on the subjective appreciation of the judge, but, more objectively, they may be related to human values already protected by positive legal principles which, taken together, reveal certain criteria of public policy. . . .'[101] The fact that the content of a norm reflects important considerations of humanity should promote its acceptance as customary law. Thus, in explaining why the Geneva Conventions can be regarded as approaching 'international legislation', Sir Hersch Lauterpacht stated that, among other reasons, 'many of the provisions of these Conventions, following as they do from compelling considerations of humanity, are declaratory of universally binding international custom.'[102]

That principles of humanity form a part of the law of war is confirmed by the authoritative field manual of the US Army: '[t]he law of war . . . requires that belligerents . . . conduct hostilities with regard for the principles of humanity and chivalry.'[103] The British Manual of Military Law recognizes the same principles.[104] Even in the US armed services, however, consensus on the specific duties derivable from the principles of humanity has been difficult to obtain. For example, another publication, which was intended to provide reference material for the military lawyer but did not

of War on Land, with Annex of Regulations (Hague Convention No. IV), signed 18 Oct. 1907, 36 Stat. 2277; TS 539; 1 Bevans 631.

[100] Restatement, above n. 17, § 702.

[101] I. Brownlie, Principles of Public International Law 29 (3rd edn. 1979). See also Abi-Saab, above n. 90, at 370-1.

[102] 1 H. Lauterpacht, International Law: Collected papers 115 (E. Lauterpacht ed. 1970).

[103] US Dep't of the Army, The Law of Land Warfare 3 (Field Manual No. 27-10, 1956).

[104] The War Office, the Law of War on Land being Part III of the Manual of Military Law 1-2 (1958).

purport to promulgate policy for the Department of the Army, emphasized that the Martens clause[105]

is characteristic of the generality of such principles of international law. Such a phrase is difficult to apply in practice. Specific obligations resulting from 'the laws of humanity . . .' are extremely difficult to agree upon. . . . Such broad phrases in international law are in reality a reliance upon moral law and public opinion.[106]

In contrast, a US Air Force publication, in a statement similarly prepared only for reference purposes, attributed to the principle of humanity such basic norms as the prohibition of the infliction of injury or destruction not actually necessary for the accomplishment of legitimate military purposes, and the prohibition against causing unnecessary suffering. The publication stated that the principles of humanity spawned the requirement of proportionality and confirmed the basic immunity of civilian populations and civilians from attack during armed conflict.[107] Although these rules were formulated at a high level of generality, they are of major importance for humanitarian law and can be regarded as legitimate offspring of the principles of humanity.

The *Nicaragua* Court's discussion of the Geneva Conventions is remarkable, indeed, for its complete failure to inquire whether *opinio juris* and practice support the crystallization of Articles 1 and 3 into customary law. Doubts about the Court's position regarding Articles 1 and 3 were expressed by judges as eminent as Sir Robert Jennings and Roberto Ago.[108] Moreover, the parties to the Geneva Conventions have built a poor record of compliance

[105] See below n. 127 and accompanying text.

[106] US Dep't of the Army, 2 International Law 15 (Pamphlet No. 27-161-2, 1962).

[107] US Dep't of the Air Force, International Law—The Conduct of Armed Conflict and Air Operations 1-6 (Pamphlet 110-31, 1976).

[108] Judge Jennings stated that there must be at least very serious doubts whether the Geneva Conventions could be regarded as embodying customary law and that the Court's view of Art. 3 'is not a matter free from difficulty'. 1986 ICJ Rep. at 537 (Jennings J. dissenting). Judge Ago observed that he was 'most ruluctant to be persuaded that any broad identity of content exists between the Geneva Conventions and certain "fundamental general principles of humanitarian law", which, according to the Court, were pre-existent in customary law, to which the Conventions "merely give expression" (para. 220) or of which they are at most "in some respects a development" (para. 218).' 1986 ICJ Rep. at 184 (Ago J. sep. op.). See generally Charney, *Customary International Law in the Nicaragua Case Judgment on the Merits*, Hague YB Int'l L. 16 (1988).

with the norms stated in Article 3,[109] and evidence of practice by non-parties is lacking. Nevertheless, it is not so much the Court's attribution of customary law character to both Articles 1 and 3 of the Geneva Conventions that merits criticism. Rather, the Court should be reproached for its near silence concerning the evidence and reasoning supporting this conclusion.

Despite the Court's pronouncements on Articles 1 and 3, the status of the Geneva Conventions remains very much as it was prior to the judgment. As in the past, the determination to which category—customary or conventional—a particular provision belongs must be made *in concreto*.

To characterize Articles 1 and 3 of the Geneva Conventions as customary law in the absence of practice dehors the Geneva Conventions, the ICJ must have both taken into account the practice of states parties to the Conventions and assessed that practice as being in substantial conformity with the Conventions. Perhaps the judgment will be invoked in support of claims to lighten the burden of proof necessary to establish the customary law character of a particular provision of the Conventions because of their humanitarian content. In this sense, the Court's judgment promotes valuable ethical considerations mentioned in Section I above, and contributes to the transformation of certain provisions into customary law.

IV. THE ANTECEDENTS TO *NICARAGUA*

The Court should not be singled out for criticism for its conclusory treatment of certain provisions of the Geneva Conventions as customary law without discussing the supporting evidence or the process by which the Conventions might be transformed into customary law. Military manuals of leading powers, such as the

---

[109] See T. Meron, above n. 14, at 43-4, 47; Obradović, *Que faire face aux violations du droit humanitaire? Quelques Réflexions sur le rôle possible du CICR*, in Swinarski (ed.), above n. 5, at 483; Farer, *Humanitarian Law and Armed Conflicts: Toward the Definition of "International Armed Conflict"*, 71 Colum. L. Rev. 37, 52–61 (1971). See also below n. 165.

United States[110] and the United Kingdom,[111] have not attempted to identify those provisions of the Geneva Conventions which are declaratory of customary international law. The few international judicial decisions on international humanitarian law reveal little, if any, inquiry into the process by which particular instruments have been transformed into customary law.

The leading case on the Hague Regulations of 1907 is the judgment of the International Military Tribunal (IMT) for the *Trial of German Major War Criminals* (Nuremberg, 1946). The argument was raised that Hague Convention No. IV did not apply because of the general participation (*si omnes*) clause—several of the belligerents not being parties to the Convention. In response, the IMT apparently acknowledged that at the time the Regulations were adopted the participating states believed that they were making new law: '[b]ut by 1939 these rules laid down in the Convention were recognised by all civilised nations, and were regarded as being declaratory of the laws and customs of war'.[112] The IMT did not even discuss the process by which the Hague Regulations had metamorphosed from conventional into customary law. The Tribunal's language (the use of the word 'regarded') suggests that the Tribunal may have looked primarily at the *opinio juris*, rather than at the actual practice of states.

Similarly, although more cautiously, the International Military Tribunal for the Far East (1948) characterized Hague Convention No. IV 'as good evidence of the customary law of nations, to be considered by the Tribunal along with all other available evidence in determining the customary law to be applied in any given

[110] The US Army manual states that the Regulations Respecting the Laws and Customs of War on Land annexed to the Hague Convention No. IV, above n. 99, and the 'general principles' of the (Geneva) Prisoners of War Convention, above n. 80, 'have been held to be declaratory of the customary law of war, to which all States are subject'. The manual observes that provisions of law-making treaties regarding the conduct of warfare 'are in large part but formal and specific applications of general principles of unwritten law'. US Dep't of the Army, The Law of Land Warfare 6 (Field Manual No. 27-10, 1956). See also 2 US Dep't of the Army, International Law 249 (Pamphlet No. 27-161-2, 1962).

[111] The War Office, The Law of War on Land being Part III of the Manual of Military Law 1, 4 (1958). The manual regards the Hague Regulations as embodying rules of customary international law. Ibid. at 4. See also Report of the Secretary-General on Respect for Human Rights in Armed Conflicts, UN Doc. A/7720, at 22 (1969).

[112] *Trial of German Major War Criminals*, 1946, Cmd. 6964, Misc. No. 12, at 65.

situation'.[113] This Tribunal, in contrast to the IMT, did not view the entirety of the Hague Regulations as necessarily an accurate mirror of customary law.

The most interesting case on the relationship between custom and treaty in the context of the Geneva Conventions is *United States* v. *von Leeb* ('The High Command Case').[114] The IMT judgment focused on the significance of the *si omnes* clause in Hague Convention No. IV 32 years after its adoption. In contrast, *von Leeb* principally concerned whether and to what extent the 1929 Geneva Prisoners of War Convention could be binding on Nazi Germany *vis-à-vis* the Soviet Union, which was not a party to the Convention, regarding actions stemming from the Nazi invasion of the USSR only 12 years after the convention was adopted.

In *von Leeb*, the Nuremberg Tribunal endorsed the principle applied by the IMT with regard to the Hague Regulations, extrapolating from that principle to the 1929 Convention. The Tribunal noted:

[I]t would appear that the IMT . . . followed the same lines of thought with regard to the Geneva Convention as with respect to the Hague Convention to the effect that they were binding insofar as they were in substance an expression of international law as accepted by the civilized nations of the world, and this Tribunal adopts this viewpoint. . . .
Most of the provisions of the Hague and Geneva Conventions, considered in substance, are clearly an expression of the accepted views of civilized nations and binding upon Germany and the defendants on trial before us in the conduct of the war against Russia.[115]

[113] *In re Hirota*, 15 Ann. Dig. 356, 366. The Tribunal stated that 'acts of inhumanity to prisoners which are forbidden by the customary law of nations as well as by conventions are to be prevented by the Government having responsibility for the prisoners.' Ibid.

[114] 11 Trials of War Criminals before the Nuernberg Military Tribunals under Control Council Law No. 10, at 462 (1948) (hereinafter cited as Trials of War Criminals).

[115] Ibid. at 534-5. The Nuernberg Tribunal cited with approval Admiral Canaris's remarkable protest against the German regulations for the treatment of Soviet prisoners of war. His protest stated that the regulations were based on a 'fundamentally different viewpoint' from that underlying the principles of international law: 'Since the 18th century these have gradually been established along the lines that war captivity is neither revenge nor punishment, but solely protective custody, the only purpose of which is to prevent the prisoners of war from further participation in the war.' The admiral concluded that while the Geneva Convention was not binding on Germany *vis-à-vis* the Soviet Union, the principles of international law on the treatment of prisoners were. Ibid. at 533.

While admitting that 'certain detailed provisions pertaining to the care and treatment of prisoners of war' could be binding only as conventional law,[116] the Tribunal cited as customary law five provisions of the 1907 Hague Regulations and nineteen provisions of the 1929 Geneva Convention, even including a provision, Article 9, requiring that '[p]risoners captured in unhealthful regions or where the climate is injurious for persons coming from temperate regions, shall be transported, as soon as possible, to a more favourable climate.' Some of the provisions of the Geneva Convention listed by the Tribunal ranged far beyond the few short principles stated in the Hague Regulations. The Tribunal did not address the process by which those provisions of the Geneva Convention that did not echo the provisions of the Hague Regulations had been transformed in just a few years into customary law.

The Tribunal was similarly silent concerning the rationale for determining which provisions were part of customary law. Baxter observed that '[a] rough-and-ready distinction may be discerned between those safeguards that are essential to the survival of the prisoner, on the one hand, and those protections that are not basic or which give depth to or implement the essential principles.'[117] He acknowledged, however, that that line is not rigorously observed. The Tribunal did refer to the Soviet Union's practice of using German POWs to construct fortifications during the war as 'evidence given to the interpretation of what constituted accepted use of prisoners of war under international law'.[118]

In another case, involving the defence of superior orders and thus unrelated to the Geneva Convention, the Tribunal noted that the recognition by states of such a defence in their manuals of military law was not a competent source of international law but might have evidentiary value.[119] This position appears to have been

116 Ibid. at 535.
117 Baxter, above n. 81, at 282.
118 *Von Leeb*, above n. 114, at 534. The Tribunal concluded that because of the 'uncertainty of international law . . . orders providing for . . . use [of prisoners of war in the construction of fortifications outside of] dangerous areas, were not criminal upon their face . . .'. Ibid.
119 'We point out that army regulations are not a competent source of international law. They are neither legislative nor judicial pronouncements. . . . [But] it is possible . . . that such regulations, as they bear upon a question of custom and practice in the conduct of war, might have evidentiary value, particularly if the applicable portions had been put into general practice. It will be observed that the

supported by an understandable reluctance to accept the defence of superior orders from German officers. Generally, however, given the difficulty of ascertaining significant state practice in periods of hostilities, manuals of military law and national legislation providing for the implementation of humanitarian law norms as internal law should be accepted as among the best types of evidence of such practice, and sometimes as statements of *opinio juris* as well. This is especially so because military manuals frequently not only state government policy but establish obligations binding on members of the armed forces, violations of which are punishable under military penal codes. For states, manuals create mutual expectations of compliance and many of the rules stated therein are good evidence of customary law.[120] Of course, the practice of states is also reflected in the adoption of such international instruments as normative declarations and, especially, in the multilateral treaty, which 'constitutes an expression of their attitude toward customary international law, to be weighed together with all other consistent and inconsistent evidence of the state of customary international law'.[121]

V. GENEVA CONVENTIONS: ASSESSING PRACTICE, *OPINIO JURIS* AND VIOLATIONS

Only a few international judicial decisions discuss the customary law nature of international humanitarian law instruments. These decisions nevertheless highlight certain trends in this area, including the tendencies to ignore, for the most part, the availability of evidence concerning state practice scant as it may have been, and to assume that humanitarian principles deserving recognition as the positive law of the international community have in fact been

determination, whether a custom or practice exists, is a question of fact.' *United States* v. *List*, above n. 114, at 1230, 1237.

The US field manual, above n. 103, at 3 (referring to the black-letter text), states that its purpose 'is to provide authoritative guidance to military personnel on the customary and treaty law applicable to the conduct of warfare on land and to relationships between belligerents and neutral States'. I agree with Baxter that such manuals provide 'telling evidence' of the practice of states. Baxter, above n. 81, at 283.

[120] Gasser, *Customary Law and Additional Protocol I to the Geneva Conventions for the Protection of War Victims: Future Directions in Light of the U.S. Decision not to Ratify*, 81 ASIL PROC. 31, 33 (1989).

[121] Baxter, above n. 28, at 52. For other evidence of state practice, see also the US field manual, above n. 103, at 6.

recognized as such by states. The 'ought' merges with the 'is', the *lex ferenda* with the *lex lata*. The teleological desire to solidify the humanizing content of the humanitarian norms clearly affects the judicial attitudes underlying the 'legislative' character of the judicial process. Given the scarcity of actual practice, it may well be that tribunals have been guided, and may continue to be guided, by the degree to which certain acts are offensive to human dignity. The more heinous the act, the more willing the tribunal will be to assume that it violates not only a moral principle of humanity but also a positive norm of customary law.

Although the Court in the *Nicaragua* case did not discuss the formation of customary law in the direct context of the Geneva Conventions, the method adopted there cannot but influence future consideration of customary law in various fields of international law, including the Geneva Conventions. Having posed all the traditional, correct questions regarding the existence of actual practice and the *opinio juris*, the Court made only perfunctory and conclusory references to the practice of states. Despite the variety of reasons which impel states to adopt their respective positions in international fora, the Court found *opinio juris* in verbal statements of governmental representatives to international organizations, in the content of resolutions, declarations, and other normative instruments adopted by such organizations, and in the consent of states to such instruments. This approach, which has important antecedents,[122] is not without doctrinal support. A scholar as respected as Judge Baxter has argued that

---

[122] 1896 ICJ Rep. at 98–108. The Court's approach has significant antecedents in earlier cases. See *Legal Consequences for States of the Continued Presence of South Africa in Namibia* (*South West Africa*) *Notwithstanding Security Council Resolution 276* (*1970*), 1971 ICJ Rep. 16, 31–2 (Advisory Opinion of 21 June); *Western Sahara*, 1975 ICJ Rep. 12, 30–7 (Advisory Opinion of 16 Oct.). See also Chapter II, Section II, below.

In discussing the Court's view (expressed in the *Nicaragua* case) that 'voting for a norm-declaring resolution is an exercise in *opinio juris*', Professor Franck warns that '[t]he effect of this enlarged concept of the lawmaking force of General Assembly resolutions may well be to caution states to vote against "aspirational" instruments if they do not intend to embrace them totally and at once, regardless of circumstance. That would be unfortunate. Aspirational resolutions have long occupied, however uncomfortably, a twilight zone between "hard" treaty law and the normative void.' Franck, *Some Observations on the ICJ's Procedural and Substantive Innovations*, 81 AJIL 116, 119 (1987).

A tendency similar to that of the ICJ can be found also in decisions of national courts on the customary law of human rights: e.g. in the emphasis by Judge Kaufman on international and domestic normative instruments prohibiting torture,

[t]he actual conduct of States in their relations with other nations is only a subsidiary means whereby the rules which guide the conduct of States are ascertained. The firm statement by the State of what it considers to be the rule is far better evidence of its position than what can be pieced together from the actions of that country at different times and in a variety of contexts.[123]

Despite perplexity over the reasoning and, at times, the conclusions of a tribunal, both states and scholarly opinion in general will accept judicial decisions confirming the customary law character of some of the provisions of the Geneva Conventions as authoritative statements of the law. Eventually, the focus of attention will shift from the inquiry into whether certain provisions reflect customary law to the conclusions of judicial decisions establishing that status.

As far as law-making is concerned, the starting-point is, of course, the practice of states. Yet in non-codifying multilateral treaties even outside the humanitarian law field, norms and values that differ from the actual practice of states are commonly asserted. For human rights or humanitarian conventions—i.e. conventions whose object is to humanize the behaviour of states, groups, and persons—the gap between the norms stated and actual practice tends to be especially wide.

The law-making process does not merely 'photograph' or declare the current state of international practice. Far from it. Rather, the law-making process attempts to articulate and emphasize norms and values that, in the judgment of some states, deserve promotion

on government statements, and on scholarly opinion, in *Filartiga* v. *Peña-Irala*, 630 F. 2d 876 (2d Cir. 1980), in the focus on normative instruments to determine the prohibition in international customary law of arbitrary detention, *Rodriguez-Fernandez* v. *Wilkinson*, 505 F. Supp. 787, 796-800 (D. Kan. 1980), *aff'd on other grounds*, 654 F. 2d 1382 (10th Cir. 1981), and in the discussion of the principle of diplomatic immunity (in the case of Raoul Wallenberg), *Von Dardel* v. *Union of Soviet Socialist Republics*, 623 F. Supp. 246, 261 (DDC 1985). Cf. Schachter's list of types of evidence adduced to support a finding that a particular human right is a part of customary law, *International Law in Theory and Practice*, 178 Recueil des cours 11, 334-5 (1982-V). See also Schrader, *Custom and General Principles as Sources of International Law in American Federal Courts*, 82 Colum. L. Rev. 751, 762-8 (1982). On practice creating customary human rights, see also Restatement, above n. 17, at §701, Reporters' note 2. See also Gerstel and Segall, *Conference Report: Human Rights in American Courts*, 1 Am. U. J. Int'l L. & Pol. 137, 162 and nn. 79-80 (1986). *For a critique of Filartiga and Rodriguez-Fernandez*, see Oliver, *Problems of Cognition and Interpretation in Applying Norms of Customary International Law of Human Rights in United States Courts*, 4 Hous. J. Int'l L. 59, 60 (1981). See also below Chapter II, Section III.

[123] Baxter, above n. 81, at 300.

and acceptance by all states, in order to establish a code for the better conduct of nations.[124] This applies in particular to instruments designed to humanize the behaviour of states in armed conflict, which is characterized by violence and violations, by the necessity of committing acts frequently not preceded by careful deliberation, by exceptional conditions, by limited third-party access to the theatre of operations, and by the parties' conflicting factual and legal justifications for their conduct. Because of these circumstances, humanitarian conventions may have lesser prospects for actual compliance than other multilateral treaties, even though they enjoy stronger moral support. Consequently, in the violent situations addressed by the humanitarian conventions, the gulf between the more enlightened norms and the actual practice of states may, to some extent, be expected to remain formidable. With regard to humanitarian instruments, the international community expects neither strict nor immediate compliance with the stated norms. Because of the requirements or perceptions of security, states are willing to accept gradual and partial compliance as fulfilling the requirements for the formation of customary law.

Far from codifying the actual behaviour of states or the mores of the international community, law-making conferences try to promulgate more protective rules of conduct,[125] stretching the consensus of the negotiating states as widely as possible. As a mixture of actual and desired practice, humanitarian instruments may thus reflect deliberate ambiguity, designed to encourage broader compliance with the stated norms and to promote the greatest possible acceptance of the norms as the general law of the international community. In the creation of international humanitarian law, the teleological component of *lex ferenda* is especially important, though often deliberately downplayed. The sound judgment of the 'legislators' and the distance between the

---

[124] Meron, *The Meaning and Reach of the International Convention on the Elimination of All Forms of Racial Discrimination*, 79 AJIL 283, 317-18 (1985).

[125] The Preamble to Hague Convention No. IV, above n. 99, expresses this approach with rare candour:

'Animated by the desire to serve, even in this extreme case, the interests of humanity and the ever progressive needs of civilization;

Thinking it important, with this object, to revise the general laws and customs of war . . . confining them within such limits as would contain their severity as far as possible;

[I]nspired by the desire to diminish the evils of war, as far as military requirements permit. . . .'

'is' and the 'ought to be' determine whether a particular instrument will raise the expectations of the international community, will be accepted in practice as the living, binding general law of the international community, or will become marginal or even fall eventually into desuetude.

In discussing the customary law character of the Geneva Conventions, two questions merit consideration. The first pertains to the status of the Conventions as declaratory of customary law at the time of their adoption, the second to the subsequent passage into customary law of norms stated in the Conventions.

As regards the first question, a further distinction is perhaps necessary. Most of the substantive provisions of Conventions Nos. I, II, and III are based on earlier Geneva Conventions, and thus have a strong claim to customary law status. Geneva Convention No. IV, in contrast, was the first Geneva Convention ever to be addressed to the protection of civilians. A product of the universal condemnation of the Nazis' treatment of civilians in occupied Europe during the Second World War, the Convention is rooted only in the few provisions on the treatment of civilians in combat zones and occupied territories found in Articles 23, 25, 27, 28, 42–56 of the Hague Regulations. The ICRC *Commentary* on Article 154 of Geneva Convention No. IV demonstrates, however, that the Convention repeats the bulk of the Hague Regulations relating to the protection of civilian persons.[126] Although in their range and depth, some of the provisions in the Geneva Convention No. IV retain only an attenuated link with the brief and fairly primitive Hague Regulations, I believe that the Hague Regulations can provide the foundation for building the customary law content of this Convention. Those involving procedures and implementation lack any such antecedents.

Nevertheless, because some provisions of Conventions Nos. I–III formed new, conventional law, and some provisions of Convention No. IV reflected customary law (e.g. the principle of protection of the physical and mental integrity of civilians, and of

---

[126] *Commentary* on Geneva Convention No. IV, above n. 79, at 620. Regarding the antecedents of Geneva Conventions Nos. I–II, see Dinstein, *Human Rights in Armed Conflict: International Humanitarian Law*, in 2 Human Rights in International Law: Legal and Policy Issues 345, 346 (T. Meron ed. 1984).

However, as regards protection of private property, the Hague Regulations provide the basic principles, while Geneva Convention No. IV states a number of supplementary rules.

sick and wounded), the significant difference between the former Conventions and Convention No. IV is quantitative, not qualitative. All of the Conventions contain a core of principles (e.g. the Martens clause)[127] that express customary law. Of course, the identification of the various provisions as customary or conventional law presents the greatest difficulties. Neither international practice nor scholarly studies provide a comprehensive foundation for identifying those rules in Geneva Convention No. IV which are declaratory of pre-existing customary law. Only an overconfident commentator would try to identify all the customary norms embodied in Geneva Convention No. IV. Nevertheless, a tentative attempt to identify some examples of such rules may be worthwhile. The relationship of the provisions of the Geneva Conventions to the Hague Regulations provides a rational guideline for such a survey.

In my opinion, the following partial list of Geneva Convention No. IV provisions exemplifies norms of which the cores, although not necessarily the specific language and details, embody customary

---

[127] See Strebel, *Martens' Clause*, [Instalment] 3 Encyclopedia of Public International Law 252 (R. Bernhardt ed. 1982); F. Kalshoven, Constraints on the Waging of War 14-15 (1987). The Martens clause reads as follows: 'Until a more complete code of the laws of war has been issued, the High Contracting Parties deem it expedient to declare that, in cases not included in the Regulations adopted by them, the inhabitants and the belligerents remain under the protection and the rule of the principles of the law of nations, as they result from the usages established among civilized peoples, from the laws of humanity, and the dictates of the public conscience.'

The Martens clause appears also, in modified form, in the common Article on the denunciation of Geneva Conventions (63/62/142/158); in Art. 1(2) of Protocol I, above n. 80; in the Preamble to Protocol II, above n. 80; and in the Preamble to the Convention on Prohibitions or Restrictions on the the Use of Certain Conventional Weapons which may be Deemed to be Excessively Injurious or to Have Indiscriminate Effects, opened for signature 10 Apr. 1981, UN Doc. A/CONF.95/15 (1980), reprinted in 19 ILM 1524 (1980).

On the Martens clause and the principles of humanity, see above nn. 101-7 and the accompanying text.

In 'the *Krupp Case*', the Martens clause was described as much more than a pious declaration:

'It is a general clause, making the usages established among civilized nations, the laws of humanity, and the dictates of public conscience into the legal yardstick to be applied if and when the specific provisions of the Convention and the Regulations annexed to it do not cover specific cases occurring in warfare, or concomitant to warfare.' *United States* v. *Krupp von Bohlen und Halbach* (Case 10, Military Tribunal III), 9 Trials of War Criminals at 1341.

Professor Dinstein highlights the 'innovations' in Art. 118 of the Geneva Convention No. III. Dinstein, *The Release of Prisoners of War*, in Swinarski (ed.), above n. 5, at 37, 44.

law: The prohibition of destruction of property, set forth in Article 53, which originates in Hague Regulations 23(g) and 46 and which may be related to the prohibition of collective penalties in Hague Regulation 50; the prohibition of enlistment and of certain types of labour of protected persons which are in conflict with their allegiance to the ousted sovereign, stated in Article 51, which is grounded in Hague Regulations 23(h) and 52; the prohibition of coercion stated in Article 31 which is derived from Hague Regulation 44 and Hague Regulation 23(h); the prohibition of murder, torture, corporal punishment, mutilation, and other measures of brutality, stated in Article 32, which is implicit in Hague Regulation 46[128] and reflects reaction to treatment of civilians by Nazi authorities during World War II; the right of protected persons to enjoy respect for their persons, honour, family rights, religious convictions and practices stated in Article 27, which is clearly derived from the Hague Regulation 46; the protection of civilian hospitals and of their personnel, set forth in Articles 18 and 20, which is rooted in the Hague Regulation 27; the prohibition of pillage, stated in Article 33, which is based on the Hague Regulations 28 and 47; the prohibitions of collective punishment, intimidation, and terrorism, and of reprisals (further discussed in Chapter III, Section XI) against protected persons and their property set forth in Article 33, which have their roots in Hague Regulation 46 and Hague Regulation 50 and the principle of individual responsibility which Regulation 50 articulates; the absolute prohibition of the taking of hostages, stated in Article 34, which may be related to the prohibition of collective penalties stated in Hague Regulation 50 and the principle of individual responsibility which underlies it. In addition to the prohibition upon the taking of hostages in international humanitarian law instruments (e.g. common Article 3 of the Geneva Conventions, Article 75(2)(c) of Protocol I and Article 4(2)(c) of Protocol II), the taking of hostages has been solemnly prohibited by the International Convention Against the Taking of Hostages, which was adopted by the UN General Assembly on 17 December 1979, and by other authoritative statements, such as treaties criminalizing hijacking of aircraft and resolutions condemning hostage-taking. I would, therefore, submit

[128] Art. 46 reads as follows: '[f]amily honour and rights, the lives of persons, and private property, as well as religious convictions and practice, must be respected . . .'.

that the norm tracking the prohibition stated in Article 1 of the Convention of 17 December 1979 is maturing into customary humanitarian and human rights law. More directly, the prohibition of hostage-taking is a result of the international community's revulsion over the Nazi practice of taking and killing hostages and the crystallization, by the time the Geneva Conventions were adopted, and since then under the influence of the evolving human rights law, of a universal *opinio juris* assessing this inhuman practice as unlawful. Hostage-taking is clearly contrary to the natural right of the human person not to be made responsible for acts which he or she did not commit.[129]

Article 49 of Geneva Convention No. IV, which prohibits, among other things, '[i]ndividual or mass forcible transfers [and] deportations of protected persons from occupied territory to the territory of the Occupying Power or to that of any other country ... regardless of their motive', has no antecedents in the Hague Regulations. Nevertheless, the ICRC *Commentary* to that Convention argues, on the basis of post-World War II trials of German war criminals, that the prohibition of deportations   has been 'embodied in international law.'[130] I believe that at least the central elements of Article 49(1), such as the absolute prohibitions of forcible mass and individual transfers and deportations of protected persons from occupied territories stated in Article 49(1), are declaratory of customary law even when the object and setting of the deportations differ from those underlying German World War II practices which led to the rule set forth in Article 49.[131] Although

---

[129] *Commentary* on Geneva Convention No. IV, above n. 79, at 231. The UN Commission on Human Rights affirmed that the taking of hostages constitutes a grave violation of human rights and censured 'the actions of all persons responsible'. Res. 1988/38, UN ESCOR Supp. (No. 2) 97–8, UN Doc. E/1988/12, E/CN.4/1988/88. See also the International Convention against the Taking of Hostages, GA Res. 345/146, 34 UN GAOR Supp. (No. 46) at 245, UN Doc. A/34/46 (1980).

[130] *Commentary* on Geneva Convention No. IV, above n. 79, at 279 and n. 3.

[131] Cohn, above n. 5 and Dinstein, above n. 5, discuss the controversy concerning the customary law content of Art. 49. In several decisions (most recently in High Court of Justice Dec. 785/87, 845/87, 27/88, of 10 Apr. 1988) the Israel Supreme Court asserted that Art. 49 was not intended to prohibit deportation of individuals on security grounds from occupied territories and that it does not embody principles of customary law. In the decision of 4 Apr. 1988 (High Court of Justice Dec. 785/87, 845/87, 27/88), Mr Meir Shamgar, the President of the Supreme Court, supported by the majority of the Court, asserted that, as a matter of treaty interpretation, Art. 49 prohibited only such, especially collective, deportations as are carried out for purposes similar to those underlying the deportations carried out by the Nazi authorities during World War II. He stated that individual,

it is less clear that individual deportation was already prohibited in 1949, I believe that this prohibition has by now come to reflect customary law.

Additionally, the core of the due process guarantees stated in Geneva Convention No. IV embodies norms constituting general principles of law. Thus, the principle *nullum crimen, nulla poena sine lege* (Article 65), the requirement that courts apply only those provisions of the applicable law 'which are in accordance with

security-motivated deportations were not prohibited by Art. 49. For an incisive criticism of this decision, see Dinstein, *Deportation from Administered Territories*, 13 Tel Aviv U. L. Rev. 403 (1988).

This interpretation of Art. 49 is, in my judgment, contrary to the rules of treaty-interpretation stated in the Vienna Convention on the Law of Treaties. Art. 31(1) of the Vienna Convention requires that a treaty be interpreted in good faith in accordance with the ordinary meaning to be given to its terms, etc. The language of Art. 49 is clear and categorical. It prohibits both individual and collective deportations, regardless of their motive. Recourse to supplementary means of interpretation (Article 32 of the Vienna Convention) was, therefore, not justified. In any event, the object and purpose of Geneva Convention No. IV, a humanitarian instrument *par excellence*, was not only to protect civilian populations against Nazi-type atrocities, but to provide the broadest possible humanitarian protection for civilian victims of future wars and occupations, with their ever-changing circumstances.

The opinion accepting the prohibition stated in Art. 49(1) as customary law finds further support in the virtually universal condemnation by the international community, reflecting *opinio juris*, of deportations from occupied territories and in the proscription of deportations of a citizen from his or her own country stated in international human rights instruments. See e.g. Arts. 12–13 of the Political Covenant and Art. 12 of the African Charter on Human and Peoples' Rights (which clearly imply such a prohibition); and Art. 3(1) of Protocol 4 to the European Convention and Art. 22(5) of the American Convention (which contain explicit prohibitions of such deportations).

Deportation is already prohibited by Art. 23 of Lieber's Code ('[p]rivate citizens are no longer murdered, enslaved, or carried off to distant parts . . .'). F. Lieber, Instructions for the Government of Armies of the United States in the Field (1863), originally published as General Orders No. 100, War Department, Adjutant General's Office, 24 Apr. 1863; reprinted in R. Hartigan, Lieber's Code and the Law of War 45–71 (1983). This Code has had a major influence on the drafting of national statutes and regulations pertaining to the law of war and of such treaties as Hague Convention No. IV and the Geneva Conventions and, of course, on the formation of customary law. The ICRC explains the silence of the Hague Regulations on the question of deportations by 'the practice of deporting persons . . . at the beginning of this century . . . having fallen into abeyance'. *Commentary* on Geneva Convention No. IV, above n. 79, at 279. It adds that the prohibition of deportations 'may be regarded to-day as having been embodied in international law.' (footnote omitted). Ibid. In *United States* v. *von Leeb*, above n. 114, at 603, the Tribunal observed that 'there is no international law that permits the deportation or the use of civilians against their will for other than on reasonable requisitions for the needs of the army, either within the area of the army or after deportation to rear areas or to the homeland of the occupying power.'

general principles of law, in particular the principle that the penalty shall be proportionate to the offence' (Article 67), and the rule stating that '[n]o sentence shall be pronounced by the competent courts of the Occupying Power except after a regular trial' (Article 71) are among provisions which the authoritative ICRC *Commentary* to these Articles of Geneva Convention No. IV considers as reflecting universally recognized legal principles and fundamental notions of justice recognized by all civilized nations. These due process provisions (due process guarantees are discussed also in Section III, above, and in Chapter II, Section I, below) therefore exemplify norms binding on states not only as treaty obligations but also as general principles of law (Article 38(1)(c) of the Statute of the ICJ).

Discussion of the second question, the development of the law of the Geneva Conventions since their adoption in 1949, should begin by noting their unparalleled success, as manifested by their acceptance as treaties by the entire international community. Because practically all the potential participants in creating customary law have become parties to the treaty, little evidence is available demonstrating that non-parties behave in accordance with the norms of the Conventions, and thereby create concordant customary law. The 'Baxter paradox' (Judge Baxter himself coined the term 'paradox' in this context) is in full blossom: 'As the number of parties to a treaty increases, it becomes more difficult to demonstrate what is the state of customary international law dehors the treaty. . . . As the express acceptance of the treaty increases, the number of States not parties whose practice is relevant diminishes. There will be less scope for the development of international law dehors the treaty. . . .'[132] In Baxter's opinion, the Geneva Conventions typify this phenomenon:

Now that an extremely large number of States have become parties to the Geneva Conventions . . . who can say what the legal obligations of combatants would be in the absence of the treaties? And if little or no customary international practice is generated by the non-parties, it becomes

[132] Baxter, above n. 28, at 64, 73. Charney points out: 'In cases where . . . widespread adherence to the agreement exists, substantial evidence of state actions taken in circumstances where the agreement is not directly applicable may be hard to obtain. As a consequence, support for new rules of customary law will have to be found in the agreement and in secondary evidence derived from writers, and perhaps in self-serving official state policy statements.' Charney, above n. 86, at 990.

virtually impossible to determine whether the treaty has indeed passed into customary international law.[133]

Does this suggest necessarily that the door is now closed to further creation of customary law regarding matters governed by the Geneva Conventions? I do not believe it does. In confronting this problem, it should be noted that Baxter's approach is supported principally by the judgment in the *North Sea Continental Shelf Cases*. The Court's denial that the practice of parties to a convention has evidentiary weight in the creation of customary law is striking in its brevity and categorical nature:

[O]ver half the States concerned, whether acting unilaterally or conjointly, were or shortly became parties to the Geneva Convention [on the Continental Shelf], and were therefore presumably . . . acting actually or potentially in the application of the Convention. From their action no inference could legitimately be drawn as to the existence of a rule of customary international law in favour of the equidistance principle.[134]

It is far from certain that the Court intended, in this context, to refer to universally accepted conventions, especially those of humanitarian character whose object is not so much the reciprocal exchange of rights and obligations among a limited number of states, as the protection of the human rights of individuals.[135] Significantly, the Court did allude briefly to the possibility of transforming widely accepted conventions into general law:

With respect to the other elements usually regarded as necessary before a conventional rule can be considered to have become a general rule of international law, it might be that, even without the passage of any

[133] Baxter, above n. 28, at 96. In the same vein, Judge Jennings observed in the *Nicaragua* case that 'there are obvious difficulties about extracting even a scintilla of relevant "practice" . . . from the behaviour of those few States which are not parties to the Charter; and the behaviour of all the rest, and the *opinio juris* which it might otherwise evidence, is surely explained by their being bound by the Charter itself.' 1986 ICJ Rep. at 531 (Jennings J. dissenting).

[134] 1969 ICJ Rep. at 43.

[135] See *The Effect of Reservations on the Entry into Force of the American Convention (Arts. 74 and 75)*, Advisory Opinion OC-2/82 of 24 Sept. 1982, Inter-American Court of Human Rights, Ser. A, Judgments and Opinions, No. 2, at 19–22 (1982); *Ireland v. United Kingdom*, 25 Eur. Ct. HR (Ser. A), para. 239 (1978); *Reservations to the Convention on Genocide*, 1951 ICJ Rep. 15, 23 (Advisory Opinion of 28 May); T. Meron, above n. 11, at 146–7.

considerable period of time, a very widespread and representative participation in the convention might suffice of itself, provided it included that of States whose interests were specially affected.[136]

It is unfortunate that the Court did not elaborate on this statement. This statement suggests, perhaps, why the 'Baxter paradox' does not present an unsurmountable obstacle to the maturation into customary law of rules stated in the universally ratified Geneva Conventions. It lends additional support to the conclusions of the Court in the *Nicaragua* case concerning the customary law character of the norms embodied in common Articles 1 and 3 of the Geneva Conventions.

Commenting on this statement, Sinclair observed that 'the Court has in terms recognised the possibility that customary international law may be generated by treaty. But it has carefully qualified this recognition by establishing a series of conditions which, in the instant case, it was found had not been fulfilled.'[137] Moreover, in the statement quoted,[138] the Court did not address the question of practice by non-parties. In a trenchant dissenting opinion, Judge Lachs pointedly referred to the practice of states that were 'both

[136] 1969 ICJ Rep. at 42. More recently, the Court stated that '[i]t is of course axiomatic that the material of customary international law is to be looked for primarily in the actual practice and *opinio juris* of States, even though multilateral conventions may have an important role to play in recording and defining rules deriving from custom, or indeed in developing them. . . . [I]t cannot be denied that the 1982 Convention [United Nations Convention on the Law of the Sea, which has not yet entered into force] is of major importance, having been adopted by an overwhelming majority of States; hence it is clearly the duty of the Court, even independently of the references made to the Convention by the Parties, to consider in what degree any of its relevant provisions are binding upon the Parties [before the Court] as a rule of customary international law.' *Continental Shelf* (Libyan Arab Jamahiriya/Malta), 1985 ICJ Rep. 13, 29–30 (Judgment of 3 June). The Court's explicit defence of the importance of practice and *opinio juris* to the establishment of customary law is not necessarily followed by a genuine effort to identify the relevant practice. Charney thus observes that the Court fails to identify 'the actual evidence of state practice upon which [it] purport[s] to rely'. Charney, above n. 86, at 995.

A recent study notes the diminishing investigation by the ICJ of the existence of practice and of *opinio juris* in the formation of customary law. Haggenmacher, *La Doctrine des deux éléments du droit coutumier dans la pratique de la Cour internationale*, 90 Rev. gén. droit int'l pub. 5, 111–14 (1986). See also Art. 38 of the Vienna Convention on the Law of Treaties; Marek, *Le Problème des sources du droit international dans l'arrêt sur le plateau continental de la mer du Nord*, Revue belge de droit international 44, 57 (1970).

[137] I. Sinclair, above n. 21, at 23 (referring, primarily, to the statement by the Court to be found in 1969 ICJ Rep. at 41–2).

[138] See above text accompanying n. 136.

parties and not parties to the Convention'[139] (in delimiting the continental shelf on the basis of the equidistance rule). However, even the Court's statement 'that no inference could legitimately be drawn' from the action of states parties to a convention does not necessarily suggest a priori that such action can *never* be taken into account for the formation of customary international law.

Acts concordant with the treaty obviously are indistinguishable from acts 'in the application of the Convention'. If it could be demonstrated, however, that in acting in a particular way parties to a convention believed and recognized that their duty to conform to a particular norm was required not only by their contractual obligations but by customary or general international law as well (or, in the case of the Geneva Conventions, by binding and compelling principles of humanity), such an *opinio juris* should be given probative weight for the formation of customary law. Such a distinction between an *opinio juris generalis* and an *opinio obligationis conventionalis* has already been suggested by Professor Cheng.[140]

Opionio Juris is thus critical for the transformation of treaties into general law.[141] To be sure, it is difficult to demonstrate an *opinio juris*,[142] but this poses a problem of proof rather than of principle. The possibility that a party to the Geneva Conventions may be motivated by the belief that a particular course of conduct is required not only contractually but by the underlying principles of humanity is not far fetched.

In any event, the 'real issue', as Sinclair stated in his discussion of Professor D'Amato's arguments, appears

to be whether treaties, considered as elements of State practice . . . need

---

[139] 1969 ICJ Rep. at 228 (Lachs J. dissenting).

[140] Cheng, *Custom: The Future of General State Practice in a Divided World*, in The Structure and Process of International Law 513, 532-3 (R. Macdonald and D. Johnston eds. 1983). In a different context (concerning the adoption of a treaty at an international conference), Professor Sohn speaks of *opinio juris* in the sense that the provisions of a convention 'are generally acceptable'. Sohn, *"Generally Accepted" International Rules*, above n. 86, at 1078. He considers a multilateral convention 'not only as a treaty among the parties to it, but as a record of the consensus of experts as to what the law is or should be'. Sohn, *Unratified Treaties as a Source of Customary International Law*, above n. 86, at 239. On customary law applicable between parties to agreements, see Bos, above n. 86, at 25.

[141] 1969 ICJ Rep. at 41.

[142] Professor D'Amato alludes to this difficulty in his article, *The Concept of Human Rights in International Law*, 82 Colum. L. Rev. 1110, 1141 (1982).

to be accompanied by *opinio juris* in the traditional sense in order to be regarded as being expressive of or as generating rules of customary international law; and, if so, how this requirement of *opinio juris* can be satisfied.[143]

How does one assess the weight of such *opinio juris*, which is not accompanied by practice of non-parties *vis-à-vis* non-parties? In the absence of practice extrinsic to the treaty, non-parties are unlikely to accept being bound by principles which the parties may consider to be custom grafted on to the treaty. On the other hand, parties to normative treaties embodying deeply felt community values have a strong interest in ensuring concordant behaviour by non-parties and, thus, in promoting the customary character of the treaty. It is well known that states and non-governmental organizations invoke provisions of human rights and humanitarian treaties characterized as customary or as general law against non-party states guilty of egregious violations of important values of the international community.

The effectiveness of this invocation may thus depend on the proof of acquiescence in the norm stated in the treaty by non-parties. The parties, striving to impose the treaty norm on non-parties,[144] may urge a lower burden of proof. Obviously, a tension exists between community interests which seek to impose the treaty norms upon third states and the sovereignty of third states. Public opinion tends to view provisions of widely ratified humanitarian and human rights treaties as authoritative statements of values binding on all states (*erga omnes*), without much concern for legal niceties.

[143] I. Sinclair, above n. 21, at 256.

[144] On acquiescence, see Baxter, above n. 28, at 73. See also Sohn, "*Generally Accepted*" *International Rules*, above n. 86, at 1074–5. On a critique of contemporary tendencies to impose conventional rules on non-parties, see Weil, *Towards Relative Normativity in International Law?*, 77 AJIL 413, 439 (1983). Professor Weil expresses the classical view: 'It has never been denied that a provision in a convention, though binding as such only on states parties thereto, could play a role in the formation of a customary rule that would also be binding on third states (provided they had not manifested any objection to it). Even so, it would still be necessary for that provision to have been corroborated by state practice, whether before or after its enactment.' Ibid. at 434. Weil's view, that state conduct is an essential element in the formation of customary rule, may be contrasted with that of Professor Bernhardt, who states that '[i]f . . . the community of States unequivocally and without any dissent considers certain acts, which have not been known before, to be illegal, the *opinio juris* might suffice even if no practice could evolve.' Bernhardt, *Customary International Law*, [Instalment] 7 Encyclopedia of Public International Law 65 (R. Bernhardt ed. 1984).

However, this question is moot with regard to the Geneva Conventions, because all the potential actors are already parties to them.

In the *Nicaragua* case, the Court held that the Charter does not subsume or supervene customary international law and that 'customary international law continues to exist and to apply, separately from international treaty law, even where the two categories of law have an identical content.'[145] In contrast to the brevity and the high level of abstraction of the principles of the Charter, the provisions of the Geneva Conventions are characterized by their extensive detail. The accretion of a significant corpus of customary law alongside the Conventions is therefore even more hampered, especially when the Conventions are applied only infrequently in the field.[146]

However, the sparse application of the Conventions by the states directly concerned is balanced, at least up to a point, by other forms of practice. Such forms include the universal acceptance of the Conventions as treaties, ICRC's and Security Council's appeals to parties to conflicts to apply the Geneva Conventions,[147] as well as Security Council resolutions stating that Geneva Convention No. IV applies to the territories occupied by Israel and requesting

---

[145] 1986 ICJ Rep. at 96. See also ibid. at 93-5.

[146] Professor Dinstein argues that because Geneva Convention No. IV had not been applied between its adoption in 1949 and the Six Day War (1967), there was no practice that could have been relied upon for the transformation of the Convention's norms into customary law. Dinstein, above n. 5, at 167-8. But see generally Roberts's discussion of the application in practice of the rules of the Convention even by states not acknowledging its applicability. Above n. 5. Consider also the Convention's application in the case of Falklands (Malvinas), ICRC Annual Report 1982, at 30 (1983); 53 Brit. YB Int'l L. 523-5 (1982). Concerning the controversy between Argentina and the United Kingdom as to whether the islands 'were occupied' by Argentina and as to the 'strict applicability' of Geneva Convention No. IV, see S. Stoyanka-Junod, Protection of the Victims of Armed Conflict Falkland-Malvinas Islands (1982) at 34 (1984).

[147] For ICRC's invocation of Geneva Conventions Nos. III and IV in the Iran-Iraq conflict, see International Committee of the Red Cross, Annual Report 1986 at 66-8 (1987). For ICRC's invocation of Geneva Convention No. IV in the case of territories occupied by Israel, see ibid. at 71-2. ICRC Press Release No. 1559 (13 Jan. 1988) contains ICRC's reaction to the recent expulsions of a number of individuals from those territories.

See also Security Council Resolution 598 which deplored the violation, in the conflict between Iran and Iraq, of international humanitarian law and other laws of armed conflict and urged the release and repatriation of prisoners of war in accordance with Geneva Convention No. III. UN Doc. S/RES/598 (1987).

Israel to abide by its obligations under that Convention.[148] The Secretary-General of the United Nations recently stated that 'even though Israel does not accept the *de jure* applicability of the Fourth Geneva Convention, the *opinio juris* of the world community is that it must be applied.'[149] Yet another type of supporting practice is to be found in the repetition of many of the humanitarian provisions of the Geneva Conventions, including Geneva Convention No. IV, and the Hague Regulations in Additional Protocol I, parts of which are widely recognized as embodying customary law.[150]

The possibility of accretion of a significant corpus of customary law alongside the Conventions should not be discounted altogether, especially with regard to practice not adequately or explicitly regulated by the Conventions, e.g. in situations of prolonged belligerent occupation, where Geneva Convention No. IV leaves some questions unanswered, or internal strife falling short of non-international armed conflict.[151] Such development of customary law in the interstices of a treaty, however, does not suggest that the treaty itself would necessarily become customary law.

Practice by states that modifies the original provisions of the Conventions may also spawn new rules of customary law. But it may prove difficult to distinguish such rules from additional layers of treaty law created by the parties through interpretation or modification as a result of practice.[152]

In addition, the emergence of customary law in other fields of international law may have an impact on the transformation of the parallel norms of the Geneva Conventions (i.e. those with an identical content) into customary norms. Consider, for instance, the developments in the human rights field that led to the recognition of the prohibitions of the arbitrary taking of life and of torture as norms of customary law.[153] The recognition as customary of norms

[148] See e.g. Security Council Resolutions 605, 607, and 608, UN Docs. S/RES/605 1987), S/RES/607 (1988), S/RES/608 (1988). Other Security Council Resolutions on this subject are listed in UN Doc. S/19443, above n. 84, at 8 (1988). Regarding the invocation of Geneva Convention No. III by the European Commission of Human Rights, see T. Meron, above n. 11, at 217.

[149] UN Doc. S/19443, above n. 84, at 9 (1988).

[150] See below Section VI(A) and Section VI(C).

[151] Meron, *Inadequate Reach*, above n. 14, at 589; Meron, *Towards a Humanitarian Declaration on Internal Strife*, 78 AJIL 859 (1984).

[152] See Vienna Convention on the Law of Treaties, above n. 20, Arts. 31 and 41. See also I. Sinclair, above n. 21, at 138.

[153] See e.g. Restatement above n. 17, at § 702 (c)–(d).

rooted in international human rights instruments will probably affect, through a kind of osmosis, or application by analogy, the interpretation, and eventually perhaps even the status, of the parallel norms in instruments of international humanitarian law, including the Geneva Conventions. Through a similar process, humanitarian norms will affect human rights. If governments, the scholarly community and the informed public opinion learn to regard as customary a particular human rights norm which has a parallel norm with an identical content in humanitarian law, in the perception of the decision-makers the latter norm will also be regarded as an embodiment of customary rules, even when not supported by significant state practice. Professor Schachter discusses a somewhat similar phenomenon which has occurred in the field of law-making:

Officials who . . . have to ascertain . . . law naturally look to the product of the process in which they or their colleagues took part. . . . Practical and bureaucratic factors help to increase the use made of the adopted texts. . . . The consequences over time are two-fold: (1) the instrument generally accumulates more authority as declaratory of customary law and (2), in cases where the declaratory nature of a particular provision is shown to be contrary to the understanding of the drafters . . . the tendency to apply that provision will in time result in custom 'grafted' upon the treaty.[154]

Finally, as suggested by the preceding discussion of the *North Sea Continental Shelf Cases*, observance of the provisions of the Conventions, especially if accompanied by verbal affirmations supporting the binding, even *erga omnes*, character of the humanitarian principles stated in the Conventions, may evince *opinio juris* facilitating the gradual metamorphosis of those conventional norms into customary law.

Both scholarly and judicial sources have shown reluctance to reject conventional norms whose content merits customary law status as candidates for that status, or to deprive those norms of customary law character because of contrary practice. This reluctance may reflect the strength of moral claims for the application and observance of the norms in instruments relating to international human rights and humanitarian law,[155] and of other norms which

[154] Schachter, above n. 122, at 97–8.
[155] See Baxter, above n. 81, at 286.

58 *Humanitarian Norms*

express basic community values and are essential for the preservation of an international public order,[156] as well as the differences in the kinds of evidence of state practice involved.[157] Nevertheless, contrary practice or violations of a norm may be so rampant and sweeping that it becomes unclear whether the 'norm' or the violations represent the true reflection of the policy and practice of states. A distinction should therefore be made between episodic breaches of the rule that do not nullify the rule's legal force, and massive, grave, and persistent violations of the rule, which amount to ' "State practice" that nullifies the legal force of [a] right'.[158] In the same vein, an official publication of the US Navy states as follows:

Occasional violations do not substantially affect the validity of a rule of law, provided routine compliance, observance, and enforcement continue to be the norm. However, repeated violations not responded to by protests, reprisals, or other enforcement actions may, over time, indicate that a particular rule of warfare is no longer regarded by belligerents as valid.[159]

Other norms which are frequently violated, such as the prohibition of torture, concern practices contrary both to national law and the official state policy. Their endurance as legal norms, despite frequent breaches, can also be explained by a deeply felt belief in the norms' importance. Lamenting the continuing incidence of torture, the UN Human Rights Commission's Special Rapporteur on Torture and Other Cruel, Inhuman or Degrading Treatment or Punishment notes that

allegations of torture have continued to come in; their number does not show a tendency to decrease. . . . How can this remarkable discrepancy

[156] Schachter, *In Defense of International Rules on the Use of Force*, 53 U. Chi. L. Rev. 113, 131 (1986).
[157] See Schachter, above n. 122, at 334-5. Schachter observes that 'value-judgments are always implicit in the recognition of practice as law'. Ibid. at 96.
[158] Ibid. at 336. Professor Schachter observes that some norms 'are so widely disregarded in practice as a matter of state policy as to be more the norm than the exception'. Ibid.
See also the exchange between Watson and Sohn on the significance of the discrepancy between human rights and the reality of state practice in Watson, *Legal Theory, Efficacy and Validity in the Development of Human Rights Norms in International Law*, 1979 U. Ill. LF 609, 626-35; and Sohn, *The International Law of Human Rights: A Reply to Recent Criticisms*, 9 Hofstra L. Rev. 347, 350-1 (1981).
[159] Department of the Navy, the Commander's Handbook on the Law of Naval Operations NWP 9, at 6.1 (1987).

between legal opinion (*opinio juris*) and practice be explained, a discrepancy which is not unknown in the field of human rights in general but is all the more remarkable with respect to torture, since here the practice is never justified by those who are alleged to have practised it but is flatly denied.[160]

As a yardstick for differentiating episodic breaches from breaches which reflect state policy, Professor Schachter proposes assessing the 'intensity and depth of the attitudes of condemnation'[161] by third parties. This criterion emphasizes the reactions of others to a particular breach rather than the statements of the actor state. (In Chapter II, Section I, we shall propose additional criteria which can be utilized to identify emerging customary human rights norms.) In the *Nicaragua* case the Court focused on the statements of the actor state:

The Court does not consider that, for a rule to be established as customary, the corresponding practice must be in absolutely rigorous conformity with the rule. In order to deduce the existence of customary rules, the Court deems it sufficient that the conduct of States should, in general, be consistent with such rules, and that instances of State conduct inconsistent with a given rule should generally have been treated as breaches of that rule, not as indications of the recognition of a new rule. If a State acts in a way prima facie incompatible with a recognized rule, but defends its conduct by appealing to exceptions or justifications contained within the rule itself, then whether or not the State's conduct is in fact justifiable on that basis, the significance of the attitude is to confirm rather than to weaken the rule.[162]

Elsewhere, the Court elaborated on this statement by considering third-party responses to a particular state's claim: 'Reliance by a State on a novel right or an unprecedented exception to the principle might, if shared in principle by other states, tend towards a modification of customary international law.'[163]

The earlier statement by the Court should be understood in light of the latter statement. Statements which states make to justify alleged breaches of international law have considerable weight in assessing the significance of the breach for the continued vitality of the customary norm in question. Account must, however, be

160 UN Doc. E/CN.4/1988/17, at 23 (1988).
161 Schachter, above n. 122, at 336.
162 1986 ICJ Rep. at 98.
163 Ibid. at 109.

taken of the fact that states bent on evading compliance with international law commonly resort to factual or legal exceptions or justifications contained in the rule itself and in the relationship of their particular case or situation to that rule. Obviously, states normally shield themselves with self-serving justifications, calculated to minimize international censure of their course of action. In infrequent situations, a state may want to challenge frontally the existence of a rule of law, but as Professor Charney observes, 'States will rarely, if ever, admit that they have violated customary international law, even in order to change it. Rather, they will argue that their behavior is consistent with the traditional law, or that the law has already changed.[164] Why should states challenge a rule head on, if less provocative conduct would better serve them?[165] Of course, because of its legitimate interest in safeguarding the stability of customary law, the international community tends to view violations as mere episodic breaches which do not directly challenge the binding character of a recognized norm.

[164] Charney, *The Power of the Executive Branch of the United States Government to Violate Customary International Law*, 80 AJIL 913, 916 (1986). See also Akehurst, above n. 23, at 8: '[A]s an alternative to changing customary law by breaking it, States can change it by repeatedly declaring that the old rule no longer exists. . . .'

[165] With some exceptions, e.g. Iran's claim that Iraqi POWs should be treated according to the dictates of the Koran, which claim implies the subordination to the Koran of Geneva Convention No. III (see UN Doc. S/16962, at 38, 42 (1985)), states tend to avoid a frontal challenge to the Conventions, preferring instead to justify their discordant practices on differences between the conflicts presently encountered and those for which these instruments were originally adopted. Aldrich, *Human Rights and Armed Conflict: Conflicting Views*, 67 ASIL PROC. 141, 142 (1973); Roberts, above n. 5, at 279–83.

Professor Henkin has cogently observed that to reduce the 'cost' of violating the law, states will often stress ambiguities about the facts and their proper characterization, as well as uncertainties about the applicable norm. See L. Henkin, How Nations Behave 70 (1968).

The recent resolution on Respect for International Humanitarian Law in Armed Conflicts and Action by the ICRC for Persons Protected by the Geneva Conventions highlighted violations of the Geneva Conventions and 'a disturbing decline in the respect of international humanitarian law' and acknowledged that 'disputes about the legal classification of conflicts too often hinder the implementation of international humanitarian law . . .'. 25th International Conference of the Red Cross, Doc. P.2/CI, Ann. 1 (1986).

ICRC President Alexandre Hay has recently complained that '[n]ot only are conflicts increasing in number and length, but practices prohibited by international humanitarian law are becoming more and more common . . .'. Hay, *Respect for International Humanitarian Law: ICRC Report on its Activities*, Int'l Rev. Red Cross, No. 256, Jan.–Feb. 1987, at 60, 61. See also Tavernier, *La Guerre du Golfe: Quelques Aspects de l'application du droit des conflits armés et du droit humanitaire*, 30 Annuaire français de droit international 43 (1984).

If states fail to observe the provisions of the Geneva Conventions in conflicts or resort to numerous reservations[166] having a significant adverse impact on the actual observance of the norms in the Conventions, naturally the claims of the Conventions' provisions to customary law status will be weakened. To illustrate, the fact that, in most cases, states fail either to prosecute or to extradite perpetrators of grave breaches of the Geneva Conventions weakens the claim of the obligations to prosecute or to extradite perpetrators of grave breaches to customary law status. Cumulatively, frequent evasions of the Conventions' norms by states through reliance on the specific circumstances of particular situations (*sui generis* claims) may erode the position of the Conventions as crucial instruments of humanitarian law and as claimants to customary, and *a fortiori* to *jus cogens*, status. Concordant practice is, of course, the best indicator of expectations about binding prescriptions on state behaviour. It must, however, be made clear that the requirement of concordant practice must not be interpreted to mean that the practice must be totally uniform. As the *Nicaragua* Court observed in the statement discussed above, it is only required that the conduct of states should, in general, be consistent with such rules.

Violations are, of course, much more visible than practice demonstrating respect for a norm. To balance the greater visibility of violations, it is therefore necessary that any inquiry into international practice should focus on cases of conduct consistent with a norm. The characteristic compliance by states with, for example, Geneva Convention No. III must be taken into account no less than the much more publicized violations of that Convention. Because the Geneva Conventions are meant to apply in exceptional situations only, in which violations abound, it is particularly difficult to quantify cases of conduct concordant with the Conventions. It is considerably easier to take into account practice consistent with human rights instruments which apply to day-to-day life.

The decisive factor is whether or not states observe the Geneva Conventions. As with other widely ratified treaties, if states parties comply with the Geneva Conventions in actual practice, verbally

---

[166] I am addressing here the question of the number and the extent of the reservations actually made rather than the question of whether a particular reservation is compatible with the purpose and object of the Convention or is prohibited. See generally Baxter, above n. 81, at 285; Baxter, above n. 28, at 48–52.

On the significance of inconsistent practice, see also Section VI(C), below.

affirm their vital normative value, and accept them in *opinio juris*, both states and tribunals will be reluctant to advance or to accept the argument that the law of Geneva is solely,[167] or even primarily, conventional. Such observance by the parties will eventually lead, in the perception of governments and scholars, to the blurring of the distinction between norms of the Conventions that are already recognized as customary law and other humanitarian provisions of the Conventions that have not yet achieved that status. In the final analysis, movement in this direction depends on whether states realize that, in the long run, bona fide compliance with the Geneva Conventions serves their best interests.

VI. ADDITIONAL PROTOCOLS OF 1977

A. Protocol I

The identification of those provisions of Protocol I[168] which are declaratory of customary international law is particularly important and timely in light of the decision by President Reagan not to seek the Senate's advice and consent to the ratification of the Protocol. This decision also provides an opportunity to examine the process whereby the US government identifies customary norms. In deciding not to recommend ratification of Protocol I, the US government expressed the opinion that certain provisions of the Protocol reflect customary international law, other provisions appear to be positive new developments, while other provisions are neither customary, nor desirable. The United States took the position that these new developments should be incorporated into the rules governing military operations, e.g. military manuals, 'with the intention that they shall in time win recognition as customary international law separate from their presence in Protocol I'.[169] The importance of

[167] Such a position has been asserted by the Supreme Court of Israel with regard to Geneva Convention No. IV. See above n. 5. *Contra Mauritius Transport Case* (Supreme Court of West Berlin) (1967): 'Although the Geneva . . . Convention concerning the protection of Civilians in Wartime was enacted on 12 August 1949, its provisions reflect only what had already been recognized previously by civilized nations. . . . ' 60 Int'l L. Rep. 208, 215 (1981).

[168] Message from the President of the United States, Transmitting the Protocol II Additional to the Geneva Conventions of August 12, 1949, and Relating to the Protection of Victims of Noninternational Armed Conflicts, Concluded at Geneva on June 10, 1977, Letter of Transmittal, S. Treaty Doc. No. 2, 100th Cong., 1st Sess. at III–IV (1987).

[169] Secretary of State George P. Shultz, Letter of Submittal, *ibid.* at X. For an analysis of Protocol I from the perspective of a legal adviser of the ICRC (presented

a norm's customary character even in the case of universally recognized conventions, such as the Geneva Conventions, has been explained in Section I, above. Because the United States has chosen not to become a party to Protocol I, and also because thus far a limited number of states have ratified this Protocol, the importance of identifying those provisions of the Protocol which reflect customary law is even greater than in the case of the Geneva Conventions.[170] The United States, which has warned that the Protocol should not be viewed as a definitive indication for expectations of future behaviour of its forces in armed conflict,[171] and other states that choose not to become parties to the Protocol, will be bound by its rules 'only to the extent that they reflect customary law, either now or as it may develop in the future'.[172]

Accordingly, the United States has not limited its study of the Protocol to pinpointing existing rules of customary law but has also looked for provisions that may be regarded as emergent rules of customary law or as 'positive' rules which may merit eventual inclusion in the corpus of customary law. This process of identifying the emergent rules of customary law and the merely 'positive' rules, as well as more general principles of humanitarian law and incorporating these into the manuals of military law, coupled with calls for other states to accord these rules similar treatment, will

in personal capacity only), see Gasser, *Protocol I to the Geneva Conventions on the Protection of War Victims: An Appeal for Ratification by the United States*, 81 AJIL 912 (1987).

[170] Seventy-three states have ratified or acceded to Protocol I as of Feb. 1988. International Committee of the Red Cross, Dissemination No. 9 (Aug. 1988). See also Chapter II, Section I, below. A UN report discussing the question whether Iran is bound by the norm stated in Art. 47 of Protocol I concerning mercenaries concludes that 'the notion of "mercenaries" is only of recent origin and cannot be invoked by States which have not ratified the First Protocol . . .'. UN Doc. S/16962 at 59 (1985).

The ICJ considered the claim that a convention is declaratory of customary international law to be weakened by the fact that it had been ratified by only a limited number of states. *Colombian-Peruvian Asylum* case, 1950 ICJ Rep. 266, 277 (Judgment of 20 Nov.).

[171] Remarks by M. Matheson (Deputy Legal Adviser, US Department of State), in panel on *Customary Law and Additional Protocol I to the Geneva Conventions for Protection of War Victims: Future Directions in Light of the U.S. Decision not to Ratify*, 81 ASIL PROC. 26, 28 (1989). For an expansive view of the customary law character of the Additional Protocols of 1977, see generally, Cassese, above n. 93, at 55-118.

[172] Matheson, above n. 171 at 29.

exercise a significant impact on the formation of customary law and on future law-making.[173]

This analysis will begin with a description of the rules of Protocol I identified by the United States as embodying customary law, and some of the rules regarded by the United States as 'positive' and thus appropriate for maturation into customary law. Secondly, I shall focus on the broader principles of humanitarian law which the United States has identified in the Protocol. Thirdly, I shall discuss those provisions of the Protocol which the United States regards as unsound or undesirable, and thus unlikely to mature into customary international law. Finally, I shall address the process underlying these developments and the relationship between general humanitarian principles and concrete rules of customary humanitarian law.

An expert who conducted a detailed study of the Protocols for the US Joint Chiefs of Staff noted that many articles of Protocol I either 'accurately reflect customary international law or are promising candidates for such status'[174] This expert identified Article 35(1) (the right of the parties to the conflict to choose methods or means of warfare is not unlimited), Article 35(2) (prohibition on employing weapons, projectiles and material, and methods of warfare of a nature to cause superfluous injury or unnecessary suffering), and Article 40 (prohibition of refusing quarter) as restatements of the Hague Regulations, which are declaratory of customary law. The definition of perfidy in Article 37 and the prohibition of direct attacks on civilians and the civilian population and of acts or threats of violence whose primary purpose is to terrorize civilians stated in Article 51(2) were likewise viewed as customary law. The definition of a military objective set forth in Article 52(2), which has been incorporated into US military manuals[175] and at least one other international instrument,[176] was

[173] Matheson notes: 'The U.S. and other governments, particularly those with significant military forces, can advance the process of recognition of principles as customary law by stating that they are prepared to observe them in armed conflict and desire them to be recognized in due course as customary law.' Matheson, above n. 171.

[174] Remarks by Lt.-Col. B. Carnahan (of the Joint Chiefs of Staff) (views presented in personal capacity only), in panel, above n. 171 at 37.

[175] US field manual, above n. 103, para. 40(*c*) (Change 1, 15 July 1976); Air Force Pamphlet 110–31, above n. 107, at para. 5–3(b).

[176] See Protocols II–III to the Convention on Prohibitions or Restrictions on the Use of Certain Conventional Weapons Which May be Deemed to be Excessively

deemed 'almost certainly' to embody rules of customary law. Further, it was pointed out that the prohibition of shooting at persons parachuting in distress (Article 42) was recognized 'as existing law' in US military manuals.[177] Article 59 (protection of non-defended localities), Article 60 (demilitarized zones), Article 57(2)(c) (duty to give advance warning of attacks which may affect the civilian population), Article 73 (protection of refugees and stateless persons), Article 75 (fundamental guarantees and human rights for persons affected by an international armed conflict who are in the power of a party to the conflict and do not benefit from more favourable treatment) and Article 79 (confirming the civilian status of journalists) were said to 'complete the list of protocol articles already part of customary law'. Another US government official stated that most, but not all, of the provisions concerning protection of the civilian population against effects of hostilities were 'useful and deserving of treatment as customary law . . .'.[178]

Other provisions were viewed by the expert of the Joint Chiefs

Injurious or to Have Indiscriminate Effects, opened for signature 10 April 1981, reprinted in 19 ILM 1523, 1530, 1535 (1980).

[177] US field manual, above n. 103, at para. 30 (1956); Air Force Pamphlet, above n. 107, at para. 4-2(e).

[178] Remarks by M. Matheson, in *The Sixth Annual American Red Cross-Washington College of Law Conference on International Humanitarian Law: A Workshop on Customary International Law and the 1977 Protocols Additional to the 1949 Geneva Conventions*, 2 Am. U. J. Int'l L. & Pol. 415, 426 (1987).

It may be noted that the provisions expressly mentioned as declaratory of customary law did not include those containing the rule of proportionality (e.g. Art. 57(2)(b)), which has previously been mentioned in a US Air Force manual as resulting from the principles of humanity. See above n. 107. The statement of the principle of proportionality in the Protocol has been characterized by the head of the US delegation to the conference which adopted the Protocols as 'the first codification ever of the customary rule of proportionality'. Aldrich, *Progressive Development of the Laws of War: A Reply to Criticisms of the 1977 Geneva Protocol I*, 26 Va. J. Int'l L. 693, 699 (1986). For a different approach, see generally Parks, *Rolling Thunder and the Law of War*, 33 Air U. Rev. 2 (No. 2, 1982).

An ICRC expert, speaking in a personal capacity, addressed the problems which arise when a general principle is transformed into a detailed rule, stating that the rule of proportionality as codified in Arts. 51(5)(b) and 57(2) has the character of customary law, but that it was possible that 'the rule as codified by the diplomatic conference slightly develops the generally agreed concept, mostly on the drafting level'. Gasser, in panel, above n. 171 at 33. Compare Fenrick, *The Rule of Proportionality and Protocol I in Conventional Warfare*, 98 Mil. L. Rev. 91 (1982). Reservations to the formulation of the principle of proportionality in Protocol I have been made by Belgium, Italy, and, upon signature, by the United Kingdom. D. Schindler and J. Toman, The Laws of Armed Conflicts 707, 713, 717 (1988). In my view the core of the principle is customary and perhaps also a general principle of law.

of Staff as 'likely candidates eventually to reflect general practice recognized as law'. These included most of the provisions stated in Articles 10, 12–15, 18–20, and 24–31 (which concern protection of the sick and wounded and medical personnel and transports), Articles 32–4 (concerning missing and deceased persons), Articles 74 (concerning family reunification), 76 (concerning protection of women), 77 (concerning protection of children), and 78 (concerning evacuation of children).

Among the provisions of the Protocol the United States found to be neither desirable nor a part of customary international law were: Article 1(4), which extends the concept of international armed conflicts covered by the Protocol to conflicts waged against colonial domination, alien occupation, and racist regimes;[179] Article 35(3), which prohibits methods of warfare which are intended, or may be expected, to cause widespread, severe, and long-term damage to the natural environment; and Article 39, prohibiting the use of enemy emblems and uniforms during military operations.[180]

The Joint Chiefs' expert took issue with the provisions concerning the denial of prisoner of war status to mercenaries (Article 47), concerning the protection of works and installations containing dangerous forces (Article 56), and concerning the presumption of civilian status (Articles 50(1) and 52(3)). The 'almost total prohibition on belligerent reprisals' (contained in Article 51 and following articles)[181] was singled out for particularly severe criticism as a provision that 'would allow the non-law abiding side in a conflict to engage in terroristic attacks against the morale of a civilian population with little fear of a reply in kind'. At least one other state, Italy, has already made a reservation to the Protocol's

---

[179] Carnahan, above n. 174, at 35–7. The United States government has recently emphasized that Arts. 1(4) and 44, i.e. the provisions on wars of national liberation and combatant and prisoner of war status, definitely do not reflect customary international law. Affidavit of Kerri L. Martin, *United States* v. *Shakur*, 82 Cr. 312, Exhibit A, at 10–11 (SDNY, 23 Mar. 1988). Professor Kalshoven observes that the Protocol's new rules with regard to guerrilla fighters do not embody customary law. Kalshoven, *Reaffirmation and Development of International Humanitarian Law Applicable in Armed Conflicts: The Diplomatic Conference, Geneva, 1974–1977*, 8 Neth. YB Int'l L. 107, 133 (1977).

[180] Statement by Matheson, above n. 178, at 424–5. Matheson referred to Arts. 44 and 45, which 'relax' for irregulars the principle of distinction and allow them to retain combatant status in certain circumstances as 'highly undesirable and potentially dangerous to the civilian population [and as neither] customary law or deserving of such status'. Ibid. at 425.

[181] Compare Aldrich, above n. 178, at 710–11.

prohibitions of reprisals. As discussed in Section II, such reservations may weaken a provision's claim to customary law status.

It should be noted that the United States has singled out relatively few provisions of the Protocol as unlikely candidates for customary law status. Although these provisions are very important, it can be suggested, *a contrario*, that the United States agrees that the bulk of the provisions of Protocol I embodies norms which either have already matured into customary law or are appropriate for maturation into customary law.

For purposes of scholarly inquiry, more information about the method followed by the United States in identifying the rules of Protocol I which embody customary law would be helpful. What acts did the US government experts regard as constituting good evidence of state practice? What acts or statements did the experts deem demonstrative of the existence of *opinio juris* regarding the customary status of Protocol I's provisions? Were the methods used to establish the customary law character of the provisions of Protocol I derived from the 'law of Geneva' different than the methods employed for those provisions rooted in the 'law of the Hague'? As regards inter-state reciprocal obligations, the burden to be met in establishing the customary law character of the provisions of Protocol I is perhaps heavier than that applicable to those provisions which implicate human rights, i.e. relations between the government and the governed. Because the contemporaneous understanding of the drafters of Protocol I is not necessarily dispositive of the question of the customary law character of its provisions, what can be learned from the practice of states since 1977? What conclusions did the US experts draw from the scarcity of practice concordant with the provisions of the Protocol?

Although the statements by US government experts did not provide adequate material for answering these questions, it would nevertheless appear that the United States experts attributed particular weight to certain factors. Their examination of state practice focused on the similarities of the Protocol provisions to the Hague Regulations of 1907. Identical or similar rules in US military manuals, particularly the black-letter provisions which carry the force of law for U.S. forces, in the military manuals of other states, and in subsequent international agreements were given added weight. The United States also examined combat practice as recorded in the official histories of the conflicts in Korea[182] and in South-East Asia.[183] In addition, the study drew upon the experiences of World War II, including that of the war crimes trials held in its aftermath, the Middle East conflicts of 1967, 1973, and 1982, the 1982 Falklands/Malvinas war, the Iran-Iraq war, the Soviet operations in Afghanistan, and even the US-Libya encounters in the Gulf of Sidra.[184] The study of the Protocol by the United States included also investigation of the combat practices of its potential adversaries. Evaluation of the often ambiguous provisions of the Protocol was carried out with due regard to the conditions prevailing on the modern battlefield, where electronic warfare plays an important role.[185]

In identifying various rules as customary, the United States was seemingly guided both by considerations of its own military interests and by policy and value judgments. For example, value judgments must have guided the government experts in their determination that Article 75 of Protocol I embodies customary law. Article 75 contains an enlightened catalogue of human rights and due process protections which, in certain respects, exceeds the short list of customary human rights norms stated in § 702 of the Restatement.[186] As previously mentioned, the recognition of norms based in international human rights as customary may affect the interpretation and even the status of the parallel norms in instruments of international humanitarian law through a sort of osmosis or application by analogy.[187] Finally, the US government experts may have deduced some of the customary rules which they identified from general humanitarian principles. The derivation of specific rules from general principles, and particularly from the principle of humanity, is an important process in the development of customary humanitarian law. This process has been utilized in the past, for instance in General Assembly Resolution 2444(XXIII),[188]

[182] See e.g. R. Futrell, The United States Air Force in Korea, 1950-1953 (rev. ed. 1983).
[183] See e.g. The United States Air Force in Southeast Asia, 1961-1973 (C. Berger ed. 1977).
[184] Information provided to the author by US officials.
[185] Ibid.
[186] Restatement, above n. 17.
[187] Above, text accompanying nn. 153-4.
[188] 23 UN GAOR Supp. (No. 18) at 50, UN Doc. A/7218 (1969). Prohibitions of use of biological and chemical weapons and of certain other weapons is sometimes derived, in addition to conventional instruments, from the principle of humanity,

which is recognized by the United States as an embodiment of international law.[189] Resolution 2444 stated the following principles:

(*a*) That the right of the parties to a conflict to adopt means of injuring the enemy is not unlimited;

(*b*) That it is prohibited to launch attacks against the civilian populations as such;

(*c*) That distinction must be made at all times between persons taking part in the hostilities and members of the civilian population to the effect that the latter be spared as much as possible. . . .[190]

The US government viewed paragraph (*a*) of the Resolution as a restatement of the principle expressed in Article 22 of the Hague Regulations,[191] and described paragraph (*b*) as derivative of 'the

Thierry in H. Thierry, J. Combacau, S. Sur, and C. Vallée, *Droit international public* 561-3 (5th edn. 1986). There is broad agreement that customary law 'proscribes the use in war of lethal chemical and biological weapons'. Baxter and Buergenthal, *Legal Aspects of the Geneva Protocol of 1925*, 64 AJIL 853 (1970); Bunn, *Banning Poison Gas and Germ Warfare: Should the United States Agree?*, [1969] Wis. L. Rev. 375, 388-9 (1969). The ICRC stated that '[t]he use of chemical weapons, whether against military personnel or civilians, is absolutely forbidden by international law.' ICRC Press Release No. 1567 (23 Mar. 1988). The customary law nature of the prohibition upon the use of chemical weapons finds further support in the language of the Preamble to the Geneva Protocol of 1925, in the widespread condemnation of the employment by Iraq of chemical weapons, and in the fact that the Geneva Protocol has been ratified by as many as 131 states. TIAS No. 8061, 94 LNTS 65, Treaties in Force, A List of Treaties and Other International Agreements of the United States in Force on January 1, 1988, at 303. It may be noted that the Security Council Resolution 620 (1988) instructed the UN Secretary-General to investigate not only allegations of violations of the Geneva Protocol, but also those of 'other relevant rules of customary international law. . . .' For the antecedents of the 1925 Geneva Protocol, see Declaration Concerning Asphyxiating Gases (Hague, July 29, 1899), 1 AJIL Supp. 157 (1907) and Hague Regulation 23(a).

[189] Letter from J. Fred Buzhardt, General Counsel of the Department of Defense, to Senator Edward Kennedy (22 Sept. 1972), reprinted in part in Rovine, *Contemporary Practice of the United States Relating to International Law*, 67 AJIL 118, 122 (1973). Carnahan, above n. 174 at 35, noted that although much verbal practice on the law of war arises in peacetime, 'verbal practice should not be completely disregarded. It is often the best evidence available that a particular practice is now "accepted as law," and it may crystallize the proper expression of a rule of customary law. U.N. Resolution 2444(XXIII) is a primary example of the latter phenomenon.'

[190] General Assembly Resolution 2444, above n. 188. See also General Assembly Resolution 2675, which emphasized the obligation to observe the principle of distinction, to protect from attack the civilian population, and to comply with fundamental human rights in situations of armed conflict. 25 GAOR Supp. (No. 28) at 76, UN Doc. A/80/28 (1971). See also Weissbrodt and Andrus, *The Right to Life During Armed Conflict: Disabled People International v. United States*, 29 Harv. Int'l LJ 59, 77 (1988).

[191] Letter from J. Fred Buzhardt, above n. 189.

universally accepted customary international law of armed conflict to the effect that attacking forces are to refrain from making civilians as such the object of armed attack'.[192] Many provisions of Protocol I elaborate on the broad principles contained in Resolution 2444.

Some of the difficulties in obtaining consensus on the specific duties compelled by the general principles of humanity were previously mentioned, as were the efforts made to derive from these principles such rules as the requirement of proportionality.[193] As has been aptly observed,

> there is no clear line drawn for all to see between those principles that are now customary law and those which have not yet attained the degree of acceptance and observance that might make them customary law. . . . [T]he judgment as to what degree of each is sufficient for establishment as customary law is inherently subjective and hard to define precisely. In addition, it may be possible in many cases to say that a general principle is an accepted part of customary law, but to have considerable disagreement as to the precise statement of that general principle.[194]

Apparently due to the difficulty the United States encountered in reaching agreement with its allies on which of the rules of armed conflict are already incorporated into customary law, the United States has been seeking agreement 'on what principles are in our common interests and therefore should be observed and in due course recognized as customary law, whether they are currently part of customary law or not. Apart from being easier to deal with, this has the added advantage of focusing attention on the substantive merits of the various rules, as opposed to their precise current legal status.'[195]

Such principles[196] overlap unavoidably with those rules stated in Protocol I that have already been acknowledged as customary.

---

[192] Ibid.
[193] Above nn. 101–7 and the accompanying text.
[194] Matheson, above n. 171 at 29.
[195] Ibid.
[196] Matheson's listing included the following principles.
'[I]n the area of protection of the wounded, sick and shipwrecked:
—That all of them be respected and protected, and not be made the object of attacks or reprisals, regardless of the party to the conflict to which they belong;
—That medical units [and medical transports], including properly authorized civilian medical units, as well as civilian medical and religious personnel, be respected and protected at all times and not be the object of attacks or reprisals . . .
[I]n the area of treatment of the missing and the remains of the dead:

B. *Protocol II*

Although the President of the United States has recommended that the Senate give its advice and consent to the ratification of Protocol II,[197] the question of the customary law character of its provisions

—That families have a right to know the fates of their relatives, and that each party to a conflict is to search areas under its control for persons reported missing . . . and,

—That each party to a conflict permit teams to search for, identify and recover the dead from battlefield areas, that the remains of the dead are to be respected, maintained and marked. . . .

[I]n the area of methods and means of warfare:

—That weapons, projectiles and materials and methods of warfare of a nature to cause superfluous injury or unnecessary suffering are not to be used;

—That individual combatants are not to kill, injure or capture enemy personnel by resort to perfidy and that internationally recognized protective emblems, such as the Red Cross, are not to be improperly used;

—That no order is to be given that there shall be no survivors, nor an adversary threatened with such an order or hostilities conducted on that basis; and,

—That persons, other than airborne troops, parachuting from an aircraft in distress are not to be made the object of attack. . . .

[I]n the area of protection of the civilian population:

—That, while civilian populations inevitably will be affected by lawful military actions, acts of violence will be directed solely against legitimate military objectives and that the civilian population is not to be used to shield military objectives or operations from attacks.

—That starvation of civilians is not to be used as a method of warfare, and, subject to the requirements of imperative military necessity, that impartial relief actions necessary for the survival of the civilian population are to be permitted and encouraged; and

—That all practicable precautions, taking into account military and humanitarian considerations, are to be taken in the conduct of military operations to minimize incidental death, injury and damage to civilians and civilian objects. . . .

[I]n the area of persons in the power of a party to the conflict:

That all persons who are in the power of a party to a conflict are to be treated humanely in all circumstances and enjoy, as a minimum, the protections specified in the conventions without any adverse distinction based upon race, sex, language, religion or belief, political or other opinion, national or social origin, or any similar criteria.

—That such persons are not to be subjected to violence to life, health or physical or mental wellbeing, outrages upon personal dignity, the taking of hostages, or collective punishments, and that no sentence is to be passed and no penalty executed except pursuant to conviction pronounced by an impartial and regularly constituted court respecting the generally recognized principles of regular judicial procedure; and

—That women and children are to be the object of special respect and protection. . . .'

Matheson, above n. 171 at 30-1.

[197] Letter of Transmittal from the President of the United States, above n. 168, at III.

remains important for non-parties[198] including, for the time being, the United States. Additionally, because Protocol II does not address most of the rules relevant to the conduct of hostilities ('Hague law') in internal wars, the identification of customary rules regulating combat in internal armed conflicts is equally important for states parties. The cruelty of internal armed conflicts, the frequent lack of regard for the principles of humanity by the parties to such conflicts, and, except for common Article 3 and the essential core of non-derogable human rights, the uncertainty as to the binding rules regulating internal armed conflicts[199] all make the identification and the development of applicable customary rules urgent and compelling. Protocol II constitutes an extremely important addition to the rules designed to humanize internal armed conflicts.

In the earlier discussion of the Martens clause, I referred to the reluctance of the states which drafted and adopted Protocol II to agree that rules of customary law governing non-international armed conflicts then existed.[200] This reluctance to recognize that

[198] Sixty-six states were parties to Protocol II as of Feb. 1988. Dissemination, above n. 170.

[199] See generally Americas Watch, Land Mines in El Salvador and Nicaragua: the Civilian Victims (1986); Americas Watch, Human Rights in Nicaragua 1986 at 13–54 (1987); Goldman, *International Humanitarian Law and the Armed Conflicts in El Salvador and Nicaragua*, 2 Am. U. J. Int'l L. & Pol. 539 (1987). It is widely accepted that, in addition to the norms stated in common Art. 3, certain basic principles of humanitarian law derived from international armed conflicts apply as customary law to non-international armed conflicts as well. Such principles include the rules recognizing civilian immunity from attack and requiring that distinction between civilians and combatants be maintained. Ibid. at 548. See also Report of the Independent Counsel on International Human Rights Situation in Afghanistan, UN Doc. A/C.3/42/8 at 12 (1987). Other such principles include the rule that 'parties to an armed conflict do not have an unlimited choice of methods and means of warfare and that the use of weapons which are calculated to cause unnecessary suffering is prohibited'. UN Doc. A/C.3/42/8 at 6 (1987).

[200] Above n. 97 and the accompanying text. See, however, the following useful comment on the significance of the Martens clause contained in Protocol II: 'If a case is "not covered by the law in force", whether this is because of a gap in the law or because the parties do not consider themselves to be bound by common Article 3, or are not bound by Protocol II, this does not mean that anything is permitted. "The human person remains under the protection of the principles of humanity and the dictates of the public conscience": this clarification prevents an *a contrario* interpretation. Since they reflect public conscience, the principles of humanity actually constitute a universal reference point and apply independently of the Protocol.'
Commentary on the Additional Protocols of 8 June 1977 to the Geneva Conventions of 12 August 1949 at 1341 (Y. Sandoz, C. Swinarski, and B. Zimmermann eds. 1987).

customary rules apply in the context of non-international armed conflicts is further indicated by the language of Article 13(1) of Protocol II, concerning the protection of the civilian population. This provision tracks the language of Article 51(1) of Protocol I, except that the words indicating that the rules expressed in Article 51 'are additional to other applicable rules of international law' are omitted. Further, Protocol II does not contain a provision which appears in common Article 1 of the Geneva Conventions and in Article 1(1) of Protocol I requiring states with regard to international armed conflicts 'to ensure respect' for the provisions of the instruments.

In addition, Protocol II includes an especially strong prohibition of intervention in the affairs of the state in whose territory the conflict occurs.[201] Taken together, these provisions strengthen the proposition that beyond the express provisions of Protocol II, regulation of internal armed conflict is relegated to the domestic law of states. However, Protocol II also contains a basic core of human rights. Some of these rights have already been recognized as customary in human rights instruments and should also be considered as such when stated in instruments of humanitarian law.[202] This is confirmed by the recent ICRC *Commentary:*

Protocol II contains virtually all the irreducible rights of the Covenant on Civil and Political Rights. . . . These rights are based on rules of universal validity to which States can be held, even in the absence of any treaty obligation or any explicit commitment on their part.[203]

Because the diplomatic conference which drafted Protocol II could not agree on the 'Hague law' rules which should apply to internal armed conflicts, and because another law-making effort is unlikely to be undertaken in the near future, the cruelty characterizing such conflicts must be tempered primarily through the advancement of customary law. However, the search for applicable customary law is impeded by the silence of military manuals on rules governing internal armed conflicts. This silence is a reflection of the insistence by states that non-international armed conflicts are, except upon recognition of belligerency, governed by national

---

[201] Art. 3. I am indebted to the late Professor Waldemar A. Solf for enlightenment on the text preceding and accompanying this note.

[202] Above text accompanying nn. 153-4 and 187.

[203] *Commentary*, above n. 200, at 1340 (footnote omitted).

rather than international law. The quest for customary law will
also be hampered by the prevalence of inhumane practices in
situations of internal armed conflict.

It is inevitable that, in developing international law for internal
armed conflicts, the central source for the rules will be the
principles of humanity. No self-respecting state would challenge the
applicability of such principles in internal armed conflict. More
specific rules, such as proportionality, the prohibition of direct
attacks on civilians, the prohibition of indiscriminate or dis-
proportionate attacks, and the prohibition of means and methods
of warfare that cause unnecessary suffering, can and should be
regarded as necessary and proper derivations from the principles
of humanity. The incorporation of such rules for internal wars in
the national manuals of military law would be a welcome first step.
Public opinion abhorring the excesses which constantly occur in
internal wars may act as a catalyst for determinations by third
states that such practices are not only immoral, but also illegal.
This, in turn, will aid in the formation of *opinio juris* and customary
rules for the humanization of such wars.

C. *Observations on Both Protocols*

Three interrelated subjects merit further observations: the state of
the ratification of the Protocols, the state of their application, and
their value in the formation of customary law. The ratification
statistics have already been cited. As of February 1988, 73 states
have ratified Protocol I and 66 states have ratified Protocol II.[204]
These ratifications should be evaluated from the perspective of the
relevance and weight of the ratifying states. This is important both
as regards the evidentiary value of the provisions of the Protocols
as customary rules, and for the generation of new customary norms
from the provisions of the Protocols. In the *North Sea Continental
Shelf Cases*, the ICJ, in discussing the emergence of customary law
from conventional norms, pointed out that

even without the passage of any considerable period of time, a very
widespread and representative participation in the convention might suffice
of itself, provided it included that of States whose interests were specially
affected.[205]

[204] Dissemination, above n. 170. See also the discussion of the *Colombian-
Peruvian Asylum* case, above n. 170.
[205] 1969 ICJ Rep. at 42.

Of course, on one level all states are, or should be, equally concerned with the application of humanitarian law. As regards international armed conflicts, this consideration is given an important expression in common Article 1 of the Geneva Conventions. On another level, it is nevertheless possible and even necessary to focus on states which are more directly concerned with the application of the Protocols. The question thus becomes what criteria should be employed to identify states whose interests are specially affected.

First, the superpowers must be mentioned, since they are effectively or potentially involved in many international and internal conflicts. Of the permanent members of the Security Council, only China has ratified Protocol I, and only France and China have ratified Protocol II. It is to be hoped that the US Senate will give its advice and consent to the ratification of Protocol II. Other major powers, such as the German Federal Republic, India, and Japan have not yet ratified either Protocol.

The other category of states whose interests are specially affected consists of those states which are either embroiled or implicated in international or non-international armed conflicts, or which may expect such involvement in the near future. With some important exceptions, major military powers, as well as countries for which the Protocols would have immediate significance, have opted not to ratify.[206] Obviously, in forming humanitarian law, acceptance of humanitarian principles by states living in conditions of tranquillity matters less than the acceptance by states implicated in armed

[206] In Africa, for example, Algeria, Chad, Egypt, Ethiopia, Morocco, Nigeria, South Africa, Sudan, Uganda and Zimbabwe have all been specially affected by armed conflict in either the recent past or the present. None of them has ratified either Protocol. Two other states specially affected by armed conflict, Angola and Mozambique, have ratified Protocol I, but, perhaps significantly, not Protocol II. Only one state specially affected by armed conflict, Libya, has ratified both Protocols.

Among the parties to conflicts in the Middle East, Jordan has ratified both Protocols. However, neither Iran, Iraq, Israel, nor Lebanon has ratified either Protocol. Turkey, a country which has recently suffered internal strife, also has not ratified either Protocol. Cyprus and Syria have only ratified Protocol I.

In Asia, neither Afghanistan, Cambodia, India, Indonesia nor Sri Lanka has ratified either Protocol. Vietnam has only ratified Protocol I. The Philippines has recently ratified Protocol II.

In South and Central America, only three countries embroiled in civil strife, El Salvador, Guatemala, and Suriname, have ratified both Protocols. Nicaragua has not ratified either Protocol, even though it is involved in a major non-international armed conflict (Section III, above). Other countries either currently or potentially involved in civil strife, such as Chile, Colombia and Peru, have also not ratified either Protocol.

conflicts. The refusal of states involved in armed conflicts to ratify the Protocols makes the transformation of the Protocols' provisions into customary law more difficult. If customary law is formed by *repetitio facti* accompanied by *opinio juris*, it is obvious that it is primarily the states implicated in conflict situations ('States whose interests were specially affected') that can supply the necessary *repetitio facti*.

Application or the observance of the provisions of the Protocols in various conflict situations, accompanied by *opinio juris*, forms customary international law. However, only one case of application of Protocol II is available, that of El Salvador.[207] Even that case is somewhat ambiguous, since, among other problems, the government of El Salvador has been reluctant to acknowledge formally the applicability of the Protocol, to which it is a party. Despite the many cruel internal armed conflicts which are raging in many parts of the world, no other cases of application of Protocol II by parties or non-parties can be identified. Protocol II is frequently cited in reports of NGOs such as Americas Watch, but not by the parties to the conflicts themselves.[208]

Protocol I has, however, been invoked both by the ICRC[209] and by the parties in the Iran–Iraq conflict.[210] Adversarial invocation of Protocol I by the belligerents in the Gulf War to score propaganda points should be treated as suspect because the states concerned have violated practically every fundamental principle of humanitarian law, whether stated in the Protocol or not. In general, however, adversarial invocation of normative rules may sensitize public opinion to humanitarian principles, raise the expectations of compliance with humanitarian principles, and facilitate the passage of humanitarian principles into customary law. Examples of this phenomenon are available, since human rights instruments have frequently been relied upon against violating states. However, in contrast to human rights instruments and the 1949 Geneva

[207] International Committee of the Red Cross, Annual Report 1983, at 29 (1984); International Committee of the Red Cross, Annual Report 1985, at 36 (1986); International Committee of the Red Cross, Annual Report 1984, at 32 (1985); International Committee of the Red Cross, Annual Report 1985, at 36 (1986); International Committee of the Red Cross, Annual Report 1986, at 36 (1987).

[208] See e.g. Americas Watch, Human Rights in Nicaragua 1985-1986 at 69–74 (Mar. 1986).

[209] International Committee of the Red Cross, Annual Report 1983, at 58 (1984).

[210] See e.g. UN Doc. S/16649 at 2 (1984); Tavernier, above n. 165, at 58.

Conventions, the invocation of the Geneva Protocols has been sporadic and infrequent.[211] Although violations are more visible and easier to count than acts concordant with international agreements, it is clear that the Protocols have often been violated and ignored.

Although the Protocols have been so disrespected, violations of a norm do not necessarily signify the demise of the norm, particularly if the norm itself is well established and recognized. A distinction should, however, be made between the survival of a well-established norm despite its recurrent violations, and the emergence of a new customary norm which is not supported by consistent practice. There is, perhaps, as Akehurst has suggested, 'a very strong presumption against change in the law'.[212] Acts inconsistent with an emerging rule must be balanced by a greater amount of concordant practice for the rule to become consolidated.[213] None the less, even allowing for a considerably less onerous burden of proof of concordant practice, an allowance justified by the humanitarian content of the Protocols, large-scale violations of and indifference to the Geneva Protocols hinder the development of customary law from their provisions.[214]

On the positive side, the Protocols have already entered the mainstream of humanitarian law concepts, terminology and scholarship. No discussion of any subject of humanitarian law without recognition of the provisions of the Protocols is imaginable. This fact in itself will probably trigger not only more frequent invocation of the Protocols in various conflicts by the parties thereto, but also the awakening of international public opinion to the necessity for compliance with the compelling humanitarian principles stated in the Protocols, and thus the growth of greater expectations of compliance with the Protocols' provisions. These factors are already contributing to the formation of customary law generated by the provisions of the Protocols.

[211] Both Protocols are occasionally mentioned by United Nations bodies, such as the Working Group on Enforced or Involuntary Disappearances, see UN Doc. E/CN.4/1492 at 67–8 (1981). For other cases of invocation of Protocol I, see above nn. 209–10.

[212] Akehurst, above n. 23, at 19.

[213] Ibid. at 20.

[214] E.g. as regards the transformation into firm custom of provisions which reflect progressive development, of provisions *de lege ferenda*, or of general principles which enjoy broad support because of their very generality but which give rise to dissent when expressed in specific language.

The formation of customary law is, to be sure, an evolutionary process which hinges on the developments, e.g. in the number and identity of ratifying states and the range of concordant practice.

Although the poor record of compliance with the Protocols so far makes state practice an insufficient means of building their provisions into customary law, other developments indicate growing support for the transformation of many, perhaps even most, of the provisions of the Protocols into customary law. The best example of this progress is the incorporation of the Protocols' provisions considered as embodying crystallized or emerging customary rules into national manuals of military law. The development of the law through military manuals may also create the danger of the greater fragmentation of humanitarian law. None the less, more common, even ubiquitous, interests may assert themselves in the future to maintain the universality of humanitarian law.

Resort to the building of customary law through military manuals would, of course, be unnecessary had the Protocols been universally ratified or generally applied through state practice. Since this has not been the case, at the present time we can only expect gradual steps, primarily through military manuals, towards the crystallization into customary law of the compelling elements of the Protocols.

II

Human Rights Instruments and Customary Law

I. THE QUEST FOR UNIVERSALITY

Some of the consequences of a norm's customary character mentioned in our discussion of the 1949 Geneva Conventions (Chapter I, Section I) are equally relevant to human rights instruments. The Geneva Conventions have been universally accepted. In contrast, human rights instruments have been ratified by far fewer states.[1] For these instruments, therefore, the fundamental

---

[1] e.g. the Convention on the Prevention and Punishment of the Crime of Genocide, done 9 Dec. 1948, 78 UNTS 277, has 97 parties, Multilateral Treaties Deposited with the Secretary-General: Status as at 31 December 1987, at 95-6, UN Doc. ST/LEG/SER.E/6 (1988); the International Convention on the Elimination of all Forms of Racial Discrimination, done 7 Mar. 1966, 660 UNTS 195, has 124 parties, Multilateral Treaties Deposited with the Secretary-General: Status as at 31 December 1987, at 103-4, UN Doc. ST/LEG/SER.E/6 (1988); the International Covenant on Economic, Social and Cultural Rights, done 16 Dec. 1966, 993 UNTS 3, has 91 parties, Multilateral Treaties Deposited with the Secretary-General: Status as at 31 December 1987, at 118, UN Doc. ST/LEG/SER.E/6 (1988); the International Covenant on Civil and Political Rights, done 16 Dec. 1966, 999 UNTS 171, has 87 parties, Multilateral Treaties Deposited with the Secretary-General: Status as at 31 December 1987, at 128, UN Doc. ST/LEG/SER.E/6 (1988); the Optional Protocol to the International Covenant on Civil and Political Rights, done 16 Dec. 1966, 999 UNTS 171, has 40 parties, Multilateral Treaties Deposited with the Secretary-General: Status as at 31 December 1987, at 152, UN Doc. ST/LEG/SER.E/6 (1988); the Convention on the Non-Applicability of Statutory Limitations to War Crimes and Crimes against Humanity, done 26 Nov. 1968, 754 UNTS 73, has 30 parties, Multilateral Treaties Deposited with the Secretary-General: Status as at 31 December 1987, at 154, UN Doc. ST/LEG/SER.E/6 (1988); the International Convention on the Suppression and Punishment of the Crime of *Apartheid*, done 30 Nov. 1973, 1015 UNTS 244, has 86 parties, Multilateral Treaties Deposited with the Secretary-General: Status as at 31 December 1987, at 157, UN Doc. ST/LEG/SER.E/6 (1988); the Convention on the Elimination of All Forms of Discrimination against Women, done 18 Dec. 1979, A/RES/34/180, has 94 parties, Multilateral Treaties Deposited with the Secretary-General: Status as at 31 December 1987, at 160-1, UN Doc. ST/LEG/SER.E/6 (1988); Convention Against Torture and Other Cruel, Inhuman or Degrading Treatment or Punishment, done 10 Dec. 1984, GA Res. 39/46, 39 UN GAOR Supp. (No. 51) at 197, UN Doc. A/39/61 (1985) has 28 parties: Multilateral Treaties Deposited with the Secretary-General, Status as at 31 December 1987, at 174, UN Doc. ST/LEG/SER.E/6 (1988).

significance of a norm's customary character is that the norm binds states that are not parties to the instrument in which the norm is stated.

Other consequences follow as well. First, for non-parties, the acceptance of a norm's customary character signifies that the subject covered by the norm, at least in principle, is governed by international law and is thus outside the domestic jurisdiction of states (discussed further below). This result is of considerable importance because international human rights overlap to a large extent with national laws and procedures and implicate important socio-cultural values. The very effectiveness of international human rights instruments depends on their observance and implementation through domestic judicial and administrative agencies. Claims that a particular subject falls within the domestic jurisdiction of states hinder or even bar the acceptance of international human rights principles for standards of behaviour. Conversely, a consensus that a particular subject has an international character facilitates the acceptance of international human rights as standards of behaviour.

Secondly, although regional or treaty human rights organs are usually authorized to apply only those norms stated in the applicable instruments, in some cases their terms of reference encompass customary law. For example, the African Commission on Human and Peoples' Rights may draw on 'African practices consistent with international norms on human and peoples' rights, customs generally accepted as law, general principles of law recognized by African states as well as legal precedents and doctrine'.[2] The International Covenant on Civil and Political Rights requires that measures derogating from the obligations of states parties under the Covenant 'are not inconsistent with their other obligations under international law . . .'.[3] Such provisions broaden the range of protections available to the human person and highlight the importance of customary law. The determination that a given rule is or is not an embodiment of customary law thus takes on practical significance.

Professor Schachter has suggested that the recognition of a

[2] African [Banjul] Charter on Human and Peoples' Rights, adopted 27 June 1981, Art. 61, reprinted in 21 ILM 58, 67 (1982).
[3] Art. 4(1). See also T. Meron, Human Rights Law-Making in the United Nations 162 n. 71, 212 n. 229 (1986); Buergenthal, *International and Regional Human Rights Law and Institutions: Some Examples of Their Interaction*, 12 Tex. Int'l LJ 321, 324–5 (1977).

human right as customary may have yet another effect: '[It] allows not only the treaty non-parties, but also the parties to have recourse to international law remedies not provided for in the treaties.'[4] This result depends, however, on the treaty in question, since some treaties, as between the parties, may exclude resort to remedies dehors the treaty. We shall return to this question in Chapter III, Section X.

Tendencies, apparent in various fields of international law, to impose treaty norms on non-parties in the guise of general international law or customary law, even in the absence of state practice dehors the treaty, have been examined and censured by Professor Weil.[5] Such trends have been especially strong in the human rights field, where they have focused not only on treaties but also on declarations and resolutions adopted by the United Nations and other international organizations. States parties to human rights instruments and supporters of declarations and resolutions promulgating human rights naturally seek to promote the universality of human rights by attempting to assure concordant behaviour by non-parties to the instruments concerned and by states which have not supported the adoption of the declarations and resolutions. But this approach generates tension between the important human rights values advocated by states parties to human rights instruments and the sovereignty of non-parties. The credibility of international human rights therefore requires that attempts to extend their universality utilize irreproachable legal methods.

One of the principal methods employed by scholars to promote concordant behaviour of non-parties with human rights instruments has been to anchor the instruments' *erga omnes* authority in the human rights provisions of the UN Charter, especially Articles 55 and 56. This method finds support in such governmental statements as that made by France (19 Feb. 1957):

---

[4] Schachter, *International Law in Theory and Practice*, 178 Recueil des cours 334 (1982-V). The same point is made by § 703(1) of the Restatement: 'A state party to an international human rights agreement has, as against any other state party violating the agreement, the remedies generally available for violation of an international agreement, as well as any special remedies provided by the agreement.' Restatement of the Law Third, Restatement of the Foreign Relations Law of the United States § 703(1) (1987). See generally ibid. Reporters' notes 2–4.

[5] Weil, *Towards Relative Normativity in International Law?*, 77 AJIL 413, 434–9 (1983). See also Chapter I n. 144.

[A]lthough these [slavery] conventions cannot be invoked [against Saudi-Arabia and Yemen, which] abstained or were absent when the United Nations General Assembly adopted the Universal Declaration of Human Rights in 1948, it nevertheless remains that slavery is prohibited under the general principles of the Charter relating to fundamental human rights.[6]

The principal advocate of this method, Professor Sohn, has eloquently argued that the weakness stemming from the excessive generality of the Charter's human rights provisions has been remedied by their authoritative interpretation through the Universal Declaration of Human Rights, the Covenants, and other UN instruments and resolutions on international human rights. In addition to law-making instruments, Professor Sohn has found support in the UN case-law on human rights violations. The derivation from the binding authority of the Charter thus gives obligatory force to the instruments amplifying and interpreting its provisions. The Charter's human rights principles, so elaborated, have become a part of customary international law: 'The Declaration, as an authoritative listing of human rights, has become a basic component of international customary law, binding on all states, not only on members of the United Nations.'[7] Professor

[6] J.O. Débats parlementaires, Conseil de la République 418 (1957); reprinted in 2 A. Kiss, Répertoire de la pratique française en matière de droit international public 641 (1966) (my translation). While some statements made by the French government recognize the normative significance of the Universal Declaration of Human Rights on grounds such as it being an embodiment of general international law (e.g. ibid. at 258) or as the interpretation of the principles of the Charter (e.g. ibid. at 650, 651, 5 ibid. at 189), other statements (e.g. 5 ibid. at 190) and the Conseil d'Etat (2 ibid. at 650-1) have played down that significance.

The normative significance of the Universal Declaration has been played down also in positivist-orientated Socialist states, as suggested by the following comment: 'In the course of the past 40 years, the basic ideas underlying the Universal Declaration of Human Rights have been further evolved by the United Nations along systematic lines and, to a great extent have been transformed [through the Covenants and other human rights treaties] into valid international law (mutual obligations of States).' *40 Years—Universal Declaration of Human Rights: From the Declaration to a Sensible Co-operation*, 14 GDR Committee for Human Rights Bulletin 83, 84 (No. 2, 1988).

[7] Sohn, *The New International Law: Protection of the Rights of Individuals Rather than States*, 32 Am. U. L. Rev. 1, 17 (1982); Sohn, *John A. Sibley Lecture: The Shaping of International Law*, 8 Ga. J. Int'l & Comp. L. 1, 18-22 (1978). Compare Buergenthal, *International Human Rights Law and Institutions: Accomplishments and Prospects*, 63 Wash. L. Rev. 1, 8-9 (1988); T. Buergenthal, International Human Rights 29-33 (1988). For discussion of the customary law character of the Universal Declaration, see also M. McDougal, H. Lasswell, and L. Chen, Human Rights and World Public Order 272-4 (1980).

Professor Sohn argues with regard to the Covenants that '[t]hough [they] resemble

Sohn's view finds important support in the ICJ's grounding of the obligatory force of the prohibition of arbitrary deprivation of personal liberty in both the Charter and the Declaration.[8] The normative force of the Universal Declaration and other declarations is recognized in principle also in national laws, in various UN reports and statements of governments,[9] although scholarly controversy traditional international agreements which bind only those who ratify them, it seems clear that they partake of the creative force of the Declaration and constitute in a similar fashion an authoritative interpretation of the basic rules of international law on the subject of human rights which are embodied in the Charter of the United Nations. This conclusion is supported by the fact that the Covenants are even more universal in their origin than the Declaration. . . . Consequently, although the Covenants apply directly to the states that have ratified them, they are of some importance, at the same time, with respect to the interpretation of the Charter obligations of the nonratifying states.' Sohn, *The Human Rights Law of the Charter*, 12 Tex. Int'l LJ 129, at 135-6 (1977).

[8] 'Wrongfully to deprive human beings of their freedom and to subject them to physical constraint in conditions of hardship is in itself manifestly incompatible with the principles of the Charter of the United Nations, as well as with the fundamental principles enunciated in the Universal Declaration of Human Rights.' *United States Diplomatic and Consular Staff in Tehran (United States of America* v. *Iran)*, 1980 ICJ Rep. 3, 42 (Judgment of 24 May). In this statement, the Court went considerably beyond its earlier recognition, which was rooted in the Charter's explicit references to distinctions on grounds of race, that the 'denial [by South Africa] of fundamental human rights is a flagrant violation of the purposes and principles of the Charter'. *Legal Consequences for States of the Continued Presence of South Africa in Namibia (South West Africa) Notwithstanding Security Council Resolution 276 (1970)*, 1971 ICJ Rep. 16, 57 (Advisory Opinion of 21 June).

[9] A 'Survey of International Law' prepared for the International Law Commission by the Secretary-General of the United Nations observes that '[d]uring the years since its adoption the Declaration has come, through its influence in a variety of contexts, to have a marked impact on the pattern and content of international law and to acquire a status extending beyond that originally intended for it. In general, two elements may be distinguished in this process: first, the use of the Declaration as a yardstick by which to measure the content and standard of observance of human rights; and, second, the reaffirmation of the Declaration and its provisions in a series of other instruments. These two elements, often to be found combined, have caused the Declaration to gain a cumulative and pervasive effect. . . . Thus most . . . of the many national constitutions adopted since 1948 embody an endorsement of the Declaration or reflect its provisions, and numerous conventions include or refer to its articles. Besides being incorporated in acts of national legislation and cited before national tribunals, it has been used in United Nations resolutions and declarations, and in the constitutive instruments of international organizations.' UN Doc. A/CN.4/245 at 196-7 (1971) (footnotes omitted).

In the context of the Declaration on the Elimination of All Forms of Intolerance and Discrimination Based on Religion or Belief (GA Res. 36/55, 36 UN GAOR Supp. (No. 51) at 171, UN Doc. A/36/51 (1981)), Elizabeth Odio Benito, Special Rapporteur of the Sub-Commission on Prevention of Discrimination and Protection of Minorities, notes that '[i]n practice, the work done for 40 years by the United Nations organs and bodies concerned with human rights has gone beyond . . .

persists over the jurisprudential rationale for its normative character and over the question which of the rights stated in it have acquired binding nature as customary law or as an authoritative interpretation of the Charter.

Notwithstanding the challenges[10] to which it has been subjected, Professor Sohn's method is perfectly legitimate. It has served the very important purpose of extending some Charter authority to UN human rights instruments. It does, however, present certain difficulties. Except for a specific mention of prohibited distinctions on grounds of race,[11] sex, language, or religion, the human rights provisions of the Charter are characterized by exceptional brevity and generality (e.g. Article 55(c) refers to 'universal respect for, and observance of, human rights and fundamental freedoms for all . . .'). In contrast, numerous human rights instruments,

restrictive interpretation of the legal effect of General Assembly resolutions. . . .

[W]hile the General Assembly's declarations do not give rise to "rights" from the strictly legal standpoint, they do unquestionably contain "values" that should govern the daily conduct of individuals and States. . . .' UN Doc. E/CN.4/Sub.2/1987/26 at 49.

Referring to the same declaration, the US government emphasized in these terms its normative character: 'It is a carefully drafted statement regarded throughout the world as articulating the fundamental rights of freedom of religion and belief.' UN Doc. E/CN.4/1988/44/Add.2 at 1.

Reynaldo Galindo Pohl, the UN Human Rights Commission's Special Representative on the human rights situation in Iran, states as follows: 'The rights and freedoms set out in the Universal Declaration have become international customary law through State practice and *opinio juris*. Even if the strictest approach is adopted to the determination of the elements which form international customary law, that is, the classical doctrine of the convergence of extensive, continuous and reiterated practice and of *opinio juris*, the provisions contained in the Universal Declaration meet the stringent standards of that doctrine. Of course, they also meet the more liberal standards of contemporary doctrines on the constitutive elements of international customary law.

The Universal Declaration, as a projection of the Charter of the United Nations, and particularly as international customary law, binds all States.' UN Doc. E/CN.4/1987/23 at 4–5 (1987).

[10] See e.g. Lane, *Demanding Human Rights: A Change in the World Legal Order*, 6 Hofstra L. Rev. 269 (1978); Lane, *Mass Killing by Governments: Lawful in the World Legal Order?*, 12 NYU J. Int'l L. & Pol. 239 (1979); Watson, *Autointerpretation, Competence, and the Continuing Validity of Article 2(7) of the UN Charter*, 71 AJIL 60 (1977).

[11] It has thus been suggested that 'the International Convention on the Elimination of Racial Discrimination is, to a large extent, declaratory of the law of the Charter, or, in other words, the basic principles of the convention lay down the law which binds also states which are not parties to the convention, but, as Members of the United Nations, are parties to the Charter.' Schwelb, *The International Court of Justice and the Human Rights Clauses of the Charter*, 66 AJIL 337, 351 (1972). See also above n. 8.

encompassing hundreds of detailed provisions, have been adopted by the United Nations. It is therefore not surprising that the grounding of the legal force of such instruments for non-parties in the theory of the authoritative interpretation of the Charter human rights provisions has sparked considerable controversy.

Professor Sohn also relies upon a process of transformation, analogous to that in United States law, in which 'vague constitutional precepts . . . [are] translated . . . into more detailed principles, which, because of their higher precision, impart a more definite character to the whole international legal order.'[12] But the US Bill of Rights is articulated in a far higher degree of specificity than the UN Charter. Moreover, the legal force of the interpretative gloss of the Constitution is rooted in the authority of the US Supreme Court, which has no exact parallel in the United Nations. In any event, to achieve maximal credibility for international human rights, interpretative theory should not be stretched too thin, especially if the objective of assuring concordant behaviour by non-parties can be furthered through alternative, even if innovative, methods which fall within the recognized process of building customary international law.

One controversial method for extending to non-parties the *ratione personae* reach of norms accepted within international organizations builds on the significance of consensus or near-consensus. A principal protagonist of this approach, Professor Cassese, has argued that consensus points to the binding nature of some provisions of Additional Protocol I to the Geneva Conventions, such as those on wars of national liberation and the status of combatants. He has contended that '[t]he adoption of the innovative provisions [following negotiations and acceptance of fundamental elements of a package deal] reflected a general conviction to the effect that they had the status of generally binding rules.'[13] The importance of the equilibrium between conflicting demands requires 'that they form the subject of general consent and give rise to customary rules'.[14] This theory, he has admitted, is designed to

---

[12] Sohn, *The International Law of Human Rights: A Reply to Recent Criticisms*, 9 Hofstra L. Rev. 347, 355 (1981).

[13] Cassese, *The Geneva Protocols of 1977 on the Humanitarian Law of Armed Conflict and Customary International Law*, 3 UCLA Pac. Basin LJ 55, 113 (1984). See also A. Cassese, International Law in a Divided World 180-5 (1986).

[14] Cassese, *The Geneva Protocols of 1977*, above n. 13, at 116 (1984).

create obligations for non-parties which participate in a law-making conference:

> [W]ere States to leave major points of agreement in the condition of conventional regulations, so that any State would be free to adhere to them by ratifying the treaty, or to hold aloof by merely withholding ratification, there would be a lack of general standards on crucial areas of international intercourse. There are therefore compelling reasons for States to bestow the imprint of *general* rules upon those standards of behavior.[15]

Similarly, Professor Sohn has argued that 'once a principle is generally accepted at an international [law-making] conference, usually through consensus, a rule of customary international law can emerge without having to wait for the signature of the convention. . . . [T]he convention['s] signature by a large number of states confirms that the provisions . . . have been generally accepted . . . and constitutes . . . an *opinio juris* that these provisions are generally acceptable. . . .'[16] The same is true of declaratory resolutions 'which, if accepted by an overwhelming majority of the General Assembly, usually by consensus or by an almost unanimous vote, can also constitute "generally accepted" principles of international law'.[17] Because the Charter does not endow most General Assembly resolutions with binding character, Professor

[15] Ibid. at 116-17 (emphasis in original). It is worth noting that Art. 18(1) of the Vienna Convention on the Law of Treaties obligates a state that has signed a treaty to refrain from acts which defeat the object and purpose of the treaty only until 'it shall have made its intention clear not to become a party to the treaty', thus denying any implication of a more comprehensive commitment. Because Art. 18 and the customary law principle of good faith do not correspond perfectly, Art. 18 is sometimes regarded, at least in part, as a progressive development of the law. I. Sinclair, The Vienna Convention on the Law of Treaties 18-19, 43-4 (2nd edn. 1984).

It is, of course, true that 'the new modes of lawmaking . . . accelerate the process of customary law formation by relying upon the unique form of state practice which occurs in multilateral organizations like the United Nations.' Blum and Steinhardt, *Federal Jurisdiction over International Human Rights Claims: The Alien Tort Claims Act after Filartiga v. Peña-Irala*, 22 Harv. Int'l LJ 53, 72 (1981).

[16] Sohn, *"Generally Accepted" International Rules*, 61 Wash. L. Rev. 1073, 1077-8 (1986) (footnotes omitted).

[17] Ibid. at 1078. Professor Abi-Saab speaks of legislative power which is subject to the possibility of contracting out of certain norms and of claiming the status of a persistent objector. Abi-Saab, *La Coutume dans tous ses états ou le dilemme du développement du droit international général dans un monde éclaté*, in 1 International Law at the Time of its Codification: Essays in Honour of Roberto Ago 53, 64 (1987).

Sohn qualifies this statement by requiring that declarations, to become binding, 'must be generally accepted as legally binding by the members of the international community, either at the time of their adoption or by subsequent practice of a reasonable number of states, evidencing their willingness to conform to the principles contained in a declaration and by general acquiescence by other states'.[18]

The passage of norms agreed upon in international conferences into customary law through the practice, including the acquiescence, of states constitutes a common, generally accepted method of building customary international law. But an attempt to endow customary law status instantly upon norms approved by consensus or near-consensus at international conferences raises serious questions. First, in some cases it is far from certain that the participating states intended to be bound. In supporting a consensus, a state may be motivated by considerations which have nothing to do with acceptance of the binding character of the norm, at least not at the moment of its adoption. Second, the statements of a representative expressing facially minor reservations to or interpretations of a norm may in fact mask more serious disagreements which the representative prefers not to highlight. Third, the immediately binding character of a norm should not be asserted on the basis of consensus without considering the authority of the representative to commit his or her state.[19] The assertion that by supporting a consensus resolution, a diplomat representing his state before an

[18] Sohn, above n. 16, at 1079. The cumulative weight of consensus resolutions of the General Assembly has an undeniable impact on the development of customary human rights, especially when supported by additional state practice. On the legal significance and consequences of declarations, see Schachter, *The Twilight Existence of Nonbinding International Agreements*, 71 AJIL 296 (1977); Schachter, *Alf Ross Memorial Lecture: The Crisis of Legitimation in the United Nations*, 50 Nordisk tidsskrift int'l ret 3 (1981); Schachter, *The Nature and Process of Legal Development in International Society*, in The Structure and Process of International Law 745, 787–95 (R. Macdonald and D. Johnston eds. 1983); Skubiszewski, *Non-Binding Resolutions and the Law-Making Process*, 15 Polish YB Int'l L. 135 (1986); Skubiszewski, *Resolutions of the U.N. General Assembly and Evidence of Custom*, in 1 International Law at the Time of its Codification, above n. 17, at 503; Sloan, *General Assembly Resolutions Revisited (Forty Years Later)*, 58 Brit. YB Int'l L. 39 (1987).

[19] Compare Arts. 7 and 46 of the Vienna Convention on the Law of Treaties. See generally the excellent discussion by Schachter of the evidentiary value of a resolution asserting that a norm which it states is legally binding despite the scarcity of concordant practice and of the concept of 'instant custom.' Schachter, above n. 4, at 114–23.

international conference for the purpose of adopting the text of a resolution may commit his state to recognize the 'instant' customary law status of the norms approved may clash with principles of democratic government under law and separation of powers. As regards resolutions interpreting either the UN Charter or other normative instruments, Article 31(3)(b) of the Vienna Convention on the Law of Treaties should also be taken into account. Circumstances surrounding the adoption of a consensus resolution, including reactions outside the parent organization, may either strengthen or weaken the resolution's normative character.

This is not to suggest that the sources of international law listed in Article 38 of the ICJ's Statute are comprehensive and immutable. It may well be that these sources will be expanded by, for example, attributing a more direct law-creating role to normative resolutions of the General Assembly. For the time being, however, recognized methods of building customary law provide the flexibility required for promoting the passage of human rights into customary law. These can and should be resorted to whenever possible.

One such method is offered by Article 38(1)(c) of the Statute of the International Court of Justice. Because normal implementation of international human rights is accomplished through national laws and tribunals and because many human rights implicate questions of due process and administration of justice, it is surprising that 'the general principles of law recognized by civilized nations' mentioned in Article 38(1)(c) have not received greater attention as a method for obtaining greater legal recognition for the principles of the Universal Declaration and other human rights instruments.[20] As human rights norms stated in international instruments come to be reflected in national laws, especially in provisions for the administration of justice and due process, Article 38(1)(c) will increasingly become one of the principal methods for the maturation of such standards into the mainstream of international law. Human rights lawyers should play an important role in promoting Article 38(1)(c) as a route for the passage of international human rights

[20] Professor Schachter has aptly noted that the Declaration has entered 'into many national constitutions, statutes and judicial decisions [and that] many of its principles are now part of the corpus of "general principles of law recognized by civilized nations" in the sense of article 38 of the Statute of the International Court of Justice and perhaps also that state practice has given to some of its provisions the character of customary law.' Schachter, *International Law Implications of U.S. Human Rights Policies*, 24 NYL Sch. L. Rev. 63, 68 (1978).

norms into general international law. As in other fields of international law, the distinction between international customary law mentioned in Article 38(1)(b) and general principles of law recognized by civilized nations (Article 38(1)(c) of the ICJ's Statute) will eventually become blurred. Decisions of national courts, such as those discussed in Section III, below, play an increasingly important role in the recognition of various human rights as custom; so also do the judgments and the advisory opinions of the ICJ, discussed in Section II, below. Of considerable value is the case-law of such quasi-judicial bodies as the Human Rights Committee established under Article 28 of the Political Covenant. Although regional human rights courts and commissions apply and interpret their constitutive instruments rather than general international law, the cumulative weight of their case-law influences and consolidates the development of customary human rights law.

Other accepted methods of building international law can also be applied in the field of human rights. For example, Professor Schachter has justified the binding nature of United Nations Charter human rights obligations *vis-à-vis* non-member states by the implicit recognition of these obligations by nearly all non-member states,[21] i.e. by the classical theory of acquiescence. As he has acknowledged, the weight of general statements of international bodies as evidence of custom cannot be assessed without considering the actual practice of states, and national constitutions and legislation incorporating international human rights also 'require a measure of confirmation in actual behaviour'.[22] Because the community values reflected in the human rights that are stated in international human rights instruments enjoy strong public support, only a slim likelihood exists that a non-party will readily face the political consequences of openly refusing to accept the norm by becoming a persistent objector to it. The non-party will very probably find itself bound by the norm. Acquiescence is thus an effective means for expanding the universality of international human rights.

The dynamic relationship between custom and treaty, discussed in Chapter I, above, also offers a means for extending human

---

[21] Ibid. at 69.

[22] Schachter, above n. 4, at 335. Compare N. Rodley, The Treatment of Prisoners under International Law 64 (1987): '[T]he best evidence for a customary rule . . . is to be found in what states say they think the rule is, and what they say they are doing (or not doing) in terms of that rule.' Inconsistent practice and violations are discussed in Chapter I, Section V, above.

rights.[23] A codificatory treaty is, of course, an embodiment of customary rules and constitutes excellent evidence of their status. Sinclair aptly observes that

[a] codifying convention will influence the content and the development of custom, to the extent that particular norms contained in the convention may be regarded by a tribunal as being expressive of, or as generating, a rule of customary law; and customary law itself, operating alongside the codifying convention, has its role to play in filling in the gaps which any exercise in codification and progressive development inevitably leaves.[24]

Normative multilateral treaties, such as those which develop rather than codify human rights law, are of equal importance. As experience shows, such treaties generate new rules of customary law and may eventually acquire probative value for establishing the customary character of the new rules. Some treaties may, of course, state provisions which neither embody existing rules of customary international law nor generate new rules. In practice, however, treaties can only seldom be categorized as either codifying existing law, crystallizing the emergent law, generating new rules of customary law, or merely creating conventional obligations. A normative multilateral treaty characteristically mixes provisions falling into each of these categories.

[23] For an excellent discussion of the relationship of codification to customary international law and a summary of the principal literature on this question, see I. Sinclair, The International Law Commission 138–45 (1987). On codification generally, see literature cited in T. Meron, above n. 3, at 269 n. 1. See also Zemanek, *Codification of International Law: Salvation or Dead End*, in 1 International Law at the Time of its Codification, above n. 17, at 581; Ago, *Nouvelles réflexions sur la codification du droit international*, 88 Revue générale de droit international public 539 (1988).

[24] I. Sinclair, above n. 15, at 258. Jiménez De Aréchaga cogently observes, with regard to the effect upon the formation of customary law of conventions adopted at UN general codification conferences, that 'this kind of customary law which finds expression in general conventions may operate in three different ways: the conventional text may merely restate a pre-existing rule of custom; it may crystallize an emergent rule *in statu nascendi*; or, finally, a treaty provision, or even a proposal at a conference, may become the focal point of a subsequent practice of States and, in due course, harden into a customary rule. These three modalities may be described as the declaratory effect; the crystallizing effect; and the generating effect.

In the 1986 case of *Nicaragua* v. *United States* the Court referred to these three modalities, saying that a rule enshrined in a treaty may also exist as a customary rule "either because the treaty had merely codified the custom, or caused it to 'crystallize', or because it had influenced its subsequent adoption".' *The Work and the Jurisprudence of the International Court of Justice 1947–1986*, 58 Brit. YB Int'l L. 1, 32–3 (1987) (footnote omitted).

Article 38 of the Vienna Convention on the Law of Treaties confirms that '[n]othing in Articles 34 to 37 precludes a rule set forth in a treaty from becoming binding upon a third State as a customary rule of international law, recognized as such.' In its *Commentary* on Article 34 (now Article 38), the International Law Commission explained that Article 38 was designed to ensure that the draft articles did not adversely affect the legitimacy of the process whereby treaty rules may become binding on non-parties as customary rules of international law. The Commission emphasized that

[t]he role played by custom in sometimes extending the application of rules contained in a treaty beyond the contracting States is well recognized. A treaty concluded between certain States may formulate a rule . . . which afterwards comes to be generally accepted by other States and becomes binding upon other States by way of custom. . . . So too a codifying convention purporting to state existing rules of customary law may come to be regarded as the generally accepted formulation of the customary rules in question even by States not parties to the convention.[25]

As a critic of this process, Professor Weil has described '[t]reaty clauses that are declaratory of preexistent customary norms, or crystallize customary norms in process of formation, or attract concordant practice [as] variant erasers of the frontier between conventional and customary norms . . .'.[26]

Given the relatively recent birth of international human rights as positive law for the international community, treaties promulgated in the early stages of UN human rights law-making naturally only rarely articulated existing customary norms of human rights. One such rare case is, of course, that of the largely codificatory[27] Convention on the Prevention and Punishment of the Crime of Genocide.[28] In contrast, most human rights instruments state largely new or conventional norms. Nevertheless, the International Law Commission's 1977 *Commentary* on Article 22 (on the

[25] [1966] 2 YB. Int'l L. Comm'n 230-1, UN Doc. A/CN.4/SER.A/1966/Add.1 (1967).

[26] Weil, above n. 5, at 438.

[27] Professor Cassese suggests that the Convention made the 'loose prohibition laid down in customary law concrete and operational' and thus 'did go well beyond existing law'. Cassese, *The Geneva Protocols of 1977*, above n. 13, at 63.

[28] Adopted 9 Dec. 1948, 78 UNTS 277. See Chapter I, Section II, above, and Chapter II, Section II, below.

exhaustion of local remedies) of its draft articles on state responsibility (part one) went too far in its emphasis on the scarcity of customary human rights norms and the almost exclusively conventional character of human rights:

[W]ithout in any way disregarding the existence of a few customary international rules on the subject, and without ruling out the possibility— even the likelihood—that such rules will increase in number, we are bound to conclude that, today, the international obligations of the State in regard to the treatment of its own nationals are almost exclusively of a conventional nature. . . .[29]

Excessive even in 1977, the ILC's statement is becoming less and less true. Through acceptance of norms stated in human rights instruments by states, especially non-parties, human rights treaties have generated new customary rules of international law. New human rights instruments have been adopted that already embody certain customary rules. The repetition of certain norms in many human rights instruments is in itself an important articulation of state practice and may serve as evidence of customary international law. This process is typical even of bilateral agreements,[30] which are based on reciprocity, and occurs with particular vitality in the case of multilateral, normative agreements, such as international human rights and humanitarian instruments.[31]

The Restatement of the Foreign Relations Law of the United States, rightly considered to be a particularly authoritative United States source, attempts to move beyond general principles and actually to identify customary human rights. Of greater interest than the identification of already accepted customary human rights are the types of evidence used to identify them and the processes used to support the maturation of a right into customary status. Here, the Restatement notes that

[29] [1977] 2 YB Int'l L. Comm'n (pt. 2) at 46, UN Doc. A/CN.4/ SER.A/1977/Add.1 (Part 2).

[30] Baxter observed that '[a]t worst, the presence of a provision in a number of bilateral treaties can strengthen the rule of international law to which it gives expression. At best the series of similar bilateral treaties can of itself establish the state of the law.' Baxter, *Treaties and Custom*, 129 Recueil des cours 25, 89 (1970-I).

[31] Baxter observed, in the context of the Geneva Conventions, that '[t]he passage of humanitarian treaties into customary international law might . . . be justified on the ground that each new wave of such treaties builds upon the past conventions, so that each detailed rule . . . is nothing more that an implementation of a more general standard already laid down in an earlier convention. . . .'. Baxter, *Multilateral Treaties as Evidence of Customary International Law*, 41 Brit. YB Int'l L. 275, 286 (1965-6).

[p]ractice accepted as building customary human rights law includes: virtually universal adherence to the United Nations Charter and its human rights provisions, and virtually universal and frequently reiterated acceptance of the Universal Declaration of Human Rights even if only in principle; virtually universal participation of states in the preparation and adoption of international agreements recognizing human rights principles generally, or particular rights; the adoption of human rights principles by states in regional organizations in Europe, Latin America, and Africa . . . general support by states for United Nations resolutions declaring, recognizing, invoking, and applying international human rights principles as international law; action by states to conform their national law or practice to standards or principles declared by international bodies, and the incorporation of human rights provisions, directly or by reference, in national constitutions and laws; invocation of human rights principles in national policy, in diplomatic practice, in international organization activities and actions; and other diplomatic communications or action by states reflecting the view that certain practices violate international human rights law, including condemnation and other adverse state reactions to violations by other states. The International Court of Justice and the International Law Commission have recognized the existence of customary human rights law. . . . Some of these practices may also support the conclusion that particular human rights have been absorbed into international law as general principles common to the major state legal systems.[32]

The Restatement's list of types of evidence to be utilized to prove customary human rights is extremely useful. Also useful are the indicators suggested by Professor Schachter, who refers to the need to assess general statements on human rights by international bodies by reference to actual state practice and the intensity and depth of third-party condemnations of violations.[33] On the basis of these indicators, Professor Schachter believes that freedom of expression, equality between men and women, the right to work, equal pay for equal work and the right to leisure, for example, have not matured into customary law as yet.

Of course, the initial inquiry must aim at the determination whether, at a minimum, the definition of the core norm claiming customary law status and preferably the contours of the norm have been widely accepted. In this context my own preferred indicators

---

[32] Restatement, above n. 4, § 701, Reporters' note 2. For a similar list of types of evidence of customary human rights, see Schachter, above n. 4, at 334–5.

[33] Schachter, above n. 4, at 335–6.

Human Rights

evincing customary human rights are, first, the degree to which a statement of a particular right in one human rights instrument, especially a human rights treaty, has been repeated in other human rights instruments, and second, the confirmation of the right in national practice, primarily through the incorporation of the right in national laws. Countering such positive indicators are the degree to which a particular right is subject to limitations (clawback clauses) and the extent of contrary practice. Human Rights Committee practice supports this approach.

In its 'General Comments' on Article 19 of the Political Covenant, the Committee observed:

[I]n order to know the precise régime of freedom of expression, in law and in practice, the Committee needs in addition [to reports that the right is guaranteed in constitutions or laws] pertinent information about the rules which either define the scope of freedom of expression or which set forth certain restrictions, as well as any other conditions which in practice affect the exercise of this right. It is the interplay between the principle of freedom of expression and such limitations and restrictions which determines the actual scope of the individual's right.[34]

Empiric studies of state practice are therefore of the highest importance in establishing whether a particular right has matured into customary law.[35] It is, of course, to be expected that those rights which are most crucial to the protection of human dignity and of universally accepted values of humanity, and whose violation triggers broad condemnation by the international community, will require a lesser amount of confirmatory evidence.

Based on the types of evidence which it mentions,[36] Section 702 of the Restatement lists a limited number of mostly civil rights, all of central importance, as norms embodying customary international law:

A state violates international law if, as a matter of state policy, it practices, encourages or condones

  (a) genocide,

  (b) slavery or slave trade,

[34] 38 UN GAOR Supp. (No. 40) at 109, UN Doc. A/38/40 (1983).

[35] See e.g. the detailed study of national practices contained in H. Hannum, The Right to Leave and Return in International Law and Practice (1987). See also the study of state practice by C. Mubanga-Chipoya, UN Doc. E/CN.4/Sub.2/1987/10/Add.1 (1987). See also below n. 45.

[36] See above, text accompanying n. 32.

(c) the murder or causing the disappearance of individuals,
(d) torture or other cruel, inhuman, or degrading treatment or punishment,
(e) prolonged arbitrary detention,
(f) systematic racial discrimination, or
(g) a consistent pattern of gross violations of internationally recognized human rights.[37]

Section 702(g) hints that there are other legally protected international human rights which are not otherwise listed in Section 702; gross, consistent violations of other internationally recognized human rights are thus considered violations of customary international law. Section 702(g) finds support in the practice of UN organs which treat gross and systematic violations of human rights *tout court* as breaches of the states' legal obligations.

As I have already observed with regard to Geneva Convention No. IV, only an overconfident observer would attempt to identify all the customary norms stated in the Political Covenant. I accept the Restatement's list as far as it goes, but I believe that it is, perhaps, somewhat too cautious, especially concerning due process

---

[37] Restatement, above n. 4, § 702. The Restatement considers rights listed in clauses (a)–(f) as peremptory norms. Ibid. Reporters' note 11. For further discussion of some of these norms, see below Section III.

Although the Restatement does not list religious discrimination as breach of customary law, it suggests that a strong case can be made for treating it as such. § 702, comment *j*. Observance of the Declaration on the Elimination of All Forms of Intolerance and of Discrimination Based on Religion or Belief (GA Res. 36/55, 36 UN GAOR Supp. (No. 51) at 171, UN Doc. A/36/51 (1981)), which was adopted by consensus, will aid in the further crystallization of the emergent customary rule prohibiting religious discrimination. See Sullivan, *Advancing the Freedom of Religion or Belief through the U.N. Declaration on the Elimination of Religious Intolerance and Discrimination*, 82 AJIL 487, 488–9 and n. 7 (1988). Such a development will also be helped by the drafting of a future convention on this subject. Practice implementing the principles of the Declaration, assisted by the efforts of the Commission on Human Rights' Special Rapporteur charged with reporting compliance with the Declaration, together with the drafting of a convention, will further define and consolidate the content of the norm of prohibition of religious discrimination, expediting its passage into the general corpus of customary law. See generally McDougal, Lasswell, and Chen, *The Right to Religious Freedom and World Public Order: The Emerging Norm of Nondiscrimination*, 74 Mich. L. Rev. 865, 897 (1976).

Of course, the basic prohibition of discrimination on grounds of race, sex, language, or religion is established as a solemn treaty obligation in the Charter of the United Nations. Concerning the question whether the prohibition of discrimination against women has already matured into customary law, see Restatement, above n. 4, § 702, comment *l* and T. Meron, above n. 3, at 54.

guarantees.[38] The right of self-determination, which the ICJ has recognized as customary, could safely have been added.[39] Among other customary human rights, or general principles of law, I would include the right to humane treatment of detainees, stated in Article 10 of the Political Covenant. In its 'General Comments' on this right, the Human Rights Committee noted that '[t]he humane treatment and the respect for the dignity of all persons deprived of their liberty is a basic standard of universal application which cannot depend entirely on material resources.'[40] There is little doubt that the prohibition of retroactive penal measures (which is non-derogable in the Political Covenant and in both the American and the European Conventions on Human Rights) stated in Article 15 of the Political Covenant is a norm of customary international law.[41] I believe that at least the core of a number of the due process guarantees stated in Article 14 of the Covenant have a strong claim to customary law status based on the indicators which I have suggested.[42] Such rights include the right to be tried by a competent, independent and impartial tribunal established by law,[43] the right to presumption of innocence, the right of everyone not to be compelled to testify against himself or to confess guilt; the right of everyone to be tried in his or her presence and to defend himself or herself in person or through legal assistance of his or her own

[38] Compare the considerable number of customary due process rights (protections against denial of justice) of aliens listed by the Restatement, above n. 4, §711, Reporters' note 2.

[39] See Section II, below. Perhaps this right has not been included because of its 'collective' or 'group'—rather than individual—character. (However, the prohibition of genocide, which is listed in the Restatement, is also a 'collective' right.) In its 'General Comments' on Art. 1 of the Political Covenant, the Human Rights Committee stated that the right of self-determination 'and the corresponding obligations concerning its implementation are interrelated with other provisions of the Covenant and rules of international law'. 39 UN GAOR Supp. (No. 40) at 142, UN Doc. A/39/40 (1984). See also H. Gros Espiell, The Right to Self-Determination: Implementation of United Nations Resolutions 11-12, UN Doc. E/CN.4/Sub.2/405/Rev.1 at 11-12 (1980) ('the principle of self-determination necessarily possesses the character of *jus cogens*').

[40] 37 UN GAOR Supp. (No. 40) at 96, UN Doc. A/37/40 (1982). See also Rodley, above n. 22, at 269-70.

[41] On the articulation of this prohibition in international human rights instruments, see P. Sieghart, The International Law of Human Rights 285-91 (1983).

[42] For a comparative discussion of principal due process guarantees, see ibid. at 268-307. A view denying the customary law character of the right to have one's conviction and sentence reviewed by a higher court was asserted by the Israel Supreme Court. High Ct. Justice Dec. No. 87/85 (7 Feb. 1988).

[43] See also common Art. 3(1)(d) of the Geneva Conventions.

choosing, the right of everyone to examine witnesses against him or her and the right to have one's conviction and sentence reviewed by a higher tribunal according to law. The principle *ne bis in idem* (discussed in Section III, below) can also be regarded as emerging customary law. A somewhat different enumeration of customary rights prepared by Professor Lillich mentions the right to equality before the law and to non-discrimination, as stated in Article 7 of the Universal Declaration, as probably customary law, as well as the right of the individual to leave any country and to return to his own country.[44]

A recent United Nations report emphasizes, on the basis of a comparative study of international instruments and national laws, that '[t]he right to leave and return is part of the whole body of human rights.'[45] It aptly states that the 'concordance of State practice and common *opinio juris* created a legal obligation according to customary international law',[46] and that '[f]reedom of movement within the State is widely accepted both in theory and in practice.'[47]

Other scholars would list as customary the principle of non-refoulement in the context of Article 3 of the Convention Against Torture and Other Cruel, Inhuman or Degrading Treatment or Punishment, some economic, social and cultural or 'second generation' rights, and possibly even some solidarity or 'third generation' rights.[48] Such economic rights as have been recognized

[44] Lillich, *Civil Rights*, in 1 Human Rights in International Law 115, 133, 151 (T. Meron ed. 1984).

[45] C. Mubanga-Chipoya, Analysis of the Current Trends and Developments Regarding the Right to Leave any Country Including One's Own, and to Return to One's Own Country, and Some Other Rights or Consideration Arising Therefrom, UN Doc. E/CN.4/Sub.2/1987/10 at 7.

[46] Ibid. at 11.

[47] Ibid. at 19.

[48] The UN Special Rapporteur on Torture, Professor Kooijmans, describes Art. 3 of the Convention Against Torture as a 'conventional specification . . . of the customary law principle of non-refoulement . . .'. UN Doc. E/CN.4/1987/13, at para. 10. See also Chapter I, text accompanying n. 61. But see Hailbronner, *Non-Refoulement and "Humanitarian" Refugees: Customary International Law or Wishful Legal Thinking?*, 26 Va. J. Int'l L. 857, 887–8 (1986). On 'third generation' rights, see Sohn, *The New International Law*, above n. 7, at 48–62; Marks, *Emerging Human Rights: A New Generation for the 1980's?*, in International Law: A Contemporary Perspective 501 (R. Falk, F. Kratochwil, and S. Mendlovitz eds. 1985); Schachter, *The Evolving International Law of Development*, 15 Colum. J. Transnat'l L. 1 (1976); Pellet, *Note sur quelques aspects juridiques de la notion du droit au développement*, in La Formation des normes en droit international du développement 71 (M. Flory ed. 1984); Alston, *Making Space for New Human Rights: The Case of the Right to Development*, 1 Harv. Hum. Rts. YB 3 (1988);

by the internal laws of most states (e.g. as a result of ratifications of ILO's international labour conventions) may have matured into general international law as general principles of law recognized by civilized nations (Article 38(1)(c) of ICJ's Statute).

In a recent decision stating that in executing two juvenile offenders, the United States violated Articles I-II of the American Declaration of the Rights and Duties of Man, the Inter-American Commission on Human Rights considered the question whether there is a norm of customary international law prohibiting the imposition of the death penalty on persons who committed capital crimes before reaching 18 years of age.[49] The Commission agreed with the US government

that there does not now exist a norm of customary international law establishing 18 to be the minimum age for imposition of the death penalty. Nonetheless, in light of the increasing numbers of States which are ratifying the American Convention on Human Rights and the United Nations Covenant on Civil and Political Rights, and modifying their domestic legislation in conformity with these instruments, the norm is emerging.[50]

Because through its proposed reservations to Articles 4-5 of the American Convention on Human Rights the United States has protested against the norm prohibiting the imposition of capital punishment on persons below the age of 18, the Commission held that such a norm, if established, could not be binding upon the

Steiner, *Political Participation as a Human Right*, ibid. at 77.

The General Assembly has declared that the right to development is 'an inalienable human right.' Declaration on the Right to Development, Art. 1, adopted on 4 Dec. 1986, GA Res. 41/128, 41 UN GAOR Supp. (No. 53) at 186, UN Doc. A/41/53 (1987), discussed in UN Doc. E/CN.4/AC.39/1988/L.2.

For recent important studies of the right to food, see A. Eide, Report on the Right to Adequate Food as a Human Right, UN Doc. E/CN.4/Sub.2/1987/23; I. Brownlie, The Human Right to Food (Commonwealth Secretariat, Human Rights Unit Occasional Paper, 1987).

[49] Res. No. 3/87, Case 9647 (United States), Annual Report of the Inter-American Commission on Human Rights, 1986-1987, OAS/Ser.L/VII.71, Doc. 9, rev. 1, at 147 (1987), discussed in Fox, *Inter-American Commission on Human Rights Finds United States in Violation*, 82 AJIL 601 (1988). Regarding the powers of the Inter-American Commission and the binding character of the American Declaration of the Rights and Duties of Man (for the official text, see Organization of American States, Basic Documents Pertaining to Human Rights in the Inter-American System 17, OEA/SER.L.V./II.71, Doc. 6, rev. 1, 23 Sept. 1987 (1988)), see Buergenthal, *The Revised OAS Charter and the Protection of Human Rights*, 69 AJIL 828 (1975); T. Meron, above n. 3, at 137-40.

[50] Para. 60.

United States, unless it has acquired the status of *jus cogens*.[51]
Invoking *sua sponte* the concept of *jus cogens*, the Commission
found that, despite the controversy as to the age of majority, 'in
the member States of the OAS there is a recognized norm of *jus
cogens* which prohibits the State execution of children. This norm
is accepted by all the States of the inter-American system, including
the United States.'[52] It is curious that the Commission did not
address the questions whether peremptory norms can exist without
a foundation of customary law, whether the parameters of the
emerging norm were sufficiently clear for it to constitute a peremptory norm, and whether regional norms can constitute *jus cogens*
in light of Article 53 of the Vienna Convention, which defines
peremptory norms as norms 'accepted and recognized by the
international community of States as a whole as . . . norm[s] from
which no derogation is permitted'.

Given the rapid, continued development of international human
rights, the list as now constituted should be regarded as essentially
open-ended. Human rights are undergoing a stage of continuing
evolution. Through a process of accretion, in which the repetition
of the articulation and the assertion of certain norms in various
resolutions and declarations and treaties plays an important role,
elements of state practice and *opinio juris* form new customary
norms of human rights. This continuing process, in which *opinio
juris* appears to have greater weight than state practice, is more
interesting than the static picture of human rights as reflected by
the Restatement. Many other rights will be added in the course of
time.

Although international human rights also implicate obligations
running from one state to another, or even from one state to all
states (obligations *erga omnes*), they primarily seek to protect
individuals, the beneficiaries of human rights, from governments
and, sometimes from other individuals or non-state actors. Unlike

[51] Ibid. at para. 54.
[52] Ibid. at paras. 56–7. In *Thompson* v. *Oklahoma*, 108 S. Ct. 2687 (1988), the
US Supreme Court concluded that the Eighth and Fourteenth Amendments to the
US Constitution prohibit the execution of a person who was under 16 years of age
at the time of his or her offence. Ibid. at 2700. In reaching this conclusion, the
Court was guided by 'evolving standards of decency that mark the progress of a
maturing society'. Ibid. at 2691. Among these standards, the Court, in a footnote,
mentioned the prohibition of death penalty for juveniles in some human rights
treaties. Ibid. 2696 n. 34.

most other fields of international law, the observance of human rights is not based on reciprocal interests of states, but on the broader goal of states to establish orderly and enlightened international and national legal orders. In human rights instruments, the contractual (interstate) elements are far less important than those which are objective and normative. The customary law of human rights is not established by a record of claims and counterclaims between the foreign ministries of countries concerned with the protection of their rights as states and the rights of their respective nationals.

The role of arbitral and international judicial decisions in the formation of customary human rights law requires further comment. The development of human rights law through judicial, quasi-judicial, or supervisory bodies such as the European Court of Human Rights, the European Commission of Human Rights, the Inter-American Court of Human Rights and the UN Human Rights Committee established under Article 28 of the Political Covenant involves primarily the application and interpretation of the provisions of the treaties establishing such bodies rather than directly general or customary international law. Nevertheless, the decisions of such organs are frequently and increasingly invoked outside the context of their constitutive instruments and cited as authoritative statements of human rights law. Interpretations of human rights conventions by quasi-judicial or supervisory bodies affects the internal and external behaviour of states. They shape the practice of states and may establish and reflect the agreement of the parties regarding the interpretation of a treaty (Article 31(3)(b) of the Vienna Convention on the Law of Treaties). Cumulatively, the practice of judicial, quasi-judicial, and supervisory organs has a significant role in generating customary rules.

Just as special rules concerning reciprocity, breach and interpretation of treaties often apply to human rights instruments, different types of evidence may be relevant to the creation of customary human rights law. The evidence of state practice in human rights is to be found primarily in the actions of and statements by state representatives to international organizations, and in internal legislative, administrative, and judicial steps implementing international human rights at the national plane.[53]

---

[53] See e.g. Schachter, above n. 4, at 334–5.

These differences do not detract from the standing of human rights as an equal and authentic branch of international law; rather, they merely indicate that different types of evidence must be gathered to establish customary human rights. The Restatement's listing of types of evidence of customary human rights law is thus an appropriate adaptation to human rights of accepted methods of building customary law. The *Nicaragua* judgment of the International Court of Justice lends important support to the method used in the Restatement.

The uniqueness of international human rights law should not be exaggerated, however. Other, more traditional, fields of international law, such as sovereign immunity of states, have been developed largely by national courts and national laws, rather than by a state to state dialectic. Similarly, general principles of law recognized by civilized nations, mentioned in Article 38(1)(c) of the ICJ's Statute, have been generated by national legislatures and courts.

In contrast to most other fields of international law, human rights law emphasizes the individual as a subject of rights and sometimes even of duties under international law. The importance of the object/subject dichotomy may have been exaggerated, however. Professor Higgins, invoking the authority of Professors McDougal, Lasswell, and Reisman, discusses a model in which

there are no subjects or objects, but only participants . . . the topics of minimum standards of treatment of aliens, requirements as to the conduct of hostilities, and human rights, are not simply exceptions conceded by historical chance within a system of rules that operate as between states. Rather they are simply part and parcel of the fabric of international law, representing the claims that are naturally made by individual participants in contradistinction to those presented by state participants.[54]

Despite certain special characteristics, such as the types of evidence marshalled to establish customary human rights, human rights cannot but be considered a subject within the theory and discipline of public international law. Undue emphasis on the uniqueness of international human rights will not advance their acceptance, on the broadest possible scale, as international law.

[54] Higgins, *Conceptual Thinking about the Individual in International Law*, 24 NYL Sch. L. Rev. 11, 16 (1978). See generally P. M. Dupuy, *L'Individu et le droit international* (*Théorie des droits de l'homme et fondements du droit international*), 32 Archives de philosophie du droit 119 (1987). See also T. Meron, Human Rights in Internal Strife: Their International Protection 33–40 (1987).

Approached from this perspective, §702 of the Restatement which limits violations by a state of the customary international law of human rights of its citizens to acts of its officials and organs carried out as a matter of state policy merits close scrutiny. In contrast to other fields of customary international law, such as responsibility for injuries to aliens, this limitation of or special requirement for violations of customary human rights excludes violations of human rights by officials and organs of a state which are not authorized, encouraged or condoned by the responsible state authorities.[55]

Thus, according to the Restatement, in the case of a citizen, a single case of a violation by a state of one of the human rights listed in §702 might constitute a violation of an applicable human rights instrument, but not of customary law.[56] As regards foreign nationals, however, the Restatement recognizes that a state is responsible for a single violation of a human right recognized by customary law[57] by an official or organ of a state even when the violation does not represent state policy.[58] The language of the Restatement would therefore materially affect the definition of customary human rights. It is doubtful whether authority can be found for maintaining that, for example, isolated cases of deprivation of life or enslavement of an individual do not breach customary human rights law of citizens, although such cases violate customary human rights of aliens as well as the often identical rights of both citizens and aliens[59] stated, as conventional obligations, in international agreements.

As long as gross violations of human rights continue unabated, states not specially affected may indeed show little inclination to make representations regarding sporadic violations, and some UN procedures for investigating human rights violations, such as those established under Economic and Social Council Resolution 1503(XLVIII),[60] may indeed be limited to the examination of a consistent pattern of gross violations of human rights. The practice

[55] Restatement, above n. 4, §702, comment *b*.

[56] See §702, comment *m*.

[57] §711, comment *c*.

[58] §702, comment *b*, §207, comments *c–d*.

[59] See generally D. Elles, International Provisions Protecting the Human Rights of Non-Citizens, UN Doc. E/CN.4/Sub.2/392 and Corr. 1 (1976), UN Publication Sales No. E.80.XIV.2; Draft Declaration of the Human Rights of Individuals Who are Not Citizens of the Country in which they Live, UN Doc. E/CN.4/1336 (1978).

[60] E.S.C. Res. 1503, 48 UN ESCOR Supp. (No. 1A) 8–9, UN Doc. E/4832/Add.1 (1970).

of states is, therefore, not necessarily inconsistent with the approach of the Restatement.[61]

Somewhat paralleling the approach of the Restatement, Professor Schachter believes that an isolated or minor infringement of a right is not regarded as a matter of international concern and thus falls within the domestic jurisdiction.[62] Professor Schachter thus raises a fundamental question of the reach of contemporary human rights. He appears to suggest that in the sensitive field of the treatment by the state of its own citizens, international human rights norms do not entirely displace the domestic jurisdiction of states, and that there may be some overlap or concurrent applicability of international human rights and of domestic jurisdiction. Other human rights scholars will assert that whether an act falls within the domestic jurisdiction of a state turns not on the frequency and the widespread nature of the act, but on whether the subject in question is regulated by the international obligations, conventional or customary, of the state concerned. They will argue that with the advent of international human rights and the recognition of very many human rights as international obligations of states, human rights have reached a critical mass which either entirely or very largely has displaced domestic jurisdiction of states. Such observers may concede that while it may well be true that for political or other considerations states will not complain of an isolated violation and will limit their intercession at the international level to systematic or gross violations, this reality concerns responsibility, not domestic jurisdiction. I believe that where the right infringed has clearly been recognized as customary even with regard to individual violations, the matter can no longer be addressed in terms of domestic jurisdiction. The problem thus lies in the drawing of the parameters of human rights norms and the achievement of consensus on the definition of specific rights.

Professor Schachter's approach finds some support in the practice of states: characteristically, state A refrains from making representations concerning an isolated case of violation by state B of

---

[61] '[C]ustomary international law prohibits the particular human rights indicated, if the violations are state policy.' Restatement, above n. 4, § 702, Reporters' note 1.

[62] Schachter, above n. 4, at 330. Professor Schachter's position is supported by Graefrath, *Human Rights and International Cooperation: 10 Years of Experience in the Human Rights Committee*, 14 GDR Committee for Human Rights Bulletin No. 1 at 5, 29–31 (1988). For a different approach, see D'Amato, *Domestic Jurisdiction*,

human rights of a citizen of state B. It is not clear, however, whether this practice reflects a restrictive approach to the scope of customary human rights and an expansive approach to domestic jurisdiction or simply political considerations which explain the preference of state A to limit its intercession to systematic and significant violations by state B of the rights of B's citizens. Moreover, international practice appears to go further. Thus, the United States occasionally has made representations to foreign governments in the case of egregious violations of human rights of certain identified individuals. This practice finds further support in the Concluding Document of the Vienna Meeting 1986 of Representatives of the Participating States of the Conference on Security and Co-operation in Europe, Held on the Basis of the Provisions of the Final Act Relating to the Follow-up to the Conference, which was adopted at Vienna on 17 January, 1989. Paragraph 2 of the section entitled 'Human Dimension of the CSCE' (Conference on Security and Co-operation in Europe) provides that participating states have decided to hold bilateral meetings with other participating states that so request, in order to examine 'situations and specific cases' concerning respect for human rights, with a view to resolving them. Such situations and specific cases may, under paragraph 3, be brought to the attention of other participating states through diplomatic channels. Although the Concluding Statement is neither a treaty nor a universal instrument, it undoubtedly both reflects and builds the international practice which recognizes that not only general situations of massive violations but also specific, individual cases of human rights violations implicate the international accountability of governments and may fall outside the domestic jurisdiction of states. The trend to expanding the reach of customary human rights will no doubt continue, limiting the reserved domain of domestic jurisdiction, and the direction is clear. The US Court of Appeals for the Fifth Circuit has thus observed that

[r]ecently, this traditional dichotomy between injuries to states and to individuals—and between injuries to home-grown and to alien individuals—

in [Instalment] 10 Encyclopedia of Public International Law 132 (R. Bernhardt ed. 1987). See also below n. 69 and accompanying text. For a recent invocation by the United Kingdom of the Vienna Concluding Statement, see *Britain Puts Vienna Accord to Test with Romania Case*, The Times, 22 Feb. 1989, at 6, col. 1.

has begun to erode. The international human rights movement is premised on the belief that international law sets a minimum standard not only for the treatment of aliens but also for the treatment of human beings generally. Nevertheless, the standards of human rights that have been generally accepted—and hence incorporated into the law of nations—are still limited.[63]

In contrast to the approach taken by the Restatement and by Professor Schachter, in its *Commentary* on Article 18 of its draft articles on state responsibility (part one), the ILC recognized, with regard to Resolution 1503, that an isolated act may also violate human rights, finding that 'in the practice of [ECOSOC], *consistent violation* of human rights . . . has come to be established as an offence in itself, distinct from the offence constituted by an isolated violation of those rights . . .'.[64] Whether in every case a single act or omission attributable to a state results in a violation of a human right and a breach of the international responsibility of that state obviously depends on the content of the primary rule in question.[65] For instance, a single action or omission by a state may not amount to a breach of an international obligation prohibiting states from engaging in a particular discriminatory practice, but a series of actions having the same purpose, content and effect, although relating to cases independent of one another, would indicate conduct constituting such a practice.[66] Similarly, although a single case of enslavement of an individual constitutes an international delict, as mentioned in Article 19(4) of the ILC's draft articles on state responsibility (part one), only 'a serious breach on a widespread scale of an international obligation of essential importance for safeguarding the human being' may qualify as an international crime (in the meaning of Article 19(2)(*c*)).[67]

[63] *De Sanchez* v. *Banco Central de Nicaragua*, 770 F. 2d 1385, 1396-7 (5th Cir. 1985).

[64] [1976] 2 YB Int'l L. Comm'n (pt. 2) at 94 n. 438, UN Doc. A/CN.4/SER.A/1976/Add.1 (Part 2) (emphasis in original).

[65] See the ILC's *Commentary* on Art. 5(2)(e)(iii) of its draft articles on state responsibility (part two), Report of the International Law Commission on the Work of its Thirty-Seventh Session, 40 UN GAOR Supp. (No. 10) at 58, UN Doc. A/40/10 (1985).

[66] Above n. 64, at 93-4.

[67] The ILC's *Commentary* observed that 'in order to avoid extending the category of international crimes beyond what is reasonable and to remain in conformity with the provisions of international law now in force, [the ILC] added the qualification that, for the breach to be characterized as an international crime, it must be "on

Elsewhere in the Restatement, the Reporters note that

[a] different formulation asserts that a state is responsible for the acts of its officials in such human rights cases as in other cases even if the action was not state policy . . . but there is no violation, and therefore no responsibility, where the state provides an effective domestic remedy.[68]

The exhaustion of domestic remedies may be relevant both to conventional and to customary law obligations. It is none the less unfortunate that the Reporters' 'different' formulation has not been adopted. The existing language of § 702 implies that customary human rights law is different from other customary norms and that establishing state responsibility for violations of human rights is more difficult than establishing state responsibility in other fields of international law. This question will be further explored in Chapter III, Section II.

II. THE INTERNATIONAL COURT OF JUSTICE AND CUSTOMARY HUMAN RIGHTS

In the *Interpretation of Peace Treaties with Bulgaria, Hungary and Romania* case, it was contended that the General Assembly's request for an advisory opinion was *ultra vires* because, in dealing with human rights in Bulgaria, Hungary, and Romania, the Assembly was intervening in matters essentially within the domestic jurisdiction of states, and that both the Assembly and the Court were bound to observe Article 2(7) of the UN Charter. Noting that the Assembly grounded its action in Article 55 of the Charter, the ICJ stated that '[t]he interpretation of the terms of a treaty . . . could not be considered as a question essentially within the domestic jurisdiction of a State. It is a question of international law which, by its very nature, lies within the competence of the Court.'[69]

a widespread scale", that is to say, it must take the form of a large-scale or systematic practice adopted in contempt of the rights and dignity of the human being.' Above n. 64, at 121.

Similarly, 'an isolated act of discrimination constituted a violation of human rights, but that did not make it an international crime.' [1976] 1 YB Int'l L. Comm'n 73, UN Doc. A/CN.4/SER.A/1976 (remarks by N. Ushakov).

[68] Restatement, above n. 4, § 702, Reporters' note 2.

[69] 1950 ICJ Rep. 65, 70-1 (Advisory Opinion of 30 Mar.). Jiménez De Aréchaga commented 'that for the Court the question of human rights and non-discrimination is not one falling within the domestic jurisdiction of member states'. Above n. 24, at 3-4.

The *North Sea Continental Shelf Cases* contain the *locus classicus* of the constitutive elements of international customary law:

[N]ot only must the acts concerned amount to a settled practice, but they must also be such, or be carried out in such a way, as to be evidence of a belief that this practice is rendered obligatory by the existence of a rule of law requiring it. The need for such a belief, i.e., the existence of a subjective element, is implicit in the very notion of the *opinio juris sive necessitatis*.[70]

After a careful examination of the facts of the cases the Court found these elements absent.

In Chapter I, Section V, the *Nicaragua* Court's treatment of state practice in its examination of the customary law nature of the principles of prohibition of the use of force and of non-intervention has already been discussed.[71] Significantly, the Court did not refer to *North Sea Continental Shelf Cases* doctrine that only practice dehors the conventions builds customary law. In forming its conclusions on customary law, the Court undoubtedly took into account the conduct of states under the UN Charter and other instruments. The Court focused not on state practice, but on *opinio juris* found in verbal statements by governmental representatives to international organizations, the content of resolutions, declarations[72] and other normative instruments adopted by such organizations, and the consent of states to such instruments.[73] The *Nicaragua* judgment simultaneously strengthens the law-making force of General Assembly resolutions[74] and de-emphasizes the importance of practice as one of the two elements necessary for the formation of customary international law.[75] Is the Court's method in *Nicaragua* a complete change of course, or merely a

[70] *North Sea Continental Shelf Cases (FRG/Den.; FRG/Neth.)*, 1969 ICJ Rep. 3, 44 (Judgment of 20 Feb.).

[71] See above Chapter I, text preceding n. 122.

[72] The Court focused especially on the Declaration on Principles of International Law Concerning Friendly Relations and Co-operation Among States in accordance with the Charter of the United Nations, GA Res. 2625, 25 UN GAOR Supp. (No. 28) at 121, UN Doc. A/8028 (1970); and the Definition of Aggression, GA Res. 3314, 29 UN GAOR Supp. (No. 31) at 142, UN Doc. A/9631 (1974).

[73] 1986 ICJ Rep. 98–108.

[74] Franck, *Some Observations on the ICJ's Procedural and Substantive Innovations*, 81 AJIL 116, 119 (1987); Morrison, *Legal Issues in the Nicaragua Opinion*, 81 AJIL 160, 161 (1987).

[75] Statute of the International Court of Justice, Art. 38(1)(b).

more pronounced evolution of tendencies already evident in earlier cases?

Over the years, the Court has inquired into the existence of state practice and of *opinio juris* with varying degrees of detail ranging from the specific, as in the *Lotus* case,[76] to the brief and conclusory, as in the *Corfu Channel* case.[77] The Court discussed and analysed state practice and its psychological significance more thoroughly in the *Colombian-Peruvian Asylum* case,[78] the *Fisheries* case,[79] the *Nottebohm* case,[80] and in the *Right of Passage over Indian Territory* case.[81] Its analysis of practice and of *opinio juris* was particularly detailed and significant in the *North Sea Continental Shelf Cases*,[82] discussed in Chapter I, Section V, above. As noted in a recent study, the ICJ's investigation of the elements forming customary law has been diminishing.[83] This development is particularly evident in cases *in pari materia*. The contrast between the serious inquiry into the existence of the constitutive elements of custom in the *North Sea Continental Shelf Cases* and the virtual absence of such inquiry in the *Continental Shelf* case of 1985[84] illustrates this phenomenon well.

To be sure, the degree of attention given by the Court to the

[76] The case of the *S.S. Lotus* (*France* v. *Turkey*), PCIJ Ser. A, No. 10, at 22–31 (Judgment of 7 Sept. 1927).

[77] Although, as shown by Haggenmacher, *La Doctrine des deux éléments du droit coutumier dans la pratique de la Cour internationale*, 90 Rev. gén droit int'l pub. 5, 73–4 (1986), the parties' pleadings in the *Corfu Channel* case addressed the psychological element of state practice in detail, the Court's statement was brief and general, referring only implicitly to the elements of customary law: 'It is, in the opinion of the Court, generally recognized and in accordance with international custom that States in time of peace have a right to send their warships through straits used for international navigation between two parts of the high seas without the previous authorization of a coastal State, provided that the passage is *innocent*.' *Corfu Channel* case (*United Kingdom* v. *Albania*), 1949 ICJ Rep. 4, 28 (Judgment of 9 Apr.) (emphasis in original).

[78] *Asylum* case (*Colombia* v. *Peru*), 1950 ICJ Rep. 266, 276–8, 286 (Judgment of 20 Nov.).

[79] *Fisheries* case (*United Kingdom* v. *Norway*), 1951 ICJ Rep. 116, 131, 133–9 (Judgment of 18 Dec.).

[80] *Nottebohm* case (*Liechtenstein* v. *Guatemala*), Second Phase, 1955 ICJ Rep. 4, 21–4 (Judgment of 6 Apr.).

[81] *Case Concerning Right of Passage over Indian Territory* (*Portugal* v. *India*), Merits, 1960 ICJ Rep. 6, 39–43 (Judgment of 12 Apr.).

[82] *North Sea Continental Shelf Cases* (*FRG/Den.; FRG/Neth.*), 1969 ICJ Rep. 3, 37–45 (Judgment of 20 Feb.).

[83] Haggenmacher, above n. 77.

[84] *Continental Shelf* (*Libyan Arab Jamahiriya/Malta*), 1985 ICJ Rep. 13, 29–30 (Judgment of 3 June). See also above Chapter I, n. 136.

analysis of the elements of customary law is affected by the nature of the claims, the circumstances of the disputes, the arguments advanced by the parties, and the norms implicated. However, a more detailed examination of these factors in relation to the above cases is not required for our purposes. Instead, this discussion will focus on those cases which implicate humanitarian law or human rights.

In the *Corfu Channel* case, the ICJ defined the applicable humanitarian obligations as follows:

The obligations incumbent upon the Albanian authorities consisted in notifying, for the benefit of shipping in general, the existence of a minefield in Albanian territorial waters and in warning the approaching British warships of the imminent danger to which the minefield exposed them. Such obligations are based, not on the Hague Convention of 1907, No. VIII, which is applicable in time of war, but on certain general and well-recognized principles, namely: elementary considerations of humanity, even more exacting in peace than in war; the principle of the freedom of maritime communication; and every State's obligation not to allow knowingly its territory to be used for acts contrary to the rights of other States.[85]

Because Albania admitted that her knowledge of the minefield's existence would have resulted in her international responsibility had she been informed of the British operation, the Court could more easily define the relevant humanitarian principles[86] briefly and generally without resort to supporting evidence. It is none the less noteworthy that this important, universally accepted and oft-quoted statement[87] lacked any citation of precedent and practice. Contrast this approach with the Court's statement in the *Nicaragua* case that concurrence among the parties regarding the content of customary international law relating to the non-use of force and non-intervention, unless expressed in a treaty, does not obviate the necessity for the Court itself to ascertain which rules of customary international law are applicable.[88] Nevertheless, as previously

[85] 1949 ICJ Rep. 4, 22. See also the Convention Relative to the Laying of Automatic Submarine Contact Mines (Hague Convention No. VIII), signed 18 Oct. 1907, 36 Stat. 2332, TS 541, 1 Bevans 669.

[86] 1949 ICJ Rep. at 22.

[87] This statement was cited, for example, in the *Nicaragua* judgment, 1986 ICJ Rep. 112.

[88] The Court stated: 'The mere fact that States declare their recognition of certain rules is not sufficient for the Court to consider these as being part of customary international law, and as applicable as such to those States. Bound as it is by

observed, the *Nicaragua* Court's emphasis on the need to establish the existence of practice was more in the nature of a verbal protestation than a serious inquiry into the presence of the necessary elements of customary international law.

Building upon its decision in the *Corfu Channel* case, the *Nicaragua* Court stated that

if a State lays mines in any waters whatever in which the vessels of another State have rights of access or passage, and fails to give any warning or notification whatsoever, in disregard of the security of peaceful shipping, it commits a breach of the principles of humanitarian law underlying the specific provisions of Convention No. VIII of 1907.[89]

A categorical approach characterizes the Court's treatment of the crime of genocide. In its advisory opinion on *Reservations to the Convention on Genocide*[90] the Court eloquently stated that the origins of the Convention, which was a major response to Nazi atrocities, reveal that the United Nations intended to punish genocide as a crime under international law, since it

shocks the conscience of mankind and results in great losses to humanity, and . . . is contrary to moral law and to the spirit and aims of the United Nations. . . . The first consequence arising from this conception is that the principles underlying the Convention are principles which are

Article 38 of its Statute to apply, *inter alia*, international custom "as evidence of a general practice accepted as law", the Court may not disregard the essential role played by general practice. Where two States agree to incorporate a particular rule in a treaty, their agreement suffices to make that rule a legal one, binding upon them; but in the field of customary international law, the shared view of the Parties as to the content of what they regard as the rule is not enough. The Court must satisfy itself that the existence of the rule in the *opinio juris* of States is confirmed by practice.' Ibid. at 97–8.

[89] Ibid. at 112. Outside the strict parameters of humanitarian law, note also the Court's reference in point 6 of its judgment to the laying of mines as a breach of US obligations under customary international law 'not to use force against another State, not to intervene in its affairs, not to violate its sovereignty and not to interrupt peaceful maritime commerce'. Ibid. at 147.

Comparing the term 'considerations of humanity' (*Corfu Channel* case) to 'principles of humanitarian law' (*Nicaragua* case), Rosemary Abi-Saab suggests that the former 'would . . . represent general principles, or an ethical or moral basis, applying in all circumstances, in times of peace as well as in times of armed conflict. The more specific "principles of humanitarian law" would be those implementing the principles of humanity in circumstances of actual or potential armed conflict.' *The "General Principles" of Humanitarian Law According to the International Court of Justice*, Int'l Rev. Red Cross, No. 259, July–Aug. 1987, at 367, 370–1.

[90] *Reservations to the Convention on Genocide*, 1951 ICJ Rep. 15 (Advisory Opinion of 28 May).

recognized by civilized nations as binding on States, even without any conventional obligation.[91]

This approach is strongly supported by General Assembly Resolution 96(I),[92] which '[a]ffirm[ed] that genocide is a crime under international law', and by Article 1 of the Convention on the Prevention and Punishment of the Crime of Genocide.[93] Article 1, by 'confirming' that genocide is a crime under international law, clearly expressed the consensus of the UN General Assembly concerning the codificatory nature of the Convention.

The Court has also addressed customary human rights norms in two cases implicating the Charter principle of self-determination. The first of these, the advisory opinion concerning *Legal Consequences for States of the Continued Presence of South Africa in Namibia (South West Africa)*,[94] involved the interpretation of the provisions of the League of Nations' Covenant and of the Mandate for South West Africa. In determining that 'the subsequent development of international law in regard to non-self-governing territories, as enshrined in the Charter of the United Nations, made the principle of self-determination applicable to all of them',[95] the Court took into account the political history of mandated territories in general. That history demonstrated that such territories were usually placed under trusteeship and then granted independence. The Court also referred to the Declaration on the Granting of Independence to Colonial Countries and Peoples (General Assembly

[91] Ibid. at 23.
[92] The Crime of Genocide, GA Res. 96(I), (11 Dec. 1946) Resolutions Adopted by the General Assembly During the Second Part of its First Session, UN Doc. A/64/Add.1 at 188, 189 (1947).
[93] Opened for signature 9 Dec. 1948, 78 UNTS 277. Treating genocide as a crime under customary law is supported by limited but important practice, *inter alia*, by the Nuernberg Charter (see Agreement for the Prosecution and Punishment of the Major War Criminals of the European Axis, 8 Aug. 1945, 59 Stat. 1544, 82 UNTS 279) and by Art. 19(3)(c) of the International Law Commission's draft articles on state responsibility (part one). [1976] 2 YB Int'l L. Comm'n (pt. 2) at 95, UN Doc. A/CN.4/SER.A/1976/Add.1 (Part 2). See also Restatement, above n. 4, § 702(a), comment *d* and Reporters' note 3. See generally Jescheck, *Genocide*, [Instalment] 8 Encyclopedia of Public International Law 255 (R. Bernhardt ed. 1981). The limited practice of states is somewhat compensated by a particularly strong *opinio juris*. Compare Schachter, above n. 4, at 114.
[94] *Legal Consequences for States of the Continued Presence of South Africa in Namibia (South West Africa) Notwithstanding Security Council Resolution 276 (1970)*, 1971 ICJ Rep. 16 (Advisory Opinion of 21 June).
[95] Ibid. at 31.

Resolution 1514(XV)).[96] In interpreting the Covenant, the Court stated that it

must take into consideration the changes which have occurred in the supervening half-century, and its interpretation cannot remain unaffected by the subsequent development of law, through the Charter of the United Nations and by way of customary law. Moreover, an international instrument has to be interpreted and applied within the framework of the entire legal system prevailing at the time of the interpretation. . . . These developments [of the last fifty years] leave little doubt that the ultimate objective of the sacred trust was the self-determination and independence of the peoples concerned. In this domain, as elsewhere, the *corpus iuris gentium* has been considerably enriched. . . .[97]

In maintaining that, with respect to Namibia, South Africa was bound by the principle of self-determination, the Court focused both on the centrality of that principle in the Charter of the United Nations and on its passage into customary law through the general practice of states and of the United Nations as reflected in such documents as General Assembly Resolution 1514(XV). Despite the brevity of the Court's reference to customary law, the practice of states with regard to self-determination of peoples clearly was significant and served as a strong rationale for the Court's conclusions. However, as regards South Africa's policy of apartheid in Namibia, the Court preferred to base the prohibition of racial discrimination on the Charter alone, rather than on both the Charter and customary law.[98]

[96] GA Res. 1514, 15 UN GAOR Supp. (No. 16) at 66, UN Doc. A/4684 (1961).

[97] 1971 ICJ Rep. 16, 31–2. In another recent case, the Court expressed the view that the application of the 19th-century Spanish American principle of *uti possidetis* by the new African states 'must be seen not as a mere practice contributing to the gradual emergence of a principle of customary international law, limited in its impact to the African continent as it had previously been to Spanish America, but as the application in Africa of a rule of general scope.' *Frontier Dispute (Burkina Faso/Republic of Mali)*, 1986 ICJ Rep. 554, 565 (Judgment of 22 Dec.).

[98] 'Under the Charter of the United Nations, the former Mandatory had pledged itself to observe and respect, in a territory having an international status, human rights and fundamental freedoms for all without distinction as to race. To establish instead, and to enforce, distinctions, exclusions, restrictions and limitations exclusively based on grounds of race, colour, descent or national or ethnic origin which constitute a denial of fundamental human rights is a flagrant violation of the purposes and principles of the Charter.' 1971 ICJ Rep. 16, 57.

This approach makes it unnecessary to consider South Africa's position as a persistent objector to the customary law prohibitions of racial discrimination and of apartheid. See generally Charney, *The Persistent Objector Rule and the Development of Customary International Law*, 56 Brit. YB Int'l L. 1 (1985).

The Court also addressed the principle of self-determination in its advisory opinion on *Western Sahara*.[99] In construing this principle as a right, the Court, without breaking new ground, based its decision on its 1971 advisory opinion on South West Africa and on certain resolutions of the General Assembly.[100]

The most recent ICJ pronouncement on principles of human rights and humanitarian law, its judgment in the *Nicaragua* case, has been discussed in Chapter I, Section III. Our discussion of the ICJ's case-law, although brief, demonstrates that the method employed by the *Nicaragua* Court in its treatment of elements of customary international law in general and of humanitarian law in particular has important antecedents in its earlier jurisprudence, especially that implicating important human and humanitarian rights.[101]

That method accords limited significance to state practice, especially to inconsistent or contrary practice, and attributes central normative significance to resolutions both of the United Nations General Assembly and of other international organizations. The Court has found evidence of *opinio juris* and/or practice in such resolutions and in their verbal acceptance by states. The burden of proof to be discharged in establishing custom in the field of human or humanitarian rights is thus less onerous than in other fields of international law. Purists may castigate this approach as an erosion of the traditional methods of establishing customary international law, but given the absence of a true international legislative body, and the enlightened interest of the international community in extending the reach and in strengthening the effectiveness of essential norms of international public order, including those protecting human dignity, the ICJ's desire to fill the normative void is understandable.

The Court has not challenged the twin elements of Article 38(1)(b) of its Statute. Instead, it continues to use those elements in formulating judgments, while ascribing to them changing degrees of importance. These developments may indicate a recognition that in the field of human rights and humanitarian norms somewhat

[99] *Western Sahara*, 1975 ICJ Rep. 12 (Advisory Opinion of 16 Oct.).

[100] See e.g. the Declaration on Principles of International Law Concerning Friendly Relations and Co-operation Among States in Accordance with the Charter of the United Nations, GA Res. 2625, 25 UN GAOR Supp. (No. 28) at 121, UN Doc. A/8028 (1971).

[101] See generally Kirgis, *Custom on a Sliding Scale*, 81 AJIL 146 (1987).

different types of evidence, like those discussed in Section I, may be used to establish norms of customary law. Provided that the norms of human rights and of humanitarian law articulated by the Court continue to be reasonable and not too far in advance of the mores of the international community, the Court's statements that certain norms embody customary law will be regarded as authoritative.

III. CUSTOMARY HUMAN RIGHTS IN SELECTED NATIONAL COURTS

Customary human rights law, like customary international law in general, is a part of the law of the United States to which both the federal and state courts must give effect.[102] American cases implicating customary human rights have attracted extensive commentary.[103] These cases (to be considered later in this section) build on the English legal principle that international law is part of the law of the land.[104] The customary law of England embraces, of course, the customary law of human rights.[105] British courts have

---

[102] Restatement, above n. 4, § 111, § 702, comment *c*. See also US Const. Art. I, § 8, cl. 10. On recognition of customary international law in national constitutions, see Cassese, *Modern Constitutions and International Law*, 185 Recueil des cours 331, 368-93 (1985-III) (who concludes that national constitutions tend to disparage customary international law).

[103] See e.g. Gerstel and Segall, *Conference Report: Human Rights In American Courts*, 1 Am. U. J. Int'l L. & Pol. 137 (1986); Schrader, *Custom and General Principles as Sources of International Law in American Federal Courts*, 82 Colum. L. Rev. 751 (1982); Bilder, *Integrating International Human Rights Law into Domestic Law—U.S. Experience*, 4 Hous. J. Int'l L. 1 (1981); Oliver, *Problems of Cognition and Interpretation in Applying Norms of Customary International Law of Human Rights in United States Courts*, ibid. at 59; Schneebaum, *International Law as Guarantor of Judicially-Enforceable Rights: A Reply to Professor Oliver*, ibid. at 65; Paust, *Litigating Human Rights: A Commentary on the Comments*, ibid. at 81; George, *Defining Filartiga: Characterizing International Torture Claims in United States Courts*, 3 Dick. J. Int'l L. 1 (1984); Blum and Steinhardt, above n. 15, at 53; Trimble, *A Revisionist View of Customary International Law*, 33 UCLA L. Rev. 665 (1986); Lillich, *Invoking International Human Rights Law in Domestic Courts*, 54 Cin. L. Rev. 367 (1985); Burke, Coliver, de la Vega, and Rosenbaum, *Application of International Human Rights Law in State and Federal Courts*, 18 Tex. Int'l LJ 291 (1983); T. Franck and M. Glennon, Foreign Relations and National Security Law 122-50 (1987).

[104] *West Rand Central Gold Mining Co. Ltd.* v. *Rex*, [1905] 2 KB 391, 406-7; See also *Chung Chi Cheung* v. *The King*, [1939] AC 160 (PC); 1 L. Oppenheim, International Law 39-47 (H. Lauterpacht 8th edn. 1955).

[105] See generally Drzemczewski, *The Applicability of Customary International Human Rights Law in the English Legal System*, 8 Hum. Rts. J. 71 (1975).

less frequently been seized of questions of customary human rights
law than have American courts, perhaps because the institutions
established under the European Convention on Human Rights (the
European Commission of Human Rights and the European Court
of Human Rights), to which the United Kingdom is a party, offer
effective fora to persons within the jurisdiction of the United
Kingdom with human rights complaints.[106] Because of the relative
scarcity of British cases implicating customary human rights, one
can only speculate on whether the burden of proof to be met for
establishing the customary law status of human rights would be
lighter than the burden of proof which British jurisprudence requires
in other fields of international law in British courts. The opinion
of Lord Macmillan in *Compania Naviera Vascongado* v. *Steamship
'Cristina'* is of interest here:

it is a recognized prerequisite of the adoption in our municipal law of a
doctrine of public international law that it shall have attained the position
of general acceptance by civilized nations as a rule of international
conduct, evidenced by international treaties and conventions, authoritative
textbooks, practice and judicial decisions. It is manifestly of the highest
importance that the Courts of this country before they give the force of
law within this realm to any doctrine of international law should be
satisfied that it has the hallmarks of general assent and reciprocity.[107]

Successful invocation of customary human rights norms requires
that a liberal approach be adopted to treaties as a source of
customary law. The criteria advanced by Lord Wilberforce for
establishing the customary law character of treaties in British courts
in *I Congreso del Partido*, where the appellants sought to invoke
an international convention against Cuba in a case concerning
Cuba's failure to deliver a cargo of sugar, may be possible to satisfy
in the case of widely accepted normative human rights treaties:

[T]he number of states bound by it [the convention] has always been
limited and has not included states important in maritime commerce. Yet
it is invoked . . . as a statement of generally accepted international law.
Now there may be cases in which a multilateral convention may become
part of general international law so as to bind states not parties (a

[106] On the status of the European Convention on Human Rights in the United
Kingdom, see F. Mann, Foreign Affairs in English Courts 15, 73, 87, 95, 131-2
(1986).
[107] [1938] AC 485, 497. See also *The Parlement Belge*, [1880] PD 197 (CA);
Owners of the ship Philippine Admiral v. *Wallem Shipping*, [1976] 1 All ER 78 (PC).

proposition not uncontroversial) but at least the convention must bear a legislative aspect and there must be a wide general acceptance of it as law-making, over a period, before this condition is satisfied.[108]

Certain British cases are of considerable importance for the recognition of human rights as customary law. In *Oppenheimer* v. *Cattermole*, Lord Cross of Chelsea considered the effect of human rights considerations upon a 1941 Nazi decree stripping expatriate German Jews of their nationality:

[W]hat we are concerned with here is legislation which takes away without compensation from a section of the citizen body singled out on racial grounds all their property on which the state passing the legislation can lay its hands and, in addition, deprives them of their citizenship. To my mind a law of this sort constitutes so grave an infringement of human rights that the courts of this country ought to refuse to recognise it as law at all.[109]

In *Ahmad* v. *Inner London Education Authority*, Scarman LJ, in referring to the obligations of the United Kingdom under the Charter of the United Nations and the European Convention on Human Rights, emphasized that statutory provisions have to be construed and applied against the background of

a multi-racial society which has accepted international obligations and enacted statutes designed to eliminate discrimination on grounds of race, religion, colour or sex. Further, it is no longer possible to argue that because the international treaty obligations of the United Kingdom do not become law unless enacted by Parliament our courts pay no regard to our international obligations [rather,] they will interpret statutory language and apply common law principles, wherever possible, so as to reach a conclusion consistent with our international obligations. . . .[110]

In *Waddington* v. *Miah alias Ullah*, the Court of Appeal quashed a conviction based on the retroactive application of a statute, and the House of Lords affirmed. The Court of Appeal emphasized that the 'presumption against retrospection applies in general to legislation of a penal character and such legislation is, in general, forbidden by [Article 7 of the European Convention on Human Rights] and by [Article 11(2)] of the Universal Declaration of

[108] [1981] 2 All ER 1064, 1069 (HL).
[109] [1976] AC 249, 278 (HL).
[110] [1977] 3 WLR 396, 406 (CA).

Human Rights . . .'.[111] In *Allgemeine Gold- und Silberscheideanstalt* v. *Customs and Excise Commissioners*, Lord Denning stated that although the European Convention on Human Rights was not part of English law, 'we do pay attention to the Convention even as it stands.'[112]

In *Ram Chand Birdi* v. *Secretary of State for Home Affairs* (1975)[113] Lord Denning declared, in the same vein, that

[i]t is to be assumed that the Crown, in taking its part in legislation, would do nothing which was in conflict with the Treaty [the European Convention of Human Rights]. . . . So must Parliament when it passed it. All concerned must be taken to have passed the Statute with the Treaty in mind. So the courts should construe it so as to be in conformity with the Convention and not against it.[114]

In this case, however, Lord Denning went even further, suggesting that if he found, which he did not, that the Act of Parliament did not conform to the Convention, he 'might be inclined to hold it invalid'.[115]

Courts of other countries have also demonstrated readiness to conform national laws to international human rights. The case of *Hussainara Khatoon and Others* v. *Home Secretary, State of Bihar* involved the detention in jail of persons too poor to afford bail, for periods ranging from three to ten years before trial for minor offences.[116] There, the Indian Supreme Court drawing upon Article 5(3) of the European Convention on Human Rights, held that 'even under our Constitution, though speedy trial is not specifically enumerated as a fundamental right, it is implicit in the broad sweep and content of Article 21 [of the Indian Constitution]'.[117] In the case of *Mullin* v. *Administrator, Union Territory of Delhi and Others*,[118] concerning the right of a detainee to have interviews

[111] [1974] 1 WLR 683, 690–1 (HL).
[112] [1980] 2 WLR 555, 561 (CA). Regarding the relationship of the customary international law of extradition to guarantees of due process by the requesting state, see Lord Simon's opinion in *Tzu-Tsai Cheng* v. *Governor of Pentonville Prison*, [1973] 2 All ER 204, 214–19 (HL). Regarding the interpretation of conventional rules consistently with customary law, see *Public Prosecutor* v. *Koi*, [1968] 1 All ER 419, 425 (PC), Chapter I, n. 10, above.
[113] 61 Int'l L. Rep. (UKCA) 250 (1981).
[114] Ibid. at 256–7.
[115] Ibid. at 258.
[116] (1980) 1 SCC 81.
[117] Ibid. at 88–9.
[118] (1981) 1 SCC 608.

with members of her family and friends, the Indian Supreme
Court held that Article 21 of the Indian Constitution implicitly
incorporated 'the right to protection against torture or cruel,
inhuman or degrading treatment which is enunciated in Article 5
of the Universal Declaration of Human Rights and guaranteed by
Article 7 of the International Covenant on Civil and Political
Rights'.[119]

In *Koowarta* v. *Bjelke-Petersen and Others* (1982),[120] the High
Court of Australia considered the international human right
prohibiting racial discrimination. After a careful review of the
codification of this prohibition in the UN Charter and other
international instruments, including the International Convention
on the Elimination of All Forms of Racial Discrimination, the
jurisprudence of the ICJ and scholarly writings, Stephen J. stated
that

[i]t was contended on behalf of the Commonwealth that, quite apart from
the Convention, Australia has an international obligation to suppress all
forms of racial discrimination because respect for human dignity and
fundamental rights, and thus the norm of non-discrimination on the
grounds of race, is now part of customary international law, as both
created and evidenced by state practice and as expounded by jurists and
eminent publicists. There is, in my view, much to be said for this
submission. . . .[121]

The *locus classicus* of the US law on customary law is found in
the 1900 *Paquete Habana* judgment of the Supreme Court, in which
Justice Gray stated: '[I]nternational law is part of our law, and
must be ascertained and administered by the courts of justice of
appropriate jurisdiction, as often as questions of right depending

[119] Ibid. at 619.
[120] 68 Int'l L. Rep. 181 (1985).
[121] Ibid. at 223. Regarding customary human rights in Canadian courts, see
generally Woloshyn, *To what Extent Can Canadian Courts be Expected to Enforce
International Human Rights Law in Civil Litigation?*, 50 Saskatchewan L. Rev. 1
(1985/6); Humphrey, *The Canadian Charter of Rights and Freedoms and International
Law*, ibid. at 13; Schwartz and Mackintosh, *The Charter and the Domestic
Enforcement of International Law*, 16 Manitoba LJ 149 (1986). Concerning the
influence of international human rights law on the interpretation of the Canadian
Charter of Rights and Freedoms, see Tarnopolsky, *The Canadian Experience with
the International Covenant on Civil and Political Rights Seen from the Perspective
of a Former Member of the Human Rights Committee*, 20 Akron L. Rev. 611,
625-8 (1987).

upon it are duly presented for their determination.'[122] That case concerned the condemnation by US authorities of Spanish-Cuban fishing boats as prizes of war. The Court explained that the rule of international law providing for immunity of such vessels was founded, *inter alia*, 'on considerations of humanity to a poor and industrious order of men . . .'.[123]

The determination of customary international law is a matter of law to be decided by judges and courts, which is appropriate for judicial notice of such rules.[124] Thus, as stated in § 113(1) of the Restatement, customary law need not be pleaded or proved. In reality, however, given the difficulties inherent in ascertaining customary rules and some judges' lack of familiarity with international law, a growing practice of considering evidence on customary international law, including expert testimony, has evolved.[125]

The following discussion of several American cases implicating human rights will focus on the evidence cited by American courts for establishing customary human rights law and the process of its creation. Emphasis will be placed on the sources relied upon by the courts in deciding whether a particular human right is embodied in customary law.

Early American cases addressed the sources and the evidence of customary law more than a century before the emergence of modern human rights law. We shall see that the tension typical of contemporary conflict between normative pronouncements and actual practice echoes earlier discussions. For example, the question of whether customary international law prohibited the slave trade

[122] 175 US 677, 700 (1900). Among sources invoked as proof of custom were national decrees, judicial decisions and admiralty instructions, treaties, and the works of jurists and commentators. Ibid. 687-700.

For the antecedents of this decision, see *United States* v. *Smith*, 18 US (5 Wheat.) 153, 160 (1820), in which the Court had to decide whether the crime of piracy violated the law of nations. Justice Story stated that the law of nations on this subject may be ascertained 'by consulting the works of jurists, writing professedly on public law; or by the general usage and practice of nations; or by judicial decisions recognizing and enforcing that law'. Ibid. at 160-1. He noted that all the writers on the common law, the maritime law, and the law of nations treated piracy as an offence against the law of nations. The conclusive proof for the proposition that piracy constituted such a crime was the practice of every nation in punishing all persons who have committed this offence regardless of their nationality. Ibid.

[123] *The Paquete Habana*, 175 US at 708.

[124] Ibid., Restatement, above n. 4, § 113(1).

[125] Restatement, above n. 4, § 113(2), comment *c*.

arose in 1822 in *United States* v. *The La Jeune Eugenie.*[126] In
declaring that the slave trade had come to be considered an offence
against the law of nations, Justice Story relied largely on the fact
that 'there is scarcely a single maritime nation of Europe, that has
not . . . [through] conferences, acts, or treaties, acknowledged the
injustice and inhumanity of this trade; and pledged itself to
promote its abolition.'[127] This rationale emphasized normative
pronouncements and *opinio juris.* Justice Story further stated that
the law of nations could be 'deduced, first, from the general
principles of right and justice, applied to the concerns of individuals . . .'.[128]

Three years later, in *The Antelope,*[129] the Supreme Court turned
back the clock in reaching the conclusion that the slave-trade was
not contrary to the law of nations. Based largely upon the same
sources considered by Justice Story in *La Jeune Eugenie,* Chief
Justice Marshall stated that the slave-trade 'has been sanctioned in
modern times by the laws of all nations who possess distant
colonies. . . . It has claimed all the sanction which could be derived
from long usage, and general acquiescence'.[130] Conceding that the
slave-trade was contrary to the law of nature, Chief Justice Marshall
observed that, in contrast to a moralist,

a jurist must search for . . . legal solution[s] in those principles of action
which are sanctioned by the usages, the national acts, and the general
assent of that portion of the world of which he considers himself as a
part. . . . If we resort to this standard as the test of international law, the
question . . . is decided in favor of the legality of the trade.[131]

Chief Justice Marshall contrasted man's natural rights to rights
under the positive law of nations, which was founded on practice
or usage: '[T]his, which was the usage of all, could not be
pronounced repugnant to the law of nations, which is certainly to
be tried by the test of general usage.'[132]

---

[126] 26 Fed. Cas. 832 (CCD Mass. 1822) (No. 15,551).

[127] Ibid. at 846.

[128] Ibid.

[129] 23 US (10 Wheat.) 64 (1825).

[130] Ibid. at 113.

[131] Ibid. at 117. Chief Justice Marshall found further that foreign courts have
been guided by the principle that the legality of the capture of a vessel engaged in
the slave trade depends upon the law of the country to which the vessel belongs
and that the opinions of lower US courts were divided on the subject. Ibid.

[132] Ibid.

Much later, some American courts started focusing on normative instruments rather than on the practice of states. An emphasis on the role of normative instruments in the creation of international law relevant to the protection of individuals thus characterized the 1974 decision of the Second Circuit Court of Appeals in *United States* v. *Toscanino*.[133] In *Toscanino*, a criminal defendant claimed that US agents had violated international law by kidnapping him from Uruguay and bringing him to the United States. The defendant relied primarily upon the principle of the territorial integrity of states, recognized in the Charter of the United Nations and in the Charter of the Organization of American States, to which both the United States and Uruguay are parties. In remanding the case to the District Court, the Court of Appeals stressed the following:

[T]hat international kidnappings such as the one alleged here violate the U.N. Charter was settled as a result of the Security Council debates following the illegal kidnapping in 1960 of Adolf Eichmann from Argentina. . . . The resolution merely recognized a long standing principle of international law that abductions by one state of persons located within the territory of another violate the territorial sovereignty of the second state. . . .[134]

In the following year, 1975, class action plaintiffs in *Nguyen Da Yen* v. *Kissinger*[135] alleged that the US Immigration and Naturalization Service and others had violated the fundamental human rights of Vietnamese children by, among other things, subjecting them to continued involuntary detention in the United States. Although the case was not decided on this issue, the court observed in a lengthy footnote[136] that the illegal seizure, removal, and detention of aliens against their will in a foreign country may well be a tort in violation of the law of nations under the Alien Tort Claims Act.[137] The evidence adduced by the Court for this tentative conclusion included Articles 24, 49, and 50 of Geneva

[133] 500 F. 2d 267 (2d Cir. 1974).
[134] Ibid. at 277–8.
[135] 528 F. 2d 1194 (9th Cir. 1975).
[136] Ibid. at 1201–2 n. 13.
[137] 28 USC § 1350. Discussion of the Alien Tort Claims Act is outside the scope of these comments regarding the evidence and application of customary human rights law.

Convention No. IV and Articles 12, 13, 15, and 16 of the Universal
Declaration of Human Rights.[138]

The leading case on human rights and customary international
law in American courts is the 1980 decision by the Second Circuit
Court of Appeals in *Filartiga* v. *Peña-Irala*.[139] In *Filartiga*, two
Paraguayan citizens brought an action in New York against a
former Paraguayan police official for the wrongful death by torture
of a third Paraguayan citizen, who was a member of the family of
the plaintiffs. Plaintiffs asserted jurisdiction under the Alien Tort
Claims Act,[140] which provides that '[t]he district courts shall have
original jurisdiction of any civil action by an alien for a tort only,
committed in violation of the law of nations or a treaty of the
United States.' Because the action did not arise directly under a
treaty, the Court had to determine whether the prohibition against
torture was embodied in customary international law. The Court
answered this question in the affirmative[141] after consulting the
work of jurists, judicial precedents,[142] and, most important, the
usage and practice of states. Citing *The Paquete Habana* for the
idea that comity matures into a settled rule of international law by
means of the general assent of civilized nations,[143] the Court
referred to Articles 55 and 56 of the Charter of the United Nations
to demonstrate that a state's treatment of its citizens is a matter
of international concern.[144] Although there was no universal

[138] The Court also cited the position taken by the US Department of State on
this issue. *Nguyen Da Yen* v. *Kissinger*, 528 F. 2d at 1201 n. 13. See also
Abdul-Rahman Oman Adra v. *Clift*, 195 F. Supp. 857, 864-5 (D. Md. 1961).

[139] 630 F. 2d 876 (2d Cir. 1980).

[140] 28 USC § 1350. A recent bill introduced in the US Congress provides that
'[e]very person who, under actual or apparent authority of any foreign nation,
subjects any person to torture or extrajudicial killing shall be liable to the party
injured . . . in a civil action,' and states that the district courts shall have jurisdiction
over such cases. HR 1417, 100th Cong., 1st Sess. (1987).

[141] '[W]e hold that deliberate torture perpetrated under color of official authority
violates universally accepted norms of the international law of human rights. . . .'
630 F. 2d at 878.

The court further found that '[i]n light of the universal condemnation of torture
in numerous international agreements, and the renunciation of torture as an
instrument of official policy by virtually all of the nations of the world (in principle
if not in practice), we find that an act of torture committed by a state official
against one held in detention violates established norms of the international law of
human rights, and hence the law of nations.' Ibid. at 880.

[142] *Ireland* v. *United Kingdom*, 25 Eur. Ct. HR (Ser. A) (1978).

[143] 175 US 677, 694 (1900).

[144] *Filartiga* v. *Peña-Irala*, 630 F. 2d at 881.

agreement among nations regarding the status of all the rights guaranteed by the Charter, there was no dissent that those accepted include, at a bare minimum, freedom from torture.[145] The proposition that this right had become part of customary law was supported by citation of the Universal Declaration of Human Rights[146] and the Declaration on the Protection of All Persons from Being Subjected to Torture and Other Cruel, Inhuman or Degrading Treatment or Punishment.[147] The Court considered these UN declarations significant 'because they specify with great precision the obligations of member nations under the Charter'.[148] As evidence for the prohibition of torture by the modern practice of nations, the Court adduced the consensus on the prohibition of torture expressed in the American Convention on Human Rights, the International Covenant on Civil and Political Rights,[149] and the European Convention on Human Rights, as well as the *amicus curiae* brief submitted by the US Department of State. The substance of these instruments was reflected in national laws, since the constitutions of more than 55 nations prohibited torture explicitly or implicitly.

The *Filartiga* decision focused sharply on *opinio juris*, normative instruments and statements of official policy in defining customary law. Although the Court acknowledged that the renunciation of torture as an instrument of official policy may have been more reflective of principle than of practice, it nevertheless did not allow violations of the norm to detract from the norm's binding nature. Adopting a perspective similar to that taken in the *Nicaragua* judgment regarding the significance of violations of norms, the Second Circuit gave greater weight to the statement of the Department of State attesting that no state has asserted a right to torture, and to the fact that states accused of practising torture have responded either with denials or with suggestions that the conduct in question was unauthorized, than to any violations of the norm prohibiting torture.[150]

[145] Ibid. at 882.

[146] GA Res. 217A, UN Doc. A/810, at 71 (1948).

[147] GA Res. 3452, 30 UN GAOR Supp. (No. 34) at 91, UN Doc. A/10034 (1976).

[148] 630 F. 2d at 883.

[149] See the important 'General Comment' of the Human Rights Committee on Art. 7 of the Political Covenant, 37 UN GAOR Supp. (No. 40) at 94-5, UN Doc. A/37/40 (1982).

[150] 630 F. 2d at 884 and n. 15.

Although the *Filartiga* decision has triggered considerable litigation invoking customary human rights law, particularly concerning allegations of prolonged arbitrary detention, only some of
the later cases have followed its method of focusing more on
normative instruments than on the actual practice of states. In one
of the rare cases implicating an economic right, namely the right
to free elementary education, the court involved did not adopt the
approach of the *Filartiga* Court. *In re Alien Children Education
Litigation*[151] in 1980 concerned a challenge to a Texas statute which
deprived 'undocumented' (illegal alien) children of access to free
elementary education. The plaintiffs argued, among other things,
that the right to free elementary education was recognized in the
Charter of the Organization of American States, the Universal
Declaration of Human Rights (Article 26), the American Declaration of the Rights and Duties of Man, the International
Covenant on Economic, Social, and Cultural Rights, the International Covenant on Civil and Political Rights and the Declaration of the Rights of the Child. They asserted that these
agreements and declarations 'should be construed as customary
international law, thus providing a rule of decision in this case'.[152]
While the Court recognized the right of the undocumented children
to free education on other grounds, it did not accept the plaintiffs'
position on customary law. Citing *The Paquete Habana* as authority,
the Court concluded that 'the right to education, while it represents
an important international goal, has not acquired the status of
customary international law. This conclusion is founded on the
nature of international law.'[153]

In an *obiter* the Court went on to state:

[T]o the extent that the United States is neglecting its pledge to promote
human rights or to exert the greatest efforts to further educational
opportunities, an alien's government may call the United States to answer
before an international tribunal. In this court, the plaintiffs have not
shown that a rule of decision arising from customary international law
should be applied.[154]

[151] 501 F. Supp. 544 (SD Tex. 1980), *aff'd sub nom.* Plyler v. *Doe*, 457 US 202
(1982).
[152] 501 F. Supp. 544, 596 (SD Tex. 1980).
[153] Ibid. In a footnote, the Court briefly explained the elements of customary
international law. Ibid. at n. 122.
[154] Ibid. at 596.

The Court thus appeared to consider the right to education as an appropriate subject for claims of one government against another, but not as a customary norm invokable in US courts. It is, of course, important to avoid conflating customary human rights law, which almost always seeks to protect both citizens and aliens and which provides rules of decision for US courts, with international law rules pertaining to the diplomatic protection of aliens.

One case which did follow the principle of *Filartiga*, *Rodriguez-Fernandez* v. *Wilkinson*,[155] concerned a claim in which a Cuban refugee challenged his prolonged arbitrary detention in a US prison as a violation of both the US Constitution and customary international law. A federal District Court concluded that the detention violated only the latter, and not constitutional standards. Citing *Filartiga*, the Court stated that principles of customary international law may be discerned from 'an overview of express international conventions, the teachings of legal scholars, the general custom and practice of nations and the relevant judicial decisions'.[156] As sources of international human rights, the Court cited the Universal Declaration of Human Rights, the American Convention on Human Rights, the European Convention on Human Rights, and the International Covenant on Civil and Political Rights.[157] Each of these contains provisions pertaining to freedom from arbitrary detention. Although the United States was not bound by these conventions, the Court found them to be 'indicative of the customs and usages of civilized nations'.[158] The Court found further that resolutions and declarations, while not technically binding, establish broadly recognized standards.[159] The Court also relied upon statements by members of Congress and of the Department of State recognizing freedom from arbitrary arrest, and an international arbitral decision supporting the principle that arbitrary detention of an alien could give rise to a claim under international

[155] 505 F. Supp. 787 (D. Kan. 1980), *aff'd on other grounds sub nom. Rodriguez-Fernandez* v. *Wilkinson*, 654 F. 2d 1382 (10th Cir. 1981). Although the case was decided on constitutional grounds, the Court of Appeals cited the Universal Declaration of Human Rights and the American Convention on Human Rights in confirming that freedom from arbitrary imprisonment constituted a fundamental principle of international law. 654 F. 2d at 1388.

[156] 505 F. Supp. at 798.

[157] Ibid. at 796-7.

[158] Ibid. at 797. See also *Thompson* v. *Oklahoma*, 108 S. Ct. 2687, 2696 n. 34 (1988).

[159] 505 F. Supp. 787 (D. Kan. 1980), at 796.

law.[160] The Court concluded that this review 'of the sources from which customary international law is derived clearly demonstrates that arbitrary detention is prohibited by customary international law . . . [and that] the indeterminate detention of an excluded alien . . . is judicially remedial as a violation of international law.'[161]

Not all courts have acknowledged international human rights instruments as a source of customary law. In 1984, in *Jean* v. *Nelson*,[162] a class action suit brought on behalf of detained Haitian aliens who were subject to deportation ('excludable aliens'), the US Court of Appeals for the 11th Circuit rejected the argument that the prohibition of arbitrary detention, articulated in several international human rights instruments, is an embodiment of customary international law. The Court's description of the process of creation of international customary law emphasized traditional criteria: exchanges between states, protests, acquiescence, and judicial decisions, rather than the international human rights instruments.[163] By contrast, a year later, in *Fernandez-Roque* v. *Smith*,[164] a district court in Georgia agreed that plaintiffs relying on international human rights instruments 'established that customary international law prohibits prolonged arbitrary detention'.[165]

[160] Ibid. at 797–8.

[161] Ibid. at 798. Sympathetic but inconclusive references to the prohibition of arbitrary detention in international human rights instruments were also made in *Ishtyaq* v. *Nelson*, 627 F. Supp. 13, 27 (EDNY 1983), and in *Soroa-Gonzales* v. *Civiletti*, 515 F. Supp. 1049, 1061 n. 18 (ND Ga. 1981).

[162] 727 F. 2d 957 (11th Cir. 1984), *aff'd on other grounds*, 105 S. Ct. 2992 (1985).

[163] 'Customary international law, however, derives not only from individual treaties, but from the "concordant and recurring action of numerous States in the domain of international relations, the conception in each case that such action was enjoined by law, and the failure of other States to challenge that conception at the time." . . . "Arbitrary" is hardly a self-defining term, but amici have pointed to no evidence in the way of diplomatic protests, international arbitrations, or court decisions that suggest that it is current international practice to regard the detention of uninvited aliens seeking admission as a violation of customary international law.' Ibid. at 964 n. 4.

[164] *Fernandez-Roque* v. *Smith*, 622 F. Supp. 887 (ND Ga. 1985), *modified sub nom. Fernandez-Roque* v. *Meese*, 781 F. 2d 1450 (11th Cir. 1986).

[165] 622 F. Supp. 887, 903 (ND Ga. 1985), discussed in Koh, *The United States as World Forum, Civil Remedies for Uncivil Wrongs: Combatting Terrorism through Transnational Public Law Litigation*, 22 Tex. Int'l LJ 169 (1987). The human rights instruments invoked by plaintiffs (662 F. Supp. 903 (1985)) as sources of customary human rights law were similar to those cited in *Filartiga* and *Rodriguez-Fernandez*. However, because the Court found a controlling executive act which superseded customary law, that law provided plaintiffs with no relief. In deciding that directives of the Attorney-General constitute a 'controlling executive act' (ibid.), the Court unfortunately gave a broad interpretation to *Paquete Habana*'s list of acts, consisting

A particularly important decision is the (1984) case of *Tel-Oren*
v. *Libyan Arab Republic*[166] brought under the Alien Tort Claims
Act by the victims of a terrorist attack on a bus in Israel, for
violations of customary international law by members of the
Palestine Liberation Organization. The District Court dismissed
the case for lack of jurisdiction, and the Court of Appeals affirmed.
Two of the opinions by the judges of the Court of Appeals are
pertinent here. Judge Harry T. Edwards adopted the *Filartiga*
principles; however, he found that the factual differences between
the cases precluded reliance on *Filartiga* because the law of nations
does not impose the same responsibility on non-state actors, such
as the PLO, as that applied to states and persons acting under
colour of state law. The Alien Tort Claims Act could therefore not
be read to cover torture by non-state actors. Judge Edwards also
held that the disagreement between states on this issue, as reflected
in UN resolutions, indicated that politically motivated terrorism
did not violate international law.

Judge Robert H. Bork found that, when the Alien Tort Claims
Act was adopted in 1789, 'there was no concept of international
human rights; neither was there, under the traditional version of
customary international law, any recognition of a right of private
parties to recover.'[167] Judge Bork further found that contemporary
international law did not provide plaintiffs with a cause of action.
Judge Bork believed that individual rights recognized in such
instruments as the Universal Declaration of Human Rights, the
International Covenant on Civil and Political Rights, and the
American Convention on Human Rights are not intended to be
judicially enforceable, because some of them are merely precatory
and some define rights at such a high level of generality as to
preclude their application by courts in a 'traditional adjudicatory
manner'.[168] Highlighting the divergence of views that persists over
the sources and evidence of customary international law, Judge
Bork questioned the value of international human rights instruments
as such evidence:

of a 'treaty[,] . . . controlling executive [Presidential?] or legislative act or judicial
decision . . .', that could displace customary law. Ibid. at 902, citing *The Paquete
Habana*, 175 US 677, 700 (1900).
[166] 726 F. 2d 774 (DC Cir. 1984), *cert. denied*, 470 US 1003 (1985).
[167] Ibid. at 813.
[168] Ibid. at 818.

It may be doubted that courts should understand documents of this sort as having been assented to as law by all civilized nations since enforcement of the principles enunciated would revolutionize most societies. For that reason, among others, courts should hesitate long before finding violations of a 'law of nations' evidenced primarily by the resolutions and declarations of multinational bodies.[169]

That *Tel-Oren* did not bring an end to the use of human rights instruments as evidence of customary law[170] was made clear one year later in *Von Dardel* v. *Union of Soviet Socialist Republics*.[171] The District Court in the District of Columbia, where *Tel-Oren* was controlling precedent, found that the Soviet Union had violated the customary international law of diplomatic immunity by holding a Swedish diplomat, Raoul Wallenberg, in incommunicado detention for more than 35 years. Because a universal consensus existed concerning the international law of diplomatic immunity, evincing a clearly applicable international standard, the Court considered that the violation fell within even the most restrictive interpretation of the Alien Tort Claims Act. Accordingly, the Court found that it had jurisdiction to consider the claim under any of the *Tel-Oren* opinions. The Court further held that the Foreign Sovereign Immunities Act[172] of 1976 did not extend immunity to clear violations of international law.[173]

The Court stated that the applicable principles of international law were defined by legal scholars, confirmed in international conventions to which the United States is a party, and codified in US law. The Court considered not only conventions pertaining to diplomatic immunity, but also such instruments as the Charter of the United Nations, the Universal Declaration of Human Rights,

---

[169] Ibid. at 819.
[170] See also *Handel* v. *Artukovic*, 601 F. Supp. 1421, 1428 (CD Cal. 1985) (acts of genocide, enslavement, and religious discrimination constituted violations of the laws of humanity during the Second World War).
[171] 623 F. Supp. 246 (DDC 1985).
[172] 28 USCA §§ 1602-11 (1976).
[173] 623 F. Supp. 246, 254 (DDC 1985). This aspect of the decision was strongly criticized in *Amerada Hess Shipping Corporation* v. *Argentine Republic*, 638 F. Supp. 73, 77 (SDNY 1986). In *Argentine Republic* v. *Amerada Hess Shipping Corporation* the Supreme Court decided that the Foreign Sovereign Immunities Act of 1976 (FSIA) provides the sole basis for obtaining jurisdiction over a foreign state in the courts of the United States, and that the Alien Tort Statute has the same effect after the passage of the FSIA as before with respect to defendants other than foreign states. 109 S. Ct. 683, 690, 692 (1989). See also *Siderman* v. *Republic of Argentina*, CV82-1772-RMT(MCx) (CD Cal. 7 Mar. 1985).

the International Covenant on Civil and Political Rights, and the Final Act of the Conference on Security and Co-operation in Europe (Helsinki 1975), and concluded that the Soviet Union has violated such instruments.[174]

In *Forti* v. *Suarez-Mason*, the Court, following the rationale and method of *Filartiga*, recognized torture, prolonged arbitrary detention, and summary executions as prohibited by customary international law. However, applying a standard of 'universal acceptance and definition', the Court denied, with regard to the prohibition of 'causing disappearance', the existence of the requisite degree of international consensus which demonstrates a customary international norm. 'Even if there were greater evidence of universality, there remain definitional problems. It is not clear precisely what conduct falls within the proposed norm, or how this proscription would differ from that of summary execution.'[175] In so finding, the Court noted the absence of any case-law confirming that causing disappearances constitutes a violation of the law of nations. For similar reasons, the Court did not recognize as a customary norm the prohibition of cruel, inhuman, and degrading treatment.[176] It is unfortunate that the Court addressed neither the significance for the maturation of this norm into customary law of its statement in human rights treaties and in national laws nor that of its application in the practice of the European Commission and Court of Human Rights and the Human Rights Committee established under Article 28 of the Political Covenant. Upon reconsideration, the Court, citing international legal experts, the Restatement, and condemnations of causing of the disappearance of

[174] 623 F. Supp. at 261.

[175] *Forti* v. *Suarez-Mason*, 672 F. Supp. 1531, 1543 (1987). See also *Martinez-Baca* v. *Suarez-Mason*, No. C-87-2057 SC, slip op. at 9, 11 (ND Cal. 11 Jan. 1988). For a listing of human rights which are violated by the causing of disappearances, see T. Meron, above n. 54, at 99–100; Meron, *Draft Model Declaration on Internal Strife*, Int'l Rev. Red Cross, No. 262, Jan.–Feb. 1988, at 59, 62–3.

[176] 'Plaintiffs do not cite, and the Court is not aware of, such evidence of universal consensus regarding the right to be free from "cruel, inhuman and degrading treatment as exists, for example, with respect to official torture." Further, any such right poses problems of definability. The difficulties for a district court in adjudicating such a claim are manifest. Because this right lacks readily ascertainable parameters, it is unclear what behavior falls within the proscription—beyond such obvious torts as are already encompassed by the proscriptions of torture, summary execution and prolonged arbitrary detention. Lacking the requisite elements of universality and definability, this proposed tort cannot qualify as a violation of the law of nations.' *Forti* v. *Suarez-Mason*, 672 F. Supp. 1531, 1543 (1987).

individuals, recognized that this offence violates several universally recognized human rights and constitutes an international tort. 'This tort is characterized by the following two essential elements: (1) abduction by state officials or their agents; followed by (2) official refusals to acknowledge the abduction or to disclose the detainee's fate.'[177]

Future judicial decisions confirming the maturation of the prohibition of the causing of disappearances into the corpus of customary law will no doubt be instructed by the recent judgment of the Inter-American Court of Human Rights in the *Velásquez Rodríguez Case*.[178] Although the Court was applying the American Convention on Human Rights rather than customary international law as such, its finding that the practice constitutes a multiple and continuous violation of several provisions of the Convention (read in conjunction with Article 1(1)) stating fundamental human rights, and that it evinces a disregard of the duty to organize the state in such a manner as to ensure the rights recognized in the Convention to all persons subject to its jurisdiction, will be invoked as an authority for customary law as well. In this context, account should be taken of the fact that the Convention does not explicitly address the prohibition of the causing of disappearances. This understanding of the judgment is supported by the universal condemnation of causing the disappearance of individuals and by the recognition that, severally, each of the rights violated embodies customary law, e.g., arbitrary deprivation of liberty through kidnapping (Article 7), violation of the inherent dignity and the integrity of the human being through torture or other cruel, inhuman, or degrading treatment (Article 5), and flagrant violation of the right to life (Article 4).

In conclusion, review of the recent US cases reveals significant,

---

[177] No. C-87-2058-DLJ, slip op. at 7 (ND Cal. 6 July 1988).

[178] Judgment of 29 July 1988, Inter-American Court of Human Rights, Ser. C, Decisions and Judgments, No. 4, paras. 149-58, 194. Compare Restatement, above n. 4, §702. In 1987, the Human Rights Committee found Colombia to be in breach of Art. 6 of the Political Covenant because of failure 'to take appropriate measures to prevent the disappearance and subsequent killings of . . . and to investigate effectively the responsibility for their murders . . .'. Communication No. 161/1983, *Herrera Rubio* v. *Colombia*, 43 UN GAOR Supp. (No. 40) at 190, 198, UN Doc. A/43/40 (1988). The Committee considered the investigations carried out in this case 'to have been inadequate in the light of the State party's obligations under article 2 of the Covenant'. Ibid. at 197. See also the Committee's General Comment on Art. 6, 37 UN GAOR Supp. (No. 40) at 93, UN Doc. A/37/40 (1982).

though uneven and uncertain, resort to international human rights instruments as evidence of customary human rights law. The instruments considered include not only the principal human rights treaties, but also important UN declarations and resolutions. Policy statements and suggestions by the Department of State, scholarly writings, the Restatement, and judicial opinions have also been found to be useful indicia for the determination of custom.

The invocation of multilateral treaties, many of which the United States has not adopted, and especially of resolutions and declarations, does not easily fit the *Paquete Habana* paradigm. Those judgments employing a liberal approach to the sources of customary human rights law, although obviously motivated by the moral value and laudatory goals of human rights norms, do not indicate any clear understanding of the theoretical problems of creating custom. Increased attention to the incorporation of human rights norms in international law through general principles of law might help to erase the lingering doubts in certain quarters concerning the legitimacy of the formation processes of human rights law. The legitimacy of that process can also be furthered by examining international human rights instruments not in isolation but in the context of supporting practice, both in the international and national contexts. Such examinations, drawing on accepted methods of building customary law, will frequently demonstrate that many human rights reflect not only verbal commitments and *opinio juris*, but actual practice as well, and that resolutions and declarations have incremental normative consequences.[179] Given the nature and the goals of human rights, the lofty community values to which they give expression, and their focus on the protection of individuals within the state rather than on the reciprocal interests of states, the burden of proof that must be discharged to demonstrate the establishment of a customary human rights norm should indeed be lighter than in other fields of international law, which are based on reciprocal interests of states. As already indicated in Section I, above, somewhat different types of evidence can be employed to prove the existence of customary human rights. This broad diversity of evidence should be recognized in proving customary human rights.

The dichotomy between the normative instruments and the

---

[179] Blum and Steinhardt, above n. 15.

practice of states has perhaps been exaggerated. The question is not whether human rights instruments must be supported by practice, a point which is obvious. Rather the relevant questions concern the scale and the type of relevant practice required. The controversy as to the weight to be given to normative instruments and to the positions asserted by states, in contrast to their internal practices, has not been resolved and will doubtless continue. Because human rights implicate primarily internal practices, scrutiny of the 'law in action' is both practically difficult and politically sensitive. An emphasis on statements of official policy, internal legislation and international human rights instruments therefore provides more accessible evidence of emerging customary norms of human rights.[180]

Past record shows that it has not been easy to extend the reach of international human rights in the United States through the application of customary law. Success depends on the understanding of the international law of human rights which the litigants and the courts possess, on the philosophical outlook of the judges, and on the speed with which principles originating in international human rights instruments, in national practices, or in general principles of law are perceived as having been transformed into mature rules of international law. Because customary law is part of the law of the land and because the United States is a party to very few human rights treaties, active reliance by US courts on rules of customary law could provide rules of decision (positive law) and thus contribute to filling the normative void, or at least supply supporting material for interpreting the national law concordantly with international standards. Because customary human rights law is self-executing in US courts, enforcing it 'through private litigation' also largely avoids the continuing controversy over the self-executing/non-self-executing effect of international agreements in US courts. Since resort to customary law is necessarily dependent on a knowledge of international human rights, scholars and international lawyers have a special role to play in promoting human rights education.

As for the Federal Republic of Germany, the use of customary international law by West German courts is important because of Article 25 of the West German Basic Law, which states that '[t]he

---

[180] See generally Schachter, above n. 4, at 334-8.

general rules of public international law form part of the federal law. They take precedence over the laws and directly create rights and duties for the inhabitants of the Federal territory.'[181] Because the Federal Republic of Germany is a party to the European Convention on Human Rights, cases implicating international human rights are only infrequently brought before German courts.

In an early case the Bundesverwaltungsgericht, or Supreme Administrative Court, found that the articles of the Universal Declaration 'are not general rules of international law and do not therefore, according to art. 25 of the Basic Law, form part of Federal Law'.[182] Instead, in a different case, the same court separately examined rights under the Universal Declaration to determine whether they had become customary norms.[183]

The position of German courts on the Universal Declaration has evolved somewhat since those early cases. In a case involving the right of foreigners to marry their partners of choice, the Bundesverfassungsgericht, or Supreme Constitutional Court, noted that the European Convention (Article 12) guaranteed such a freedom.[184] Significantly, the Court found further that '[b]eyond the sphere of application of the [European] Convention, there is a consensus under international law that freedom of marriage is one of the fundamental human rights.'[185] To support this statement, the Court cited Article 16(1) of the Universal Declaration, which states a similar freedom.[186]

German courts have also used other human rights instruments to determine a norm's customary status. A 1987 case before the Supreme Constitutional Court involved a Turk sentenced to three years in a Greek prison by a Greek court for smuggling drugs into Greece.[187] While serving his Greek sentence, a Turkish court

[181] Grundgesetz [GG] Art. 25 (W. Ger.).
[182] Fontes iuris gentium, ser. a, sec. II, vol. 4, at 119 (1970), analysing BVerwG 29.6.1957 (BVerwG II C 105.56) BVerwGE 5, 153.
[183] The Court found that '[a]rt. 13 para. 2 of the . . . Universal Declaration . . . conferring on every individual the right to leave any State including his own and to return to his home State has programmatic importance, but contains no general rule of international law and, therefore, has not become part of federal law by virtue of art. 25 of the Basic Law.' Fontes iuris gentium, ser. a, sec. II, vol. 4, at 119–20 (1970), analysing BVerwG 22.2.1956 (BVerwG I C 41.55) BVerwGE 3, 171.
[184] 31 BVerfGE 58, 67-8 (1971).
[185] 31 BVerfGE 68, 72 Int'l L. Rep. 298 (1987).
[186] 31 BVerfGE 68.
[187] 1987 Neue juristische Wochenschrift [NJW] 2155.

sentenced him to eighteen years imprisonment in Turkey for the same offence.[188] After serving his Greek sentence, the Turk went to West Germany, where the Turkish government began extradition proceedings against him.[189] The Supreme Constitutional Court, based on the requirements of the Basic Law (Article 25), had to decide whether customary international law prevented the Turk's extradition because it would cause him to serve two sentences for the same offence.[190]

In deciding this issue, the Supreme Constitutional Court analysed Article 14(7) of the Political Covenant, which states that '[n]o one shall be liable to be tried or punished again for an offence for which he has already been finally convicted or acquitted in accordance with the law and penal procedure of each country.' The Court first noted that over 80 states from all major legal systems of the world had ratified the Covenant, and that reservations to Article 14(7) did not significantly decrease its effect. Further noting that Article 8(4) of the American Convention and Article 4 of the Seventh Protocol to the European Convention provided similar rights, the Court found that

[a]ll of these circumstances justify in any case the conclusion that, in the sense of article 25 of the Basic Law, the principle *ne bis in idem* is a general rule of international law which prohibits a second conviction of a defendant in *the same* state based on the same facts.[191]

Despite some early rulings of the Supreme Administrative Court to the contrary, the West German Supreme Constitutional Court has shown that it will rely on customary human rights law to decide cases to which they are relevant, and that it will examine a variety of evidence, including international human rights instruments, to establish the existence of that law.

In conclusion, it is clear that customary human rights law already plays an important role in the courts of many countries. These countries will eventually serve as a model to be emulated by others. By raising human rights issues before national courts, human rights lawyers can contribute to the acquisition of additional expertise in

188 Ibid.
189 Ibid.
190 Ibid. at 2157.
191 Ibid. at 2158 (emphasis in original). The Court then used the same analytical methods to decide that the customary rule *ne bis in idem* does not prevent *different* states from punishing an offender for the same offence. Ibid.

human rights law by judges, lawyers, and by the public at large, and to the expansion of the role of international human rights in the protection of the individual.

III

Responsibility of States for Violations of Human Rights and Humanitarian Norms

I. MAPPING RECOURSE OPTIONS

Past scholarly comments on the relationship between human rights and state responsibility have focused largely on the historical origins and the jurisprudential underpinnings of these two fields of international law.[1] Our discussion proceeds from a different perspective. It is based on the fundamental, and obvious, proposition that a breach of conventional or customary human rights or humanitarian norms generates the international responsibility of states. Our object is to examine the relationship between, and the meshing of, the contemporary and the rapidly developing law of human rights and humanitarian norms and the law of state responsibility. This examination of the place of human rights and humanitarian norms in the discipline of international law and of the relationship of human rights and humanitarian norms with state responsibility should contribute to the acceptance of human rights as an authentic and legitimate branch of international law and, through emphasis on responsibility and remedies, to the

---

[1] See e.g. L. Sohn and T. Buergenthal, International Protection of Human Rights 1–136 (1973); R. Lillich, The Human Rights of Aliens in Contemporary International Law 1–40 (1984); Lillich, *The Current Status of the Law of State Responsibility for Injuries to Aliens*, in International Law of State Responsibility for Injuries to Aliens 1–60 (R. Lillich ed. 1983); Restatement of the Law Third, Restatement of the Foreign Relations Law of the United States, vol. 2 at 144–46 and §711, Reporters' notes 1–2 (1987); Carbonneau, *The Convergence of the Law of State Responsibility for Injury to Aliens and International Human Rights Norms in the Revised Restatement*, 25 Va. J. Int'l L. 99 (1984).

In his thoughtful reports prepared for the ILC, García-Amador argued that the international recognition of human rights and fundamental freedoms 'constitutes precisely a synthesis of the two principles': the principle of equality between nationals and aliens, and the principle of the international standard of justice. [1956] 2 YB Int'l L. Comm'n 173, 203, UN Doc. A/CN.4/SER.A/1956/Add.1 (1957), reprinted in F. García-Amador, L. Sohn, and R. Baxter, Recent Codification of the Law of State Responsibility for Injuries to Aliens 1, 5 (1974).

securing of greater respect for international human rights and
humanitarian norms and the strengthening of their effectiveness.
Due to the scarcity of practice dehors human rights treaties, our
discussion will frequently be largely theoretical.

Because the draft articles on state responsibility adopted by the
International Law Commission (ILC), the commentaries thereto
and the reports of the special rapporteurs often give a useful
indication of customary law and of trends in the formation of *lex
ferenda*, they provide a useful framework for our discussion. The
Commission's work exemplifies the 'teachings of the most highly
qualified publicists of the various nations, as subsidiary means for
the determination of rules of law'.[2] Professor Brownlie writes that
'[s]ources analogous to the writings of publicists, and at least as
authoritative, are the draft articles produced by the International
Law Commission . . .'.[3] However, the work of the ILC should not
be regarded only as a manifestation of teachings of publicists.
Additionally, it constitutes a stage in the UN work of codification
and progressive development of international law and as such it may
demonstrate practice of states and of international organizations.

A recent study observes that the process of codification very
often produces a text 'which presents a clearer picture of the content
of the law than the fuzzier image suggested by a consideration of
the underlying customary rules [and that the ILC's work thus]
certainly involves elements of law-molding or law-ascertainment'.[4]
Obviously, the authority of the ILC's work depends on the quality
of the ILC's members, which is at present uneven and appears to
be on the decline, and of its special rapporteurs, and on the degree
of support given by the members of the Commission and states to
particular draft articles. The considerable authority of the draft
articles on state responsibility derives both from the crucial nature
of the subject and from the eminent scholarship of the past special

[2] Art. 38(1)(d) of the Statute of the International Court of Justice.
[3] I. Brownlie, Principles of Public International Law 26 (3rd edn. 1979).
Villiger observes that ILC's work 'exerts influence on the legal opinion of States,
courts and writers long before States have ratified the resulting conventions. Of
course, the ILC Drafts and other materials prepared within the ILC cannot amount
to State practice, since the ILC members act in their independent capacity.
Nevertheless, already the close ties between the Commission and States lend to
these materials a special status going beyond that of studies of learned writers.' M.
Villiger, Customary International Law and Treaties 79 (1985) (footnote omitted).
[4] I. Sinclair, The International Law Commission 127 (1987).

rapporteurs on state responsibility, Professors Roberto Ago and Willem Riphagen.

Although our examination will focus on the general principles of state responsibility implicated in breaches of human rights and humanitarian norms, regardless of whether the origin of the norm lies in customary law, in conventional law, or in a general principle of law of civilized nations, it is necessary to survey briefly the wide range of existing recourse options for securing respect of such rights.[5] Treaty provisions concerning implementation and responsibility for breaches are not, in most cases, comprehensive and exclusive. Only rarely do such provisions constitute self-contained regimes. General principles of state responsibility continue to be relevant and applicable. While taking into account the relevant treaty provisions, the invocation, in appropriate cases, of the general principles of state responsibility enhances the efficacy of international human rights.

To begin with, in some states individual victims of human rights violations may sue the perpetrators in a civil action under customary international law (as discussed in Chapter II, Section III), under international agreements where these are part of the law of the land, or under municipal law. In a number of states governmental agencies have the standing, under statutory law, to pursue a remedy for victims of violations of human rights. In certain circumstances criminal law may be invoked against the perpetrators (Section VII, below).

Certain international human rights agreements require states to provide remedies under national law for individual victims of violations of norms stated in those agreements. These include: Article 13 of the European Convention on Human Rights;[6] Article 25 of the American Convention on Human Rights, which reaches fundamental rights recognized both by the national law of the state concerned and by the American Convention on Human Rights[7] (Article 29(c) prohibits interpreting the Convention as precluding rights or guarantees which are inherent in the human personality

---

[5] See the excellent report by Bernhardt, *The International Enforcement of Human Rights: General Report*, in International Enforcement of Human Rights 143 (R. Bernhardt and J. Jolowicz eds. 1985).

[6] (European) Convention for the Protection of Human Rights and Fundamental Freedoms, signed 4 Nov. 1950, 213 UNTS 221, Eur. TS No. 5.

[7] For the official text, see Organization of American States, Basic Documents Pertaining to Human Rights in the Inter-American System 25, OEA/SER.L.V/II.71,

or derived from representative democracy while Article 29(d) prohibits interpretations excluding or limiting the effect that the American Declaration of the Rights and Duties of Man and other international acts of the same nature may have); Article 2(3) of the Political Covenant,[8] which creates the obligation of states parties to provide an effective remedy to victims of violations of rights stated in the Covenant; Article 9(5) of the Political Covenant, which grants victims 'an enforceable right to compensation' in the specific context of unlawful arrest or detention; Article 14(6) of the Political Covenant, which concerns compensation for miscarriage of justice; Article 6 of the International Convention on the Elimination of All Forms of Racial Discrimination, which requires states to provide effective remedies and confirms the right of everyone to seek from national tribunals 'just and adequate reparation or satisfaction for any damage suffered as a result of . . . discrimination';[9] and Article 14 of the Convention Against Torture and Other Cruel, Inhuman or Degrading Treatment or Punishment, which provides victims with an 'enforceable right to fair and adequate compensation, including the means for as full rehabilitation as possible'.[10] The right to a remedy is also implicit in Article 7(1)(a) of the African Charter of Human and Peoples' Rights.[11] The duty of a state to provide remedies under its national law for violations of human rights is perhaps implicit in human rights treaties which require national implementation and whose effectiveness depends on the availability of municipal remedies. To be sure, explicit provisions establishing the right of victims to such remedies and the duty of the state to provide them enhance their effectiveness in protecting human rights.[12] Where a breach of a remedies provision stated in

Doc. 6, rev. 1, 23 Sept. 1987 (1988); OAS TS 36; reprinted in 9 ILM 673 (1970).

[8] Opened for signature 16 Dec. 1966, GA Res. 2200, 21 UN GAOR Supp. (No. 16) at 52, UN Doc. A/6316 (1967); 999 UNTS 171.

[9] Opened for signature 7 Mar. 1966, 660 UNTS 195; reprinted in 5 ILM 352 (1966).

[10] Opened for signature, 10 Dec. 1984, GA Res. 39/46, 39 UN GAOR Supp. (No. 51) at 197, UN Doc. A/39/51 (1985).

[11] Adopted 27 June 1981, reprinted in House Comm. on Foreign Aff., Human Rights Documents: Compilation of Documents Pertaining to Human Rights 155 (Comm. Print 1983), 21 ILM 59 (1982). Art. 7(1)(a) states that every individual shall have the right to an appeal to competent national organs against acts violating his fundamental rights.

[12] The preparatory work of the Political Covenant is of some interest here: 'An opinion was expressed that there was no need to specify the obligations of States parties in the event of a violation of the covenant, since it was obvious that if the

a human rights treaty occurs, a state may be charged with cumulative violations, for the breach both of the material provision of the convention and of the remedies clause.[13]

Where domestic remedies cannot be obtained, or are inadequate, international redress takes on special importance. Some agreements explicitly address the authority of international bodies to afford relief measures wherever domestic remedies fall short of that required by human rights treaties and fail to redress violations of human rights. Article 63 of the American Convention[14] confers on

States undertook to abide by the covenant, they would have to provide for effective remedies against infringements. It was also likely that provisions of that kind might be too broad and sweeping to be of much value. The view was accepted, however, that the proper enforcement of the provisions of the covenant depended on guarantees of the individual's rights against abuse, which comprised the following elements: the possession of a legal remedy, the granting of this remedy by national authorities and the enforcement of the remedy by the competent authorities.' Draft International Covenants on Human Rights, Annotation Prepared by the Secretary-General, UN Doc. A/2929 at 52 (1955); M. Bossuyt, Guide to the "Travaux Préparatoires" of the International Covenant on Civil and Political Rights 64 (1987).

[13] The Human Rights Committee, acting under the Optional Protocol to the International Covenant on Civil and Political Rights, thus determined that one state, Zaire, has violated not only certain material provisions of the Covenant, but also 'article 2(3), because there was no effective remedy under the domestic law of Zaire against the violations of the Covenant complained of'. Communication No. 90/1981, *Magana* v. *Zaire*, 38 UN GAOR Supp. (No. 40) at 197, 200, UN Doc. A/38/40 (1983).

In its advisory opinion on *Judicial Guarantees in States of Emergency (Arts. 27(2), 25 and 8 American Convention on Human Rights)*, the Inter-American Court stated that according to the principle reflected in Art. 25(1) of the American Convention, 'the absence of an effective remedy to violations of the rights recognized by the Convention is itself a violation of the Convention by the State Party in which the remedy is lacking. In that sense, it should be emphasized that, for such a remedy to exist, it is not sufficient that it be provided for by the Constitution or by law or that it be formally recognized, but rather it must be truly effective in establishing whether there has been a violation of human rights and in providing redress. A remedy which proves illusory because of the general conditions prevailing in the country, or even in the particular circumstances of a given case, cannot be considered effective. That could be the case, for example, when practice has shown its ineffectiveness; when the Judicial Power lacks the necessary independence to render impartial decisions or the means to carry out its judgments; or in any other situation that constitutes a denial of justice, as when there is an unjustified delay in the decision; or when, for any reason, the alleged victim is denied access to a judicial remedy.' Advisory Opinion OC-9/87 of 6 Oct. 1987, Inter-American Court of Human Rights, Ser. A, Judgments and Opinions, No. 9, at 33.

[14] Regarding execution of judgments of the American Court which stipulate compensatory damages, see Art. 68 of the American Convention, discussed in Buergenthal, *The Inter-American System for the Protection of Human Rights*, in 2 Human Rights in International Law 439, 464-5 (T. Meron ed. 1984). Regarding the American Court's authority to award temporary injunctions, see ibid. at 465-6

the Inter-American Court of Human Rights the right to decide on appropriate remedies, including declaratory judgments and fair compensation to be paid to the injured party. Similarly, Article 50 (to be further discussed below) of the European Convention on Human Rights provides that the European Court of Human Rights may afford just satisfaction to the injured party. Some other international human rights agreements appear implicitly to accord international supervisory organs the authority to recommend[15] appropriate relief for victims. Such authority is consistent with the purposes and objects of human rights treaties, which establish the obligation of states to provide effective remedies within their national legal systems and which authorize treaty organs to consider violations. To deny such authority through interpretation would render central provisions of human rights treaties 'devoid of purport or effect'.[16]

Professor Schachter correctly observes that although Article 2(3) of the Political Covenant does not specify the nature of domestic remedies, one may assume 'that undoing, repairing, and compensating for violation constitute appropriate remedies [and that] injunctive relief . . . may be required'.[17] The Human Rights Committee has demonstrated the readiness to scrutinize the adequacy of domestic remedies awarded to a victim for violations of the Political Covenant, applying the provisions of Article 2(3).

and Art. 63(2) of the American Convention. In Jan. 1988, the American Court adopted, for the first time, provisional measures ordering the government of Honduras to prevent new assassination attempts against those that had testified before the Court or had been summoned to do so. Inter-American Court of Human Rights, Press Release (28 Jan. 1988); *Velásquez Rodriguez Case*, Judgment of 29 July 1988, Inter-American Court of Human Rights, Ser. C, Decisions and Judgments, No. 4, paras. 41-5. In this judgment, the Court applied for the first time Art. 63(1) concerning the award of fair compensation to the party injured by a breach of a right protected by the Convention. The Court reserved its right to approve the agreement between the parties (the Inter-American Commission on Human Rights and the government of Honduras) on the damages and, in the event no agreement is reached, to set the amount and order the manner of payment. The recipients of the award would be the next-of-kin of the victim. Ibid. at paras. 189-92.

[15] See e.g. Art. 14(7)(b) of the International Convention on the Elimination of All Forms of Racial Discrimination.

[16] See the ICJ's discussion of its competence to decide the amount of compensation under the special agreement concluded between Albania and the United Kingdom, *The Corfu Channel Case* (Merits), 1949 ICJ Rep. 4, 26 (Judgment of 9 Apr.).

[17] Schachter, *The Obligation to Implement the Covenant in Domestic Law*, in The International Bill of Rights: the Covenant on Civil and Political Rights 311, 325 (L. Henkin ed. 1981).

None the less, perhaps because the Covenant does not explicitly authorize the Human Rights Committee to award relief where domestic remedies fall short of what Article 2(3) requires, the Committee's jurisprudence is characterized by a lack of specificity and the tendency to grant states a wide margin of discretion.[18] Thus, in one of its earlier 'views', having found a breach of several provisions of the Political Covenant, the Committee's response was limited to a declaration that 'the State Party is under an obligation to take immediate steps to ensure strict observance of the provisions of the Covenant and to provide effective remedies to the victims.'[19] Even the more recent decisions which call upon the state to remedy violations, to 'grant compensation', and to ensure that similar violations do not occur in the future, leave to the state the determination of both the specific remedy appropriate and the amount of compensation.[20] Nonetheless, the Committee is moving toward a more specific and assertive articulation of remedies which the violating state must provide and implement, including injunctive relief. For example, the Committee has directed that similar violations not occur in the future, that the violating state return the complainant's property (*restitutio in integrum*),[21] and that it punish the perpetrators of certain egregious violations of human rights. Recently, the Committee has resorted to interim measures.[22] The Committee's readiness to afford injunctive relief in the absence

[18] For a discussion of the limited competence of the Human Rights Committee in relation to the national law and the decisions of domestic courts, see de Zayas, Möller, and Opsahl, *Application of the International Covenant on Civil and Political Rights under the Optional Protocol by the Human Rights Committee*, 28 Germ. YB Int'l L. 9, 27–30 (1985).

[19] Communication No. R.1/5, *Valentini de Bazzano* v. *Uruguay*, 34 UN GAOR Supp. (No. 40) at 124, 129, UN Doc. A/34/40 (1979).

[20] Communication No. 156/1983, *Solórzano de Peña* v. *Venezuela*, 41 UN GAOR Supp. (No. 40) at 134, 141, UN Doc. A/41/40 (1986); Communication No. 16/1977, *Monguya Mbenge* v. *Zaire*, 38 UN GAOR Supp. (No. 40) at 134, 140, UN Doc. A/38/40 (1983).

[21] *Magana* v. *Zaire*, above n. 13.

[22] See e.g. Communication No. 107/1981, *Almeida de Quinteros* v. *Uruguay*, 38 UN GAOR Supp. (No. 40) at 216, 224, UN Doc. A/38/40 (1983); *Muteba* v. *Zaire*, 39 UN GAOR Supp. (No. 40) at 182, 188, UN Doc. A/39/40 (1984); Communications Nos. 146/1983 and 148–154/1983, *Baboeram-Adhin* v. *Suriname*, 40 UN GAOR Supp. (No. 40) at 187, 194, UN Doc. A/40/40 (1985). The Committee has recently requested states parties, under rule 86 of its provisional rules of procedure, not to carry out death sentences of persons who claimed to be innocent of the crimes of which they were convicted and to have been denied a fair hearing. Stays of execution have been granted. Moreover, the Committee appointed one of its members to take rule 86 decisions on behalf of the

of textual authority is especially significant in light of the reluctance of the European Court of Human Rights to do so (see below).

In comparison with the Human Rights Committee's rudimentary jurisprudence on remedies, the European Commission and Court of Human Rights have built a rich and complex body of case-law applying and interpreting Articles 13[23] and 50 of the European Convention. Detailed discussion of this case-law is neither necessary for our purposes nor feasible in the confines of this study. Our study will not address the role of the Committee of Ministers under Articles 32 and 54 of the European Convention on Human Rights.

An authoritative commentator has observed that

[a]lthough the Court has held that neither Art. 13 nor the Convention in general lays down for States Parties any given manner for ensuring within their internal law the effective implementation of the Convention, the Court has interpreted Art. 13 as requiring that, where an individual has an arguable claim to be the victim of a violation of the rights set forth in the Convention, he must have a remedy before a national authority which can both decide his claim and, if appropriate, afford redress. While such an authority need not be a judicial authority, its powers and the guarantees which it affords are relevant in determining whether the remedy before it is effective.[24]

In contrast to the Human Rights Committee's lack of explicit

Committee. 43 UN GAOR Supp. (No. 40) at 154, UN Doc. A/43/40 (1988). Provisional rule 86 reads as follows: 'The Committee may, prior to forwarding its final views on the communication to the State Party concerned, inform that State of its views whether interim measures may be desirable to avoid irreparable damage to the victim of the alleged violation. In doing so, the Committee shall inform the State Party concerned that such expression of its views on interim measures does not imply a determination on the merits of the communication.' International Covenant on Civil and Political Rights, Human Rights Committee: Selected Decisions Under the Optional Protocol (Second to Sixteenth Sessions) 155, UN Doc. CCPR/C/OP/1 (1985).

[23] For the summary of the jurisprudence on Art. 13 until 1982, see Council of Europe, 4 Digest of Strasbourg Case-Law relating to the European Convention on Human Rights 1-39 (1985). For comments on Art. 13, see J. Frowein and W. Peukert, Europäische MenschenRechtsKonvention 298-304 (1985); Gray, *Remedies for Individuals under the European Convention on Human Rights*, 6 Hum. Rts. Rev. 153-5 (1981); Lillich, *Civil Rights*, in 1 Human Rights in International Law 115, 135-6 (T. Meron ed. 1984). Regarding the Committee of Ministers, see Eur. Comm'n Hum. Rts., Stock-Taking of the European Convention on Human Rights, Supp. 1986, at 117-18.

[24] Jacobs, *The European Convention on Human Rights*, in International Enforcement of Human Rights, above n. 5, at 31, 52.

authority to determine international remedies when domestic remedies fall short of the Covenant's requirements, the European Court is authorized by Article 50 of the Convention to afford 'just satisfaction' to a party injured by a state's breach of the Convention, if the internal law of that state permits only partial reparation. In accordance with this provision, the Court has granted pecuniary compensation for material and non-material (or moral) damage, and approved reimbursement of costs and expenses, especially lawyers' fees.[25] In other cases, the Court has held that its conclusion that a violation has occurred, i.e. a declaratory judgment, in itself constitutes adequate and just satisfaction.[26] Although a broad range of remedies is consistent with the language of Article 50 ('just satisfaction'), the Court to date has not gone beyond financial compensation and declaratory judgment to accord injunctive relief or specific performance.[27] In a discussion concerning article 50, the Court explained that its 'judgments leave to the Contracting State concerned the choice of the means to be utilised in its domestic legal system for performance of its obligation under Article . . . 53'.[28] In a number of recent cases, applicants have requested injunctive relief. The Court has refused on various grounds to accede to these requests, without directly addressing the question of its competence to grant injunctive relief.[29]

[25] Ibid. at 40; Gray, above n. 23, at 155-71. The case-law on Art. 50 up to 1982 is summarized in 5 Digest, above n. 23, at 521-72. In the *Baraona Case*, the Court has awarded compensation for non-pecuniary damage and, separately, for reimbursement of costs and expenses. It rejected the claim for pecuniary damage. 122 Eur. Ct. HR (Ser. A) 22-23 (1987).

[26] See e.g. *Deumeland Case*, 100 Eur. Ct. HR (Ser. A) 31 (1986). See also Jacobs, above n. 24, at 40.

[27] Gray, above n. 23, at 171.

[28] *Case of Campbell and Cosans*, 60 Eur. Ct. HR (Ser. A) 9 (1983). The Court therefore decided that it had no power to direct the United Kingdom to give the undertaking sought by Mrs Campbell that her children would not be subjected to any form of corporal punishment at British schools. Ibid.

[29] In one case, an applicant urged the Court to 'recommend' to the government of Italy a presidential pardon or the reopening of the criminal proceedings of his case on the ground that '[t]he words "just satisfaction" appeared to him "vague" enough to cover "any type of reparation".' The government maintained that 'the Court had no power to take such a course of action'. *Bozano Case*, 111 Eur. Ct. HR (Ser. A) 28 (1986). In another case the applicant sought employment in the civil service. The Government answered that 'the Court did not have jurisdiction to order that [the government] should take a specific measure such as the engagement of an individual as an employee.' *Milasi Case*, 119 Eur. Ct. HR (Ser. A) at 48 (1987). See also Gray, *Is there an International Law of Remedies?*, 56 Brit. YB Int'l L. 25, 40 (1985).

Decisions regarding injunctive relief tend to generate tension between international authority and state sovereignty.[30] While the Strasbourg Court's practice of denying its own competence to order injunctive relief is understandable for this reason,[31] this restraint perhaps exceeds that compelled by the language of Article 50. The Court's jurisprudence on this question reflects, perhaps, an attempt to balance concern for state sovereignty with the effective exercise of international judicial functions.

In contrast to injunctive relief, a declaration of a right by an international judicial body does not significantly clash with the right of a sovereign state to choose the necessary remedies. Declaratory judgments have the advantages of reducing both tension between state sovereignty and the judicial organ and stress on the friendly relations of the parties to the litigation. As Professor Sunderland perceptively noted in the municipal law context:

When you ask for a declaration of right only, you treat [the other party] as a gentleman. When you ask coercive relief you treat him as a wrongdoer. That is the whole difference between diplomacy and war. . . .[32]

[30] The ICJ has ordered significant measures of specific performance in a number of cases. See e.g. *United States Diplomatic and Consular Staff in Tehran (United States of America* v. *Iran),* 1980 ICJ Rep. 3, 44–5 (Judgment of 24 May). Gray observes that the *Hostages Case* was the first case in which an order to the parties rather than merely a declaratory judgment was given in the absence of a reference to remedies in the agreements between the parties. She emphasizes the rise of the declaratory judgment in ICJ's jurisprudence as a remedy in itself for a breach of international law. Gray, above n. 29, at 37–8.

[31] The Court stated that it was not competent to direct Belgium to annul certain disciplinary sanctions and sentences passed in criminal proceedings. *Case of Le Compte, Van Leuven and De Meyere,* 54 Eur. Ct. HR (Ser. A) 7 (1982). See also *Case of Albert and Le Compte,* 68 Eur. Ct. HR (Ser. A) 6, 8 (1983). The preparatory work of Art. 50 of the European Convention demonstrates that the drafters did not intend the jurisprudence of the Court to introduce 'any new element or one contrary to existing international law' and that, in particular, the Court was not to 'have the power to declare null and void or amend Acts emanating from the public bodies of the signatory States'. Report to the Committee of Ministers Submitted by the Committee of Experts Instructed to Draw Up a Draft Convention of Collective Guarantee of Human Rights and Fundamental Freedoms, Doc. No. CM/WP I (50) 15, A 924 (1950), reprinted in 4 Collected Edition of the "Travaux Préparatoires" of the European Convention on Human Rights 44 (1977).

Even when violations of the Conventions stem directly from contested legislative provisions, the Court's 'decision cannot of itself annul or repeal these provisions: the Court's judgment is essentially declaratory and leaves to the State the choice of the means to be utilised in its domestic legal system for performance of its obligation under Article 53.' *Marckx Case,* 31 Eur. Ct. HR (Ser. A) 25 (1979).

[32] Sunderland, *A Modern Evolution in Remedial Rights: The Declaratory Judgment,* 16 Mich. L. Rev. 69, 76 (1917). See also I. Zamir, The Declaratory Judgment 3–4

The unwillingness of the Strasbourg Court to award injunctive relief emphasizes the central role of declaratory judgments in judicial resolutions of human rights violations.[33]

Specific authority under human rights treaties to decide on relief measures admittedly should be supported by the jurisdictional standing of victims before international bodies. Some international agreements confer standing on the individual victims of human rights violations, regardless of their nationality, to complain against the offending governments before international fora. Article 44 of the American Convention permits not only individual victims but also any person, group of persons, or non-governmental body recognized in one or more member states of the Organization of American States to lodge with the Inter-American Commission on Human Rights petitions complaining of the violation of the Convention by a state party. By becoming a party to the Convention, a state accepts *ipso facto* this competence of the Commission.[34] Articles 55-9 of the African Charter on Human and Peoples' Rights seemingly authorize the African Commission on Human and Peoples' Rights to consider, subject to certain conditions, communications from authors other than states parties, including individual victims, without an additional act of acceptance by a state party. It is unclear, however, whether the Commission will, as I hope, consider all the individual communications which meet the criteria stated in Article 56, i.e. even sporadic breaches, or only (and in pursuance of a request from the Assembly of Heads of

(1962).

[33] The judicial restraint characteristic of the Strasbourg Court contrasts sharply with the assertive jurisprudence of the Luxembourg Court. The latter, which possesses a stronger institutional setting but lacks explicit textual authority, has incorporated fundamental human rights within the legal values which it protects. See Treaty Establishing the European Economic Community, Arts. 164, 173, 175, signed 25 Mar. 1957, 298 UNTS 11, discussed by Weiler, *Protection of Fundamental Human Rights within the Legal Order of the European Communities*, in International Enforcement of Human Rights, above n. 5, at 113, 119-21; T. Meron, Human Rights Law-Making in the United Nations: A Critique of Instruments and Process 160-1 (1986). Bernhardt emphasizes the strength of the procedural rights conferred on the individual by the law of the European Communities. Bernhardt, above n. 5, at 156. Concerning the award of remedies by the European Court of Justice under Arts. 185-6 of the EEC Treaty, see C. Gray, Judicial Remedies in International Law 137-44 (1987).

[34] Buergenthal, above n. 14, at 454.

State and Government) 'special cases which reveal the existence of a series of serious or massive violations' (Article 58).[35]

In other instruments, the victim's standing to complain against a state to judicial or quasi-judicial bodies[36] or supervisory organs depends on a special acceptance by the state of the organ's compulsory jurisdiction. Such provisions are found in the Optional Protocol to the International Covenant on Civil and Political Rights, Article 25 of the European Convention,[37] Article 14 of the International Convention on the Elimination of All Forms of Racial Discrimination,[38] and Article 22 of the Convention Against Torture, and Other Cruel, Inhuman or Degrading Treatment or Punishment.[39]

[35] Gittleman, *The African Commission on Human and Peoples' Rights: Prospects and Procedures*, in Guide to International Human Rights Practice 153, 157-8 (H. Hannum ed. 1984); Mbaya, *La Charte Africaine en tant que mécanisme de protection des droits de l'Homme*, in International Enforcement of Human Rights, above n. 5, at 77, 91-2; Bernhardt, above n. 5, at 149.

[36] The quasi-judicial role of the Human Rights Committee established under Art. 28 of the Political Covenant is discussed by Ramcharan, *The Emerging Jurisprudence of the Human Rights Committee*, 6 Dalhousie LJ 7, 8-9, 38 (1980).

[37] Higgins, *The European Convention on Human Rights*, in 2 Human Rights in International Law, above n. 14, at 495, 505-11. Art. 25 authorizes petitions not only from individual victims but also from non-governmental organizations or groups of individuals. On the scope of this provision, see T. Meron, above n. 33, at 100. Gray observes that the proceedings under the European Convention 'are not designed solely for the benefit of injured individuals but rather to secure compliance with its provisions'. C. Gray, above n. 33, at 151. Out of 22 member states of the Council of Europe (San Marino has joined the Council of Europe in November 1988), all the 21 parties to the European Convention on Human Rights have recognized the competence of the Commission as of 3 Jan. 1989. Council of Europe, Chart Showing Signatures and Ratifications of Conventions and Agreements Concluded within the Council of Europe (1989).

[38] Only 12 states have recognized the competence of the Committee on the Elimination of Racial Discrimination under this Article. 43 UN GAOR Supp. (No. 18) at 1, UN Doc. A/43/18 (1988).

[39] An innovative and useful approach is suggested by Art. 20 of the Convention Against Torture, opened for signature 10 Dec. 1984, GA Res. 39/46, 39 UN GAOR Supp. (No. 51) at 197, UN Doc. A/39/51 (1985), which grants the Committee Against Torture competence extending to all states which have not opted out of Art. 20 by entering reservations under Art. 28. Under Art. 20 the Committee is permitted, on the basis of reliable information received, to undertake *proprio motu* an inquiry into allegations of a systematic practice of torture by a state party.

For instruments denying a state party the right to refuse access to international agents investigating allegations of torture, see Draft Optional Protocol to the Draft International Convention Against Torture and Other Cruel, Inhuman or Degrading Treatment or Punishment (proposed by Costa Rica), UN Doc. E/CN.4/1409 (1980); European Convention for the Prevention of Torture and Inhuman or Degrading Treatment or Punishment, opened for signature 26 Nov. 1987, Council of Europe Doc. H (87) 4 (1987), discussed by Cassese, *A New Approach to Human Rights:*

Complaint procedures separate from those based on treaties have been established on the authority of the constitutive instruments and resolutions of international organizations. Individuals may submit communications regarding a state's consistent pattern of gross and reliably attested violations of human rights to the UN Secretary-General for consideration by a working group of the Sub-Commission on Prevention of Discrimination and Protection of Minorities under UN Economic and Social Council Resolution 1503 (XLVIII).[40]

Finally, the possibility of one state submitting complaints against another for human rights violations must be considered. The premiss of such complaints may be contrasted to the rules governing international responsibility of states for injury to aliens, which predicate a state's right to espouse the claim of its national on the victim's status as a national of the complaining state and on the supposition that the defendant state has broken an obligation towards the plaintiff state in respect of its nationals.[41] Complaints for human rights violations, whether based on multilateral human rights treaties or customary law, are based on the notion that violations of human rights offend the international legal order. As such, they injure the 'legal' interest of each and every party to a human rights treaty and, with respect to customary human rights, of all states (see Sections V–VI, below). Unless a treaty provision otherwise provides or implies, a claim alleging a violation of human rights may therefore be submitted by one state against another even if the individual victim possesses the nationality of the defendant state and not of the complaining state. To be sure, the question of the *locus standi* must be distinguished from that of the

The European Convention for the Prevention of Torture, 83 AJIL 128 (1989).

[40] ESC Res. 1503, 48 UN ESCOR Supp. (No. 1A) at 89, UN Doc. E/4832/Add.1 (1970), discussed in Sohn, *Human Rights: Their Implementation and Supervision by the United Nations*, in 2 Human Rights in International Law, above n. 14, at 369, 386–8, 391. See also Bossuyt, *The Development of Special Procedures of the United Nations Commission on Human Rights*, 6 Human Rights LJ 179 (1985).

An extraconventional procedure for consideration of communications alleging violations of human rights has been established under UNESCO Decision 104/EX/ 3.3. See UNESCO Doc. 104/EX/3.3, para. 10 (1978); UNESCO Doc. 23 C/17 (1985); T. Meron, above n. 33, at 219–20.

[41] This traditional theory of diplomatic protection was reaffirmed by the International Court of Justice in *Barcelona Traction, Light and Power Company, Limited*, (New Application) (*Belgium* v. *Spain*), 1970 ICJ Rep. 3, 32 (Judgment of 5 Feb.). See generally Leckie, *The Inter-State Complaint Procedure in International Human Rights Law: Hopeful Prospects or Wishful Thinking?*, 10 Hum. Rights Q.

content and scope of a particular human right. While most human rights equally protect nationals and non-nationals, some rights may benefit nationals only or aliens only.[42]

A number of treaties do regulate the submission by one state party against another of complaints or communications alleging violations of norms stated in human rights treaties. Article 11 of the International Convention on the Elimination of All Forms of Racial Discrimination, which is binding, *ipso facto*, on every state party to the Convention by virtue of their acceptance of the Convention, permits each state party to submit communications against other states parties. The competence of the Committee on the Elimination of Racial Discrimination, to which the communications are submitted, extends only to conciliation, however. Articles 47–54 of the African Charter on Human and Peoples' Rights govern the consideration by the African Commission on Human and Peoples' Rights of complaints of violations submitted by one state party against another. The competence of the Commission to consider such complaints does not depend on a special acceptance of jurisdiction by the states concerned, but in dealing with these complaints, the Commission only has the power to conciliate, report, and recommend.

Perhaps the most far-reaching jurisdictional clause in any UN human rights treaty is Article IX of the Convention on the Prevention and Punishment of the Crime of Genocide.[43] This Article, which provides for the compulsory jurisdiction of the ICJ over disputes 'relating to the interpretation, application or fulfillment of the present Convention, including those relating to the responsibility of a State for genocide . . .', is exceptional in its reference to state responsibility. The broad *ratione personae* reach of the prohibition to commit genocide is indicated by Article IV of the Convention, which requires that persons committing genocide be punished, 'whether they are constitutionally responsible rulers,

249 (1988).

[42] Art. 48(b) of the European Convention concerns *locus standi*. See also below n. 47. Regarding rights which are predicated on different treatment of citizens and aliens, see e.g. Arts. 13 and 25 of the Political Covenant; Arts. 5(1)(f) and 16 of the European Convention; Art. 1 of Protocol 1 to the European Convention (note the reference to 'general principles of international law', discussed in *Lithgow Case*, 102 Eur. Ct. HR (Ser. A) 48 (1986)); Arts. 3–4 of Protocol 4 to the European Convention; Arts. 22(5)–(9) and 23 of the American Convention; Arts. 12(4)–(5) and 13(1)–(2) of the African Charter on Human and Peoples' Rights.

[43] Opened for signature 9 Dec. 1948, 78 UNTS 277.

150   *Responsibility for Violation of Rights*

public officials or private individuals'. The Convention Against
Torture and Other Cruel, Inhuman or Degrading Treatment or
Punishment similarly provides, in Article 30 (to which reservations
are authorized), for the compulsory jurisdiction of the ICJ over
disputes 'concerning the interpretation or application of this
Convention'. The International Convention on the Elimination of
All Forms of Racial Discrimination provides in Article 22 for the
compulsory jurisdiction of the ICJ with respect to disputes involving
the interpretation or application of that Convention. A similar
provision is found in the International Convention on the Elimination of All Forms of Discrimination Against Women, in Article
29.[44] In contrast, under Article 24 of the European Convention on
Human Rights, the European Commission of Human Rights,
a quasi-judicial body, has compulsory jurisdiction in interstate
complaints over 'any alleged breach of the provisions of the
Convention by another' party. This broad language makes it clear
that the plaintiff state's standing is not limited to breaches of the
Convention caused to its citizens. Article 24 is of particular
importance in cases where a state has failed to declare in accordance
with Article 25 that it recognizes the right of the Commission to
receive petitions from individuals, groups, or non-governmental
organizations.

Under other UN human rights treaties, consideration of interstate
complaints depends on an additional act of special acceptance of
the supervisory organs' competence. The compulsory interstate
jurisdiction of these organs can only be invoked if it has been
accepted by both the complaining state and the state against which
a complaint has been submitted. Under Article 41 of the Political
Covenant, the Human Rights Committee has a conciliatory role
with regard to interstate complaints, which may be entertained as
between states that have recognized the competence of the Committee under that Article.[45] Article 21 of the Convention Against
Torture and Other Cruel, Inhuman or Degrading Treatment or
Punishment grants similar competence to the Committee Against
Torture.

Two major regional human rights treaties establish the compulsory jurisdiction of judicial organs derived from a special,

[44] Opened for signature 18 Dec. 1979, GA Res. 34/180, 34 UN GAOR Supp.
(No. 46) at 193, UN Doc. A/34/46 (1980).
[45] 22 states have recognized such competence. 43 UN GAOR Supp. (No. 40) at

optional acceptance. Such jurisdiction is conferred on the European Court of Human Rights by Article 46 of the European Convention on Human Rights 'in all matters concerning the interpretation and application of the present Convention'.[46] Where such jurisdiction has been accepted, Article 48 permits complaints against a state party to be submitted to the European Court of Human Rights either by the European Commission or by certain categories of states, but not by individuals.[47] Jurisdiction of the quasi-judicial Inter-American Commission on Human Rights over interstate disputes is established under Article 45 of the American Convention as between states which have made special declarations of acceptance.[48] Article 62 similarly provides for compulsory jurisdiction over interstate disputes by the Inter-American Court of Human Rights for states which have made special declarations of acceptance.[49] Under Article 61 of the American Convention, cases may be submitted to the Court not only by states, but also by the Inter-American Commission on Human Rights, though not by individuals. Additionally, the Inter-American Court has the important competence to render advisory opinions under Article 64,[50] which permits every member of the Organization of American States (whether or not party to the Convention) and OAS organs within their spheres of competence to 'consult the Court regarding the interpretation of [the] Convention or of other treaties concerning the protection of human rights in the American states'. Because states are often reluctant to present formal complaints against other

1, UN Doc. A/43/40 (1988).

[46] 20 states have accepted the compulsory jurisdiction of the European Court as of 3 Jan. 1989, Chart, above n. 37.

[47] Art. 48(b) makes the submission of a claim by a state dependent on the link of nationality between that state and the victim. Such a link is not required for submission of complaints by states to the European Commission under Art. 24 of the Convention, or to the Court under Art. 48(c) and (d).

[48] As of Nov. 1987, out of 20 states parties to the American Convention on Human Rights, 8 states have accepted this jurisdiction of the Inter-American Commission. Inter-American Treaties and Conventions, TS No. 9 at B-32 (Rev. 12 Nov. 1987). On the powers of the Inter-American Court and the Inter-American Commission, see Buergenthal, above n. 14, at 453–87; Buergenthal, *Implementation in the Inter-American Human Rights System*, in International Enforcement of Human Rights, above n. 5, at 57.

[49] As of Nov. 1987, 10 states have accepted the compulsory jurisdiction of the Inter-American Court of Human Rights. TS No. 9, above n. 48; Inter-American Court of Human Rights, Press Release CDH-S/287 (17 Nov. 1987).

[50] Buergenthal, *The Advisory Practice of the Inter-American Human Rights Court*, 79 AJIL 1 (1985).

152   *Responsibility for Violation of Rights*

states, the power of the Commission to submit to the Court
contentious cases in relation to states which have accepted the
Court's jurisdiction,[51] the right of the victims themselves to petition
the Commission under Article 44, and even the Court's advisory
jurisdiction take on a special significance for ensuring respect of
human rights.

This is equally true of other international procedures which allow
individuals or organs to submit complaints of violations, rather
than relying on states to do so. Consider, for example, the
importance of the standing of individuals (albeit dependent on the
optional acceptance by the state) to submit complaints to the
European Commission and the right of the European Commission
to bring cases before the European Court against states which have
accepted the Court's compulsory jurisdiction. Of particular interest
is the right of international civil servants employed by various
international organizations to submit complaints of breach of their
terms of employment, including such human rights as the prohibition
of discrimination on grounds of race, sex and religion, to international administrative tribunals.[52]

The institutional mechanisms for presenting complaints which
are already in place have been underutilized, both because many
states have thus far not accepted the compulsory jurisdiction of
human rights organs to consider such complaints and because most
states are reluctant to risk antagonizing other states by bringing
formal complaints of human rights violations by other states
to international judicial, quasi-judicial, and supervisory organs.
Significantly, despite the existing interstate institutional machinery
in the OAS system, no contentious case has yet been submitted by
one state against another. Only about a score of interstate
complaints have been submitted to the European Commission of

[51] See American Convention, Arts. 61-2, Basic Documents, above n. 7, Regulations of the Inter-American Commission on Human Rights, Art. 50, Basic
Documents, above n. 7, at 75. Three contentious cases submitted by the Commission
were pending before the Inter-American Court of Human Rights in June 1988. See
Velásquez Rodríguez Case, Preliminary Objections, Judgment of June 26, 1987,
Decisions and Judgments, No. 1; *Fairén Garbi and Solís Corrales Case*, ibid. No.
2; *Godínez Cruz Case*, ibid. No. 3.
[52] See generally 1 C. Amerasinghe, The Law of the International Civil Service
(1988); T. Meron, The United Nations Secretariat 159-71 (1977); Meron and Elder,
The New Administrative Tribunal of the World Bank, 14 NYU J. Int'l L. & Pol. 1
(1981).

Human Rights under Article 24 of the European Convention.[53] In no case has a provision granting the ICJ compulsory jurisdiction to determine the interpretation or application of a human rights treaty been invoked before the ICJ.

The complaints procedure founded in international human rights instruments should not be viewed in isolation, however. States have been far less reluctant to submit complaints of violations to international deliberative organs, such as the UN General Assembly and the UN Commission on Human Rights, for consideration, condemnation, or examination by various investigatory organs. Such steps are no longer considered interference in the domestic jurisdiction of states. Additionally, states have shown greater readiness to place human rights violations on the agenda of their bilateral or multilateral negotiations. These practices find critical support both in the human rights provisions of the United Nations Charter and in the growing corpus of conventional and customary human rights and humanitarian law.

Moreover, there remains the possibility of redressing breaches of human rights treaties by using the jurisdictional provisions of other international treaties in force for the states concerned; e.g. the compulsory jurisdiction of the ICJ under Articles 36(1) and 36(2) of its Statute.[54] Violations of customary rather than conventional norms of human rights present still other recourse possibilities. Since customary human rights norms impose obligations *erga omnes*, our discussion (Section V, below) will examine whether every state, not only states parties to a particular human rights treaty, may sue the violating state by utilizing jurisdictional provisions provided by bilateral or multilateral treaties. Finally, states may resort to countermeasures (discussed in Section XI, below) to ensure the enforcement of human rights.

Although a discrete section (Section IX) focuses on problems of international humanitarian law, a brief mention of its provisions

[53] See also J. Frowein and W. Peukert, above n. 23, at 351; Council of Europe, Eur. Comm. of Human Rights, Survey of Activities and Statistics 1987, at 7 (1987). Contrast the twenty odd state complaints so far submitted with the 860 individual applications registered by the Commission in 1987 alone. Ibid. at 12. Most state complaints were motivated by the special ethnic or religious relationship of the complaining states with the victims of the alleged violations rather than by the common interest in vindication of human rights. Bernhardt, above n. 5, at 148-9.

[54] The relationship between remedies under human rights treaties and remedies under other treaties or customary law will be considered in Section X, below.

bearing on responsibility and implementation may be useful here. Humanitarian conventions contain provisions bearing both on the responsibility of states and on the individual responsibility of persons who have committed breaches of their provisions.

The basic principle of the liability of states to pay compensation for breach of the Hague Regulations is contained in Article 3 of Hague Convention No. IV and repeated in Article 91 of Protocol I. Relevant provisions are contained in common Article 51/52/131/148 of the Geneva Conventions. A party to the conflict may request that an inquiry be instituted concerning any alleged violation of the Convention (52/53/132/149, Protocol I, Article 90).

The Conventions also contain important provisions regarding repression of breaches, the duty of states to enact the necessary legislation to provide effective penal sanctions for persons responsible for grave breaches of the Conventions, and the obligation to prosecute such persons or to extradite them to another state (49-50/50-1/129-30/146-7, Protocol I: Articles 85-6).

The Conventions contain extensive provisions on implementation. Common Article 1 (discussed in Chapter I, Section III) requires states parties to respect and to ensure respect for the provisions of the Conventions. A similar provision is contained in Article 1(1) of Protocol I. Article 1 of Hague Convention No. IV provides that parties shall issue instructions to their armed forces which shall be in conformity with the Hague Regulations. Article 45 of Geneva Convention No. I and Article 46 of Geneva Convention No. II provide for the detailed execution of the Conventions. A similar provision is contained in Article 80 of Protocol I. Provisions concerning the appointment and the functions of protecting powers are contained in common Article 8/8/8/9 and Article 5 of Protocol I. 'Substitutes' for protecting powers are discussed in common Article 10/10/10/11. The humanitarian role of the ICRC is addressed in common Article 9/9/9/10. Common Article 47/48/127/144 requires parties to disseminate the texts of the Conventions. A similar provision is contained in Article 83 of Protocol I and, cursorily, in Article 19 of Protocol II. It is unfortunate that in practice most of these provisions have not been implemented and have remained largely a dead letter.

II. ACTS OF STATE, IMPUTABILITY, PRIVATE ACTS

The international responsibility of a state is generated when conduct attributable to the state under international law constitutes a breach of the international obligations of the state;[55] e.g. those obligations encompassed within customary or conventional human rights law. Because a state is a legal person whose acts must be performed through natural persons, only an act or omission by an individual person or a group of persons[56] constitutes an act of state, i.e. conduct attributable to the state. (The international legal concept of 'act of state' differs from that under US law.) It is therefore necessary to 'establish when, according to international law, it is the State [as a subject of international law] which must be regarded as acting . . .'.[57]

Subject to various refinements and exceptions, the following are the basic principles evolved by international law. A state is responsible neither for all acts or omissions taking place in its territory[58] nor for acts or omissions of private individuals not acting on the state's behalf.[59] However, a state is responsible for

[55] Art. 3 of the ILC's draft articles on state responsibility (part one) reads as follows: 'There is an internationally wrongful act of a State when: (*a*) conduct consisting of an action or omission is attributable to the State under international law; and (*b*) that conduct constitutes a breach of an international obligation of the State.' [1975] 2 YB Int'l L. Comm'n 60, UN Doc. A/CN.4/SER.A/1975/Add.1 (1976).

For the ICJ's recent discussion of imputability, see *United States Diplomatic and Consular Staff in Tehran* (*United States of America* v. *Iran*), 1980 ICJ Rep. 3, 29-30 (Judgment of 24 May); *Military and Paramilitary Activities in and against Nicaragua* (*Nicaragua* v. *United States of America*), Merits, 1986 ICJ Rep. 14, 62-5 (Judgment of 27 June). See also ibid. at 187-90 (Ago J. sep. op.).

[56] See [1973] 2 YB Int'l L. Comm'n at 181, UN Doc. A/CN.4/SER.A/1973/Add.1 (1975).

Note the following statement from an important arbitral award: '[R]ules of international law, though primarily conceived in terms of conduct of and relationships between States, are ultimately concerned, like all rules of law, with the reality of physical persons, objects and activities in their interrelationship within human society.' *Case Concerning the Air Services Agreement of 27 March 1946* (*United States* v. *France*), 54 Int'l L. Rep. 304, 323-4 (1979).

[57] [1973] 2 YB Int'l L. Comm'n, above n. 56, at 189.

[58] *Corfu Channel Case* (*United Kingdom* v. *Albania*), 1949 ICJ Rep. 4, 18 (Judgment of 9 Apr.).

[59] See e.g. [1973] 2 YB Int'l L. Comm'n, above n. 56, at 189. Art. 11 of the ILC's draft articles on state responsibility (part one) reads as follows:

'1. The conduct of a person or a group of persons not acting on behalf of the State shall not be considered as an act of the State under international law.

2. Paragraph 1 is without prejudice to the attribution to the State of any other conduct which is related to that of the persons or groups of persons referred to in

the acts or omissions of members of its internal apparatus or organization; i.e. its organs and agents. Article 5 of the ILC's draft articles on state responsibility (part one) reads as follows:

For the purposes of the present articles, conduct of any State organ having that status under the internal law of that State shall be considered as an act of the State concerned under international law, provided that organ was acting in that capacity in the case in question.[60]

Under international law, independently of imputability under a country's national law, the conduct of bodies having the status of organs of state under the internal law of a state is, in principle, attributable to the state as an act of state. By describing an act of state as the conduct of an organ acting in its capacity as an organ of the state, Article 5[61] of the ILC's draft provides a tautological definition[62] in lieu of a clear standard or criteria for distinguishing between action taken in an official's private capacity, which is not attributable to the state,[63] and action taken as an agent of the state, which is attributable to the state. Acts performed by an official in his or her capacity as an organ of the state or under the cover of official status are difficult to distinguish from acts performed as a private person, especially when the official breaches the state's internal law by, for example, committing murder or torture.[64] The flaws of draft Article 5 impact on Article 10 of the ILC draft articles on state responsibility (part one), which provides as follows:

The conduct of an organ of a State, of a territorial governmental entity or of an entity empowered to exercise elements of the governmental

that paragraph and which is to be considered as an act of the State by virtue of articles 5 to 10.' [1975] 2 YB Int'l L. Comm'n, above n. 55. See also ibid., Arts. 5-10.

[60] [1975] 2 YB Int'l L. Comm'n, above n. 55.

According to draft Arts. 7-9, a state is responsible also for acts of other persons or organs, such as organs of territorial entities, *de facto* organs, and organs put at its disposal by other states.

[61] Art. 5, above text accompanying n. 60, is regarded as embodying customary law. [1973] 1 YB Int'l L. Comm'n 46, UN Doc. A/CN.4/SER.A/1973 (1974).

[62] I. Brownlie, System of the Law of Nations: State Responsibility Part I 36-7, 147-8 (1983). The drafting of Art. 10 was criticized on other grounds by Special Rapporteur Riphagen, in W. Riphagen, Seventh Report on State Responsibility, UN Doc. A/CN.4/397 at 25 (1986).

[63] [1973] 2 YB Int'l L. Comm'n, above n. 56, at 192.

[64] Distinguishing between acts of a state and private acts would perhaps be facilitated by placing the burden of proof on the state involved. An act of an official would be presumptively attributed to the state unless the state could establish that the official acted as a private individual.

authority, such organ having acted in that capacity, shall be considered
as an act of the State under international law even if, in the particular
case, the organ exceeded its competence according to internal law or
contravened instructions concerning its activity.[65]

Article 10 refers to acts which have already been identified as
official acts, i.e. acts carried out by a state organ in its capacity as
a state organ. It addresses the question whether all such acts are
to be attributed to the state. The Article reflects the well-established
principle of customary law that the conduct of a state organ is
attributable to the state even if the organ has exceeded its
competence or contravened its instructions according to the state's
internal law.[66] The ILC thus clearly recognizes the principle that
the conduct of a state organ functioning as such but acting *ultra
vires* is attributable to the state.[67]

Because the individuals comprising the organs of the state may
act not only as organs of the state, but also as private individuals,
the capacity in which they have acted in the specific case where
their activity is impugned must be determined. International
case-law and scholarly writings have developed several criteria,
some more useful than others, for determining whether an act of
state is implicated. Examples include whether an agent of the state
has employed or abused either the means or the coercive power
placed at his or her disposal by the state, and whether an agent of
the state has acted within the scope of his or her actual or apparent
authority or functions.[68]

[65] [1975] 2 YB Int'l L. Comm'n, above n. 55.
[66] Regarding the grounding of Art. 10 in customary international law, see [1975]
2 YB Int'l L. Comm'n, above n. 55, at 61, 66. The ILC emphasized that 'as practice
and international decisions become clearer and more consistent, modern international
jurists have almost unanimously come to consider it as established that actions or
omissions of organs of the State, irrespective of whether they conform or are
contrary to the legal provisions governing their conduct, must be considered as acts
of the State from the standpoint of juridical relations between States.' Ibid. at 66
(footnotes omitted).
[67] [1973] 2 YB Int'l L. Comm'n, above n. 56, at 193.
[68] F. García-Amador, L. Sohn and R. Baxter, above n. 1, at 247-9; Meron,
International Responsibility of States for Unauthorized Acts of their Officials, 33 Brit.
YB Int'l L. 85 (1957). See also Condorelli, *L'imputation à l'Etat d'un fait
internationalement illicite: solutions classiques et nouvelles tendances*, 189 Recueil des
cours 7 (1984-VI); Christenson, *The Doctrine of Attribution in State Responsibility*,
in International Law of State Responsibility, above n. 1, at 321; For other scholarly
writings on attribution to states of *ultra vires* acts of state organs, see [1975] 2 YB
Int'l L. Comm'n, above n. 55, at 66 nn. 71-2.

The ILC decided that the rule attributing such unauthorized conduct to the state must apply 'even in the case of manifest incompetence of the organ perpetrating the conduct complained of, and even if other organs of the State have disowned the conduct of the offending organ'.[69] In adopting this position, the ILC grounded its rationale both in existing case-law and in the principle of effectiveness. Emphasizing that in the majority of cases 'the fact of knowing that the organ engaging in unlawful conduct is either exceeding its competence, or contravening its instructions, will not enable the victim of such conduct to escape its harmful consequences',[70] the Commmission refused to provide the state 'with an easy loophole in particularly serious cases where its international responsibility ought to be affirmed . . .'.[71] If only that conduct which conforms to a state's internal law were attributable to a state, a defendant state could easily evade its international responsibility given the difficulty of proving that

> the organ of the defendant State had not contravened the municipal law of that State. . . . that the organ was not [sic] acting on superior orders or that, although officially disavowed, the conduct was in fact encouraged by the other organs of the State.[72]

This principle of international law attributing the authorized as well as the unauthorized conduct of its organs to the state is important in all fields of international law, but acquires particular vitality in the protection of international human rights. In the vast majority of cases, acts comprising the most egregious violations of human rights, such as torture, murder, or causing the disappearance of individuals, would also breach the internal law of the state where they were committed.[73] States in which such outrages against

---

[69] [1975] 2 YB Int'l L. Comm'n, above n. 55, at 61.

[70] Ibid. at 69 (footnote omitted).

[71] Ibid. at 69 (footnote omitted).

[72] Ibid. at 67.

[73] See *Filartiga* v. *Peña-Irala*, 630 F. 2d 876, 878, 889; *Forti* v. *Suarez-Mason*, No. C-87-2058 DLJ, slip op. at 30 (ND Cal. 6 Oct. 1987) ('the acts, if committed, were illegal even under Argentine law at all relevant times').

That the principle of effectiveness instructs the rule stating that the state is responsible for *ultra vires* acts of state organs and officials violating human rights appears clearly from the judgment of the Inter-American Court of Human Rights in the *Velásquez Rodriguez Case*. The Court declared that if acts of public power that are either *ultra vires* or violate the internal law are not considered breaches of that state's obligations under the Convention, the system of protection which it provides would be illusory. The Court concluded that such acts are, in principle,

human dignity occur either deny the facts outright or characterize the violations as contrary to their own laws and policy. Under the principle attributing to the state the unauthorized acts of its organs, expressed in the ILC's Article 10, a defence of *ultra vires* would not exonerate the state from international responsibility for the violation.

Doubts have been expressed, however, regarding whether this principle of customary law, which is rooted in the law governing the responsibility of states for injuries to aliens, is confined to that law or applies also to violations by the state of the human rights of its own nationals. While recognizing that a plea of *ultra vires* provides no defence for breaches of norms governing the responsibility of states for injuries to aliens, including the violation of their human rights,[74] the Restatement of the Foreign Relations Law of the United States takes the position that the principle excluding the defence of *ultra vires* does not apply to the violations by a state of the customary human rights of its own nationals.[75]

The US Restatement accepts, however, that a state is responsible for *ultra vires* breaches of treaty human rights.[76] This position is in accord with the approach adopted by the European Commission of Human Rights in *Ireland* v. *United Kingdom*.[77] Under the heading of 'State responsibility and "official tolerance"' the Commission rejected the argument that an individual violation by a person

---

imputable to the state. Judgment of 29 July 1988, Inter-American Court of Human Rights, Ser. C, Decisions and Judgments, No. 4, paras. 170–2.

Professor Kooijmans, the Special Rapporteur on torture of the UN Commission on Human Rights, expresses particular concern over situations where torture has become 'a more or less normal element of daily life. In such situations the authorities have either lost control over the security or law-enforcement personnel and condone the practice of torture . . . or cast a benevolent eye on such practices. . . .' UN Doc. E/CN.4/1987/13 at 23.

Professor Felix Ermacora, UN Human Rights Commission's expert on the question of the fate of missing and disappeared persons in Chile, established that certain disappearances were imputable to the government of Chile which was, therefore, responsible under international law for the fate of the missing persons. UN Doc. A/34/583/Add.1 at 87–92 (1979).

[74] Restatement, above n. 1, vol. 1 §207(c), comment *d* and Reporters' note 4, vol. 2, §711(a), comments (*a*)–(*c*).

[75] Ibid. at §702, comment *b*, Reporters' note 2. It is noteworthy that the draft bill introduced in the US Congress to provide for a civil action for recovery from persons engaging in torture extends to acts committed under the 'apparent authority of any foreign nation . . .'. Above Chapter II, n. 140.

[76] Ibid. at §702, comment *b*.

[77] 1976 YB Eur. Conv. Hum. Rts. 512 (Eur. Comm'n of Hum. Rts.).

acting in an official capacity only entails state responsibility if the state did not provide the remedy required under Article 13 of the Convention. The obligations of the state, the Commission stated, 'can be violated also by a person exercising an official function vested in him at any, even the lowest level, without express authorisation and even outside or against instructions'.[78]

The Restatement's rule hinges on the distinction between nationals and aliens, rather than on the substantive rules of conduct implicated; i.e. human rights. The Restatement is silent regarding both the rationale and the authority for its special rule of non-responsibility for unauthorized violations of human rights. That this rule would adversely affect the effective protection of human rights is clear. This approach is especially difficult to reconcile with those norms of human rights which impose obligations of result on the state. Although the ILC's Special Rapporteur Riphagen recognized that the consequences of various breaches of international law may differ,[79] the ILC rules of attribution were intended to apply across the board to all fields of international law, including both customary and conventional human rights law. The ILC thus made clear in its commentary on Article 10 that

under the system adopted by the Commission, no conduct of State organs or of the other entities mentioned in article 7 is excluded from attribution to the State *qua* subject of international law.[80]

More explicitly, Special Rapporteur Ago stated that the ILC should

formulate a really general rule to cover all cases of violation of international obligations, and especially of the basic obligations of the State, whether they concerned security, peace, the sovereignty and the independence of States, *or the protection of fundamental human rights*.[81]

[78] Ibid. at 758.
[79] W. Riphagen, Fifth Report on the Content, Forms and Degrees of International Responsibility (part two of the draft articles), [1984] 2 YB Int'l L. Comm'n (pt. 1) at 2, UN Doc. A/CN.4/SER.A/1984/Add.1 (Part 1) (1986).
[80] [1975] 2 YB Int'l L. Comm'n, above n. 55, at 61.
[81] [1975] 1 YB Int'l L. Comm'n 16, UN Doc. A/CN.4/SER.A/1975 (1976) (emphasis added).
In the *Velásquez Rodríguez Case*, the Inter-American Court of Human Rights stated that according to Art. 1(1) of the American Convention on Human Rights, any exercise of public power that violates the rights stated in the Convention is illegal. Judgment of 29 July 1988, Inter-American Court of Human Rights, Ser. C, Decisions and Judgments, No. 4, para. 169. The Court appeared to suggest that this principle reflected not only a conventional obligation, but a general principle of international law. The Court explained that its conclusion was independent of

The general customary international rule on attribution does not preclude the creation of *lex specialis* in international treaties for particular topics or categories of actors. Such a special rule is contained, for example, in Article 139 of the United Nations Convention on the Law of the Sea and in Article 3 of the Hague Convention No. IV Respecting the Laws and Customs of War on Land (to be further discussed in Section IX, below),[82] which provides that a belligerent party 'shall be responsible for all acts committed by persons forming part of its armed forces'. This provision, now accepted as customary law,[83] goes beyond the generally applicable rules governing international responsibility of states, which are based on the official capacity/private capacity distinction, to establish a more stringent standard for members of the armed forces. Article 3 constitutes 'a veritable guarantee covering all damage that might be caused by armed forces, whether they had acted as organs or as private persons'.[84] This special rule

whether the organ or official has contravened the internal law or acted *ultra vires*, because it is a principle of international law that the state is responsible for the acts and omissions of its agents in their official capacity, even if committed outside of the sphere of their authority or in violation of internal law. Ibid. para. 170.

[82] For the text of the Hague Convention No. IV, see 36 Stat. 2277, TS No. 539, 1 Bevans 631, 1910 Gr. Brit. TS No. 9 (Cmd. 5030). For discussion of responsibility of states under Art. 3, see *Affaire des Biens Britanniques au Maroc Espagnol* (*Spain v. United Kingdom*), Report III (23 Oct. 1924), at 2 UNRIAA 645 (1949), discussed in Condorelli, above n. 68, at 147-8. For the text of the United Nations Convention on the Law of the Sea, opened for signature 10 Dec. 1982, see UN Doc. A/CONF.62/122 and Corr. 1-11 (1982), reprinted in 21 ILM 1261 (1982), discussed in Condorelli and Dipla, *Solutions traditionnelles et nouvelles tendances en matière d'attribution à l'Etat d'un fait internationalement illicite dans la convention de 1982 sur le droit de la mer*, in 3 International Law at the Time of its Codification: Essays in Honour of Roberto Ago 65, 84-97 (P. Ziccardi ed. 1987).

[83] Professor Reuter observed that '[i]t was now a principle of codified international law that States were responsible for all acts of their armed forces.' [1975] 1 YB Int'l L. Comm'n, above n. 81, at 7.

[84] Ibid. at 16 (comments by Special Rapporteur Roberto Ago). See also 1 L. Oppenheim, International Law 363 at n. 1 (8th edn. H. Lauterpacht 1955). Art. 3 was in fact intended to apply also to cases 'in which negligence cannot be attributed to the government itself', i.e. violations committed 'without the knowledge of governments, or against their will'. Sandoz, *Unlawful Damage in Armed Conflicts and Redress under International Humanitarian Law*, Int'l Rev. Red Cross, No. 228, May-June 1982, at 131, 136-7.

Compare Art. 29 of Geneva Convention No. IV which provides that '[t]he Party to the conflict in whose hands protected persons may be, is responsible for the treatment accorded to them by its agents, irrespective of any individual responsibility which may be incurred', discussed in Commentary on the Geneva Conventions of 12 August 1949: Geneva Convention Relative to the Protection of Civilian Persons in Time of War 211-13 (O. Uhler and H. Coursier eds. 1958) and in UN Doc.

addresses the consequences of acts by a particular category of state agents rather than the question of attributing their acts to the state.[85] Because Article 3 appears in a text which is limited to international armed conflicts, its relevance (to be discussed in Section IX, below) to human rights violations perpetrated by soldiers outside such conflicts is less clear.

Under customary international law, as reflected in Articles 14 and 15 of ILC's draft articles on state responsibility (part one), the conduct of an insurrectional movement which is established in the territory of a state is not considered an act of that state (Article 14), but an act of an insurrectional movement which becomes the new government of a state is considered as an act of that state (Article 15). The rule of non-attribution to the state of acts of an insurrectional movement which continues to exist or has been brought down leaves, of course, a large gap in the law of state responsibility, which adversely affects the possibility of individuals obtaining remedy from insurrectional movements for breaches of human rights or humanitarian norms.

Although contemporary human rights law focuses on the duty of governments to respect the human rights of individuals, human rights violations committed by one private person against another (e.g. deprivation of life and liberty or the perpetration of acts of egregious discrimination) cannot be placed outside the ambit of human rights law if that law is ever to gain significant effectiveness. The ICJ acknowledged this reality when, in a different context, it deplored '[t]he frequency with which at the present time the principles of international law . . . are set at naught by individuals or groups of individuals . . .'.[86] Because the purpose of human

A/34/583/Add.1, at 89 (1979). Although the word 'agents' covers a broader group than that addressed in Art. 3 ('persons forming part of its armed forces'), Art. 29 does not appear to modify the general rules on imputability and responsibility. See above *Commentary*, at 212-13.

[85] Note the opinion of Professor Brownlie that '[i]mputability would seem to be a superfluous notion, since the major issue in a given situation is whether there has been a breach of duty: the content of "imputability" will vary according to the particular duty, the nature of the breach, and so on.' I. Brownlie, above n. 62, at 36.

[86] *United States Diplomatic and Consular Staff in Tehran* (*United States of America v. Iran*), 1980 ICJ Rep. 4, 42 (Judgment of 24 May).

Replying to a question of the Argentine government as to why the Inter-American Commission on Human Rights (IACHR) concerns itself exclusively with actions attributable to governments and does not investigate terrorists acts, the IACHR stated 'that the task of the Commission—as, in general, that of all other intergovernmental bodies set up for the protection of human rights—is to investigate only those actions imputable to governments'. OAS, IACHR, Report on the Situation of Human Rights in Argentina at 25, OEA/Ser.L/V/II.49, Doc. 19, Corr. 1 (1980). While this statement is correct *de lege lata,* I believe that the shape of *lex ferenda* is reflected in the observation made by a recent UN report: 'In recent decades it has been implicitly or explicitly accepted that organized or semi-organized political groups, particularly those engaged in insurgency or insurrection, may be responsible for violations of human rights and freedoms, mainly in respect of the right to life and personal freedom.' R. Galindo Pohl, Report on the Human Rights Situation in the Islamic Republic of Iran, UN Doc. E/CN.4/1987/23 at 5. See also below, text following n. 104.

In *Tel-Oren* v. *Libyan Arab Republic,* Judge Edwards aptly observed that 'the trend in international law is toward a more expansive allocation of rights and obligations to entities other than states . . .'. 726 F. 2d 774, 795 (1984).

It may, perhaps, be useful to suggest here several propositions regarding the relationship of terrorist acts to human rights of individuals.

First, terrorist acts which are organized, supported or condoned by states, and can thus be imputed to governments, violate human rights of the victims to the extent that such acts are prohibited by the international obligations of the governments concerned. Accordingly, such acts generate the international responsibility of the state. This is true of acts committed both within and outside the territory of the state concerned. For discussion of the *ratione loci* applicability of the International Covenant on Civil and Political Rights, see T. Meron, above n. 33 at 106-9. Regarding the international responsibility of states 'for nonlocal terrorism', see Lillich and Paxman, *State Responsibility for Injuries to Aliens Occasioned by Terrorist Activities,* 26 Am. U. L. Rev. 217, 251-76 (1977). Additionally, the state has an obligation to attempt to prevent acts of terrorism (discussion of the appropriate standard of care is beyond the scope of this study) and to do its best to apprehend, punish, or extradite the perpetrators.

The second proposition is that in so far as most human rights involve obligations of states towards individuals, terrorist acts committed by individuals or groups which cannot be imputed to a certain government do not amount to violations of human rights of the victims, but only to breaches of the criminal law of the state concerned. Such acts can, however, breach other norms of international law, especially of international criminal law.

The third proposition (to be discussed in the text further below) is that whether a particular human right stated in an international human rights instrument must be respected not only by governments or other public actors but also by private or non-governmental actors, that is groups whose acts cannot be attributed to governments, depends on the content and the interpretation of the provision; i.e. its language, purpose, and object.

Some prohibitions are addressed not only to states. Here, norms of international law have been intended to apply directly to the perpetrators of the prohibited acts. These norms thus have a dual character. They impose upon the states the obligation to attempt to prevent terrorist acts and to punish or extradite the perpetrators and upon non-governmental organizations and their members to respect the norms implicated. See e.g. Dinstein, *International Criminal Law,* 20 Israel L. Rev. 206, 217, 218, 219, 223 (1985). On obligations of individuals under international law, see T. Meron, Human Rights in Internal Strife: Their International Protection 33-40 (1987); E. Daes, The Individual's Duties to the Community and the Limitations on Human Rights and Freedoms under Article 29 of the Universal Declaration of Human Rights, UN Doc. E/CN.4/Sub.2/432/Rev.2 at 41-7 (1983).

rights law is to protect human dignity, and because some essential human rights are often breached by private persons, the obligation of states to observe and ensure respect for human rights and to prevent violations cannot be confined to restrictions upon governmental powers but must extend to at least some private 'interferences' with human rights.[87] States should exercise due diligence to prevent violations by non-governmental actors; the standard of care required would depend on the character and the importance of the norm protected. When prevention fails, states should resort to criminal proceedings against the perpetrator of human rights violations and should ensure that their internal law provides the victim with effective civil remedies against the responsible private actor. In the *Velásquez Rodríguez Case*, which involved causing the disappearance of individuals, the Inter-American Court of Human Rights, *obiter*, interpreted the obligation of Honduras 'to ensure to all persons subject to [its] jurisdiction' the rights recognized in the American Convention of Human Rights as encompassing the obligation to punish the perpetrators of violations of such rights.[88] The requirement that the government of Honduras employs all means within its power to investigate the assassinations of witnesses before the Court, identify the perpetrators and impose the punishment provided by the law was also included in the Court's provisional measures order of 15 January 1988. Because of the similarity of Article 1 of the American Convention to Article 2 of the Political Covenant and, in this context, to Article 1 of the European Convention, the jurisprudence of the American Court is of general importance for the international law of human rights. It demonstrates that this evolving law aims at the prevention of violations of human rights by private or unofficial actors or groups within the state and that punishment is a necessary component of an effective policy of prevention.

Human rights obligations stated in international humanitarian and human rights instruments increasingly extend to private individuals and to private action. In some areas of international

---

[87] Forde, *Non-Governmental Interferences with Human Rights*, 56 Brit. YB Int' L. 253 (1985). Note particularly the discussion of the practice of the European Commission of Human Rights and the European Court of Human Rights with respect to non-governmental interference with human rights. Ibid. at 271–8.

[88] *Velásquez Rodríguez Case*, Judgment of 29 July 1988, Inter-American Court of Human Rights, Ser. C, Decisions and Judgments, No. 4, para. 166. See also ibid., para. 41, and Sohn, *The New International Law: Protection of the Rights of*

law, such as that governing labour rights and conditions of work, the relevant international labour conventions routinely regulate relations between private employees and employers. The prohibitions of slavery and genocide (discussed in Section I, above) apply, of course, also to private persons and groups. So does the prohibition of hostage-taking (discussed in Chapter I, Section V).

Other examples can be found in humanitarian law. Common Article 3 of the Geneva Conventions (discussed in Chapter I, Section III) imposes also on the non-governmental party to the conflict the obligation to comply with important humanitarian norms. Members of the non-governmental party to the conflict, whose acts could not be imputed to the government concerned, may themselves be responsible for breach of such humanitarian norms as violence to life and person, murder, mutilation, cruel treatment, torture and hostage-taking. Article 27(2) of Geneva Convention No. IV, which provides that women shall be protected against 'any attack on their honour, in particular against rape, enforced prostitution, or any form of indecent assault', appears to require states to provide protection from both public and private actors.

The 'to respect and to ensure to all individuals' clause of Article 2(1) of the Political Covenant implies the duty of states to ensure compliance by private persons with some of the Covenant's norms, or, at a minimum, to adopt measures 'against private interference with enjoyment of the rights . . .'.[89] This interpretation is supported by the practice of the Inter-American Court of Human Rights in application of Article 1 of the American Convention of Human Rights and of the European Commission and Court of Human Rights in application of Article 1 of the European Convention (which provides that the 'High Contracting Parties shall secure to everyone within their jurisdiction the rights and freedoms defined in Section I of this Convention') and other provisions of the European Convention on Human Rights.

In its judgment in the *Velásquez Rodríguez Case*, the Inter-American Court has construed similar language contained in Article

Individuals Rather than States, 32 Am. U. L. Rev. 1, 31–2 (1982).

[89] Buergenthal, *To Respect and to Ensure: State Obligations and Permissible Derogations*, in The International Bill of Rights, above n. 17, at 72, 77–8; Sohn, above n. 88; Sperduti, *Responsibility of States for Activities of Private Law Persons*, in [Instalment] 10 Encyclopedia of Public International Law 373, 375 (R. Bernhardt ed. 1987).

1(1) of the American Convention on Human Rights.[90] The Court stated that the obligation to ensure the free and full exercise of the rights recognized in the Convention to every person subject to its jurisdiction implies the duty of every state to organize the governmental apparatus in such a way that this goal could be juridically ensured. States must, therefore, prevent, investigate, and punish any violation of such rights, and, if possible, attempt to restore the right violated and provide for compensation. Such a robust interpretation of Article 1(1) may inspire other commissions and courts to give a broad *ratione personae* construction to the provisions of other human rights treaties and should help to discourage violations of human dignity even in those cases where no governmental officials are involved (as they were in the *Velásquez Rodríguez Case*) in the violations. This interpretation of Article 1(1) helps, to be sure, to overcome difficulties of proving state complicity in the violations. It made it possible for the Court to state (para. 182) that it found Honduras in breach of Article 1(1) even had the fact not been proved that the disappearance was carried out by agents acting under cover of public authority.

In the *Young, James and Webster Case* (*Closed Shop Case*) (1981)[91] the European Court of Human Rights, applying Articles 1 and 11 (which guarantee the rights of peaceful assembly and freedom of association, including the right to form and to join trade unions), found that Article 11 had been violated, stating that

[a]lthough the proximate cause of the events giving rise to this case was the 1975 agreement between British Rail and the railway unions, it was the domestic law in force at the relevant time that made lawful the treatment of which the applicants complained. The responsibility of the respondent State for any resultant breach of the Convention is thus engaged on this basis. Accordingly, there is no call to examine whether, as the applicants argued, the State might also be responsible on the ground that it should be regarded as employer or that British Rail was under its control.[92]

In the *National Union of Belgian Police Case*, Application 4464/70 (1974),[93] the European Commission of Human Rights interpreted

---

[90] Judgment of 29 July 1988, Inter-American Court of Human Rights, Ser. C, Decisions and Judgments, No. 4, para. 166.

[91] 62 Int'l L Rep. 359 (1982). 44 Eur. Ct. HR (Ser. A) (1981).

[92] 62 Int'l. L. Rep. 376-7 (1982).

[93] 17 Eur. Ct. HR (Ser. B) (1976).

Article 11 by taking into account UN human rights instruments
and ILO Conventions Nos. 87 and 98. It concluded that the latter
Conventions

> reflect widely accepted labour law standards which are elaborated
> and clarified by the competent organs of the ILO. As they are a
> body of special rules binding also on European States, they should
> not be ignored in the interpretation of Article 11, particularly if
> the European Convention is to keep pace with the rules of
> international labour law and if its concepts are to remain in
> harmony with the concepts used in international labour law and
> practice.[94]

On this broad international law basis, the Commission concluded
that freedom of association stated in Article 11 'may be legitimately
extended to cover State responsibility in the sphere of labour-
management relations'.[95]

The Commission followed the same approach in *Swedish Engine
Drivers' Union Case*, Application No. 5614/72 (1974).[96] Taking
into account once more UN human rights instruments and the
ILO's Conventions, the Commission rejected the assertion that
Article 11 provided protection only against governmental interference. On the contrary, the Article was 'designed to protect
unions against all kinds of interference, including interference by
employers'.[97] Invoking the principle of effectiveness in treaty
interpretation, the Commission concluded that

> [i]f it is the role of the Convention and the function of its interpretation
> to make the protection of individuals effective, the interpretation of Article
> 11 should be such as to provide, in conformity with international labour
> law, some protection against 'private' interference.[98]

More recently, the Court addressed the duty of states to conform
to the Convention by adopting legislative measures governing
certain relations between private individuals. In the *Case of X and
Y v. The Netherlands* (1985),[99] the applicant claimed that the right
of both his daughter and himself to respect for their private life,

[94] Ibid. at 51. See also ibid. at 49–51.
[95] Ibid. at 52.
[96] 18 Eur. Ct. HR (Ser. B) 42–6 (1977).
[97] Ibid. at 45.
[98] Ibid. at 46.
[99] 91 Eur. Ct. HR (Ser. A) (1985).

guaranteed by Article 8 of the European Convention, had been infringed and that Article 8 required that parents must be able to have recourse to remedies in the event of their children being the victims of sexual abuse. Finding that Article 8 had in fact been breached, the Court stated:

The Court recalls that although the object of Article 8 is essentially that of protecting the individual against arbitrary interference by the public authorities, it does not merely compel the State to abstain from such interference: in addition to this primarily negative undertaking, there may be positive obligations inherent in an effective respect for private or family life. . . . These obligations may involve the adoption of measures designed to secure respect for private life even in the sphere of the relations of individuals between themselves.[100]

The International Convention on the Elimination of All Forms of Racial Discrimination requires states to bring an end to 'racial discrimination by any persons, group or organization'[101] (Article 2(1)(d)), and imposes on states far-reaching obligations to criminalize racist theorizing and the setting up of racist organizations by private actors (Article 4).[102] Similarly, with regard to women, Article 2(e) of the Convention on the Elimination of All Forms of Discrimination against Women targets discriminatory behaviour by 'any person, organization or enterprise'.[103] Finally, Article 13(3) of the American Convention on Human Rights prohibits restricting the exercise of the freedom of expression through 'private controls' over means of dissemination. In the advisory opinion on *Compulsory Membership in an Association Prescribed by Law for the Practice of Journalism (Arts. 13 and 29 of the American Convention on Human Rights)*, the Inter-American Court of Human Rights declared that Article 13(3)

does not only deal with indirect governmental restrictions, it also expressly prohibits 'private controls' producing the same result. This provision must be read together with the language of Article 1 of the Convention wherein the States Parties 'undertake to respect the rights and freedoms recognized (in the Convention) . . . and to ensure to all persons subject to their

---

[100] Ibid. at 11.
[101] For discussion of the private and public reach of this Convention, see T. Meron, above n. 33, at 18–23. Compare Forde, above n. 87, at 262.
[102] See also Political Covenant, Art. 20, discussed in T. Meron, above n. 33, at 23–35.
[103] Discussed in T. Meron, above n. 33, at 59–60.

jurisdiction the free and full exercise of those rights and freedoms . . .'. Hence, a violation of the Convention in this area can be the product not only of the fact that the State itself imposes restrictions of an indirect character which tend to impede 'the communication and circulation of ideas and opinions,' but the State also has an obligation to ensure that the violation does not result from the 'private controls' referred to in paragraph 3 of Article 13.[104]

The extension of such human rights as the prohibition of egregious discrimination on grounds of race or sex to encompass private action is impelled by significant community values. This expansion inevitably generates tension with other human rights, such as the freedom of association and the right to privacy, and requires a careful balancing of these values. The alternative, limiting the reach of human rights to public life, would diminish their effectiveness and is thus clearly unacceptable. It is significant that international public opinion, NGOs, and UN organs condemn violations of human rights and humanitarian law even by groups that cannot be considered 'parties' to the conflict under common Article 3 of the Geneva Conventions. The UN Commission on Human Rights, for example, has recently affirmed in Resolution 1988/38 that 'the taking of hostages constitute[s] a grave violation of human rights' and censured 'the actions of all persons responsible'.

Whether a particular human right stated in an international human rights instrument must be respected not only by public but also by private actors depends on the interpretation of the provision, i.e. its language, context, purpose, and object. Because the object of human rights treaties is to ensure effective protection of human dignity, due weight must be given to the principle of effectiveness in construing human rights treaties. When a human rights treaty establishes an obligation of result, and that result may be frustrated by private action, the arguments for an interpretation reaching private action are compelling.

A number of provisions which explicitly target private as well as public action have been mentioned. Others address only public action.[105] Still others are silent with regard to their reach, but their

---

[104] Advisory Opinion OC-5/85 of 13 Nov. 1985, Inter-American Court of Human Rights, Ser. A, Judgments and Opinions, No. 5, at 110–11. See also ibid. at 114.

[105] See e.g. Art. 1 of the Convention Against Torture and Other Cruel, Inhuman or Degrading Treatment or Punishment, which covers acts inflicted 'by or at the instigation of or with the consent or acquiescence of a public official or other person acting in an official capacity', above n. 39. For a discussion of a similar provision

purpose requires that they be extended to private action. As Forde points out, 'certain rights, [e.g. prohibitions of slavery, servitude and murder] by their very nature must envisage governmental responsibility for failure to ensure that they are respected by private individuals and organizations.'[106] Subject to the rules stated in Articles 31-2 of the Vienna Convention on the Law of Treaties, broad interpretations of rights are necessary for the effective protection of human dignity, which is the goal of human rights law.

To be sure, the applicability of some human rights instruments to private actors does not imply that the conduct of private persons when not carried out in fact on behalf of a state (Article 8 of ILC's draft articles on state responsibility (part one)) in breach of such instruments is attributable to the state. Rather, the breach is generated by the fact that the state itself violates its obligations under international law by tolerating the occurrence of the prohibited acts.[107] Thus in the *Velásquez Rodríguez Case* (discussed

in the UN Declaration on the Protection of All Persons from Being Subjected to Torture and Other Cruel, Inhuman or Degrading Treatment or Punishment, see Forde, above n. 87, at 263. This definition of torture thus applies only to governmental actors. Tardu, *The United Nations Convention against Torture and other Cruel, Inhuman or Degrading Treatment or Punishment*, 56 Nordic J. Int'l L. 303, 306 (1987). Whether Art. 7 of the Political Covenant incorporates the same limitation is open to question. Tardu suggests that 'global treaties leave the modalities of combating private torture much to the discretion of the state.' Ibid.

In *Forti* v. *Suarez-Mason*, above n. 73, the court stated that while 'purely private torture will not normally implicate the law of nations, since there is currently no international consensus regarding torture practiced by non-state actors', ibid. at 16, torture practiced by military and police personnel under the supervision and control of superior officials falls 'within the international tort first recognized in *Filartiga*', ibid. at 17 (footnote omitted), even if in breach of Argentine law. Ibid. at 30.

Personal responsibility of the individual torturer is, of course, not dispositive of the question whether the state itself is internationally responsible for tolerating the occurrence of acts of torture.

[106] Forde, above n. 87, at 262. See also Sohn, above n. 88.

[107] See [1975] 2 YB Int'l L. Comm'n, above n. 55, at 71. See also draft Art. 11(2), above n. 59. In its commentary on that Article, the ILC explains that 'although the international responsibility of the State is sometimes held to exist in connexion with acts of private persons its sole basis is the internationally wrongful conduct of organs of the State in relation to the acts of the private person concerned.' Ibid. at 82.

Arts. 4-5 of Hague Convention No. V Respecting the Rights and Duties of Neutral Powers and Persons in Case of War on Land, signed 18 Oct. 1907, 36 Stat. 2310, TS 540, 1 Bevans 654, which prohibit the opening on the territory of a neutral power of recruiting agencies to assist the belligerents, obviously reach agencies operated by private individuals. But Art. 6 provides that '[t]he responsibility of a neutral Power is not engaged by the fact of persons crossing the frontier separately

above in this Section), the Inter-American Court of Human Rights suggested (paras. 172-3) that acts of public authority which are imputable to the state do not exhaust all the circumstances in which a state is obligated to prevent, investigate, and punish human rights violations, nor the cases in which the state itself might be responsible for violations. A breach of human rights which is initially not imputable to a state, having been committed by either a private or by an unidentified person, can generate state responsibility not because of the act itself, but because of the lack of due diligence to prevent the violation or to respond to it according to the requirements of the American Convention. The critical question, therefore, is whether the state has demonstrated lack of due diligence by allowing the act to take place either with its support or acquiescence or by not taking measures designed to prevent the act or to punish those responsible.

To be sure, the fact that a particular human right may not impose obligations on a private person or a private group does not mean that the acts contemplated are lawful. In practice, such acts often constitute breaches of the national law of the state concerned.

III. EXHAUSTION OF LOCAL REMEDIES

The requirement of exhaustion of local remedies is a principle of customary law applicable to the protection of aliens,[108] which has been frequently confirmed or modified by international agreements.[109] An alien alleging a breach by the host country of his or her international legal (including human) rights must exhaust all of the remedies available in the host country before his or her

to offer their services to one of the belligerents.' Acts of individuals addressed by Art. 6 are thus not to be imputed to the state.

Professor Brownlie points out that acts of private persons generate state responsibility when a particular rule of international law is breached by the state itself, as, for example, in the case of breach of duty to exercise due diligence in control of private persons. I. Brownlie, above n. 62, at 160-3.

[108] [1977] 2 YB Int'l L. Comm'n (pt. 2) at 31, UN Doc. A/CN.4/ SER.A/1977/Add.1 (Part 2) (1978). The ILC observed that all of the cases decided by the international courts in which the principle of exhaustion of local remedies was recognized involved 'the breach or alleged breach of international obligations concerning the treatment accorded by a State in its territory to aliens or their property'. Ibid. at 32. In this comment, the ILC appears to refer to cases in which the courts applied customary law, rather than to cases in which international tribunals, applying treaty provisions, recognized the duty to exhaust local remedies in connection with human rights obligations.

[109] Ibid. at 31.

state of nationality may espouse his or her claim on the international plane.[110] A question arises, however, regarding whether the requirement of exhaustion of local remedies extends to those relations between the state and its own nationals which are governed by international human rights. In other words, must local remedies be exhausted before the victim of the violation may present a complaint to an international authority? Is exhaustion required before a state which is not directly affected may submit a claim of a victim who is not its national either to an international authority or to the state which committed the violation?

The requirement that local remedies be exhausted before a claim against a state may be submitted to an international forum[111] is stated in all of the principal human rights treaties, both with respect to complaints submitted against states by individual victims[112] of

[110] Art. 22 of the ILC's draft articles on state responsibility (part one) reads as follows: 'When the conduct of a State has created a situation not in conformity with the result required of it by an international obligation concerning the treatment to be accorded to aliens, whether natural or juridical persons, but the obligation allows that this or an equivalent result may nevertheless be achieved by subsequent conduct of the State, there is a breach of the obligation only if the aliens concerned have exhausted the effective local remedies available to them without obtaining the treatment called for by the obligation or, where that is not possible, an equivalent treatment.' Ibid. at 11. The question of whether the exhaustion requirement applies both to obligations of means and to obligations of result will be discussed in Section IV, below.

[111] For our purposes there is no need to discuss the controversial question of whether the requirement of the exhaustion of local remedies is a substantive principle which generates the international responsibility of the state, or merely a procedural condition for the admissibility of the claim. See ibid. at 34–42. The ILC interprets the jurisprudence of the European Commission of Human Rights as lending support to the former position; i.e. that 'the principle of the exhaustion of local remedies [essentially] lays down a condition for generation of the international responsibility of the State . . .'. Ibid. at 40.

[112] See e.g. the Optional Protocol to the International Covenant on Civil and Political Rights, Art. 5(2)(*b*); American Convention on Human Rights, Art. 46(1)(*a*); European Convention on Human Rights, Art. 26; African Charter on Human and Peoples' Rights, Art. 56(5)–(6); International Convention on the Elimination of All Forms of Racial Discrimination, Art. 14(7)(*a*); Inter-American Convention to Prevent and Punish Torture, signed 9 Dec. 1985, Art. 8, OAS Doc. OEA/Ser.A/42(SEPF); Convention Against Torture and Other Cruel, Inhuman or Degrading Treatment of Punishment, Art. 22(5)(*b*).

The requirement of exhaustion of local remedies is also stated in ECOSOC Resolution 1503, Art. 6(*b*)(i). ESC Res. 1503, 48 UN ESCOR Supp. (No. 1A) 8–9, UN Doc. E/4832/Add.1 (1970).

In contrast, the League of Nations' Minorities Treaties were construed to allow the Council of the League to consider either individual or collective petitions even where the petitioners have not exhausted local remedies. International Protection of Human Rights, above n. 1, at 255–78.

violations, and with respect to complaints brought by states.[113] Such treaties routinely describe the requirement of exhaustion of local remedies as a general, i.e. a customary, principle of law,[114] and exclude its application in cases where exhaustion of local remedies is unreasonably prolonged[115] or where local remedies are ineffective or unavailable.[116] In so far as claims concerning breaches of humanitarian law normally involve direct injuries caused by one state to another, the requirement of exhaustion of local remedies does not concern humanitarian law.

Several issues merit discussion in this context. First, the advantages and disadvantages of the rule of exhaustion of local remedies in the field of human rights should be weighed. Second, the significance and impact of provisions in human rights treaties which characterize the rule of exhaustion of local remedies as customary law should be evaluated. Third, the scope and applicability of the requirement of exhaustion of local remedies stated in human rights treaties requires clarification. Finally, the applicability of the requirement to human rights claims governed by customary law should be explored.

[113] See e.g. the International Covenant on Civil and Political Rights, Art. 41(1)(c); American Convention on Human Rights, Art. 46(1)(a); European Convention on Human Rights, Art. 26; African Charter on Human and Peoples' Rights, Art. 50; International Convention on the Elimination of All Forms of Racial Discrimination, Art. 11(3); Convention Against Torture and Other Cruel, Inhuman or Degrading Treatment or Punishment, Art. 21(1)(c).

[114] See e.g. the International Covenant on Civil and Political Rights, Art. 41(1)(c) ('in conformity with the generally recognized principles of international law'); American Convention on Human Rights, Art. 46(1)(a) ('in accordance with generally recognized principles of international law'); International Convention on the Elimination of All Forms of Racial Discrimination, Art. 11(3); ('in conformity with the generally recognized principles of international law'); Convention Against Torture and Other Cruel, Inhuman or Degrading Treatment or Punishment, Art. 21(1)(c) ('in conformity with the generally recognized principles of international law').

[115] See e.g. the International Covenant on Civil and Political Rights, Art. 41(1)(c); Optional Protocol to the International Covenant on Civil and Political Rights, Art. 5(2); American Convention on Human Rights, Art. 46(2)(c); African Charter on Human and Peoples' Rights, Arts. 50 and 56(5); International Convention on the Elimination of All Forms of Racial Discrimination, Arts. 11(3) and 14(7)(a); International Convention Against Torture and Other Cruel, Inhuman or Degrading Treatment or Punishment, Arts. 21(1)(c) and 22(5)(b).

[116] See e.g. the American Convention on Human Rights, Article 46(2)(a)-(b); African Charter on Human and Peoples' Rights, Art. 50 ('all local remedies, if they exist') and Art. 56(5) ('local remedies, if any'); International Convention Against Torture and Other Cruel, Inhuman or Degrading Treatment or Punishment, Arts. 21(1)(c) and 22(5)(b) ('this shall not be the rule where the application of the remedies . . . is unlikely to bring effective relief to the person who is the victim of

First, several advantages of the rule may be identified. One of these is that it serves to eliminate claims which can be resolved through national agencies, thus protecting international agencies from inundation by a flood of claims. By giving the state an opportunity to redress an alleged breach of international human rights through its own apparatus and under its national law before the claim becomes admissible for consideration by an international authority,[117] the rule aids the continuing process of acceptance of international human rights obligations by states. The exhaustion requirement facilitates the balancing of human rights goals against both state sovereignty and the reluctance of states to accept third-party involvement in relations between government and citizens, which have traditionally been viewed as matters of national

the violation of this Convention'). Other instruments refer to the duty to exhaust 'available remedies'.

[117] '[T]he real reason for the existence of the principle of the exhaustion of local remedies must always be kept in mind: it is *to enable the State to avoid the breach of an international obligation by redressing, through a subsequent course of conduct adopted on the initiative of the individuals concerned, the consequences of an initial course of conduct contrary to the result required by the obligation.*' *Commentary* on Art. 22 of the draft articles on state responsibility (part one), [1977] 2 YB Int'l L. Comm'n (pt. 2), above n. 108, at 47 (emphasis in original).

Discussing the requirement of exhaustion of local remedies in the context of Art. 46(1)(a) of the American Convention on Human Rights, the Inter-American Court of Human Rights stated: '[U]nder the generally recognized principles of international law and international practice, the rule which requires the prior exhaustion of domestic remedies is designed for the benefit of the State, for that rule seeks to excuse the State from having to respond to charges before an international body for acts imputed to it before it has had the opportunity to remedy them by internal means. The requirement is thus considered a means of defense and, as such, waivable. . . .' *In the Matter of Viviana Gallardo et al.*, No. G 101/81, Inter-American Court of Human Rights, Decisions and Judgments, Ser. A at 88 (1984).

In the same vein, the Inter-American Court has recently observed that the rule of exhaustion allows the state to resolve the problem under its internal law before being brought before an international jurisdiction and that in the human rights field, the international jurisdiction reinforces or complements the domestic jurisdiction of states. *Velásquez Rodríguez Case*, Judgment of 29 July 1988, Inter-American Court of Human Rights, Ser. C, Decisions and Judgments, No. 4, para. 61.

The government of Colombia has argued, with respect to complaints pertaining to disappearances in Colombia, that the UN Working Group on Enforced or Involuntary Disappearances should apply the rules pertaining to the examination of communications under the Optional Protocol to the Political Covenant, which contained norms which were 'universally accepted'. Although Colombia did not insist on prior exhaustion of domestic remedies, 'cases of disappearances should at least be filed with national authorities before being admitted by the Working Group', so that the government could conduct its own investigations. UN Doc. E/CN.4/1988/19 at 18.

jurisdiction.[118] Commentators have therefore considered exhaustion as 'a reasonable rule which is predicated both on practicality and on due respect for the sovereignty of States'.[119] Special Rapporteur Ago emphasized that

the minds most heedful of today's problems and of the difficulties in solving them realize that compliance with this essential requirement may well be the best guarantee of further substantial progress in the acceptance of new obligations with regard to human rights. In the circumstances, the Special Rapporteur considers that it would be injudicious to tamper with the existing general scope of the principle in the name of an alleged progressive development which others might regard as a step backwards in the matter of guarantees of equal sovereignty for all States.[120]

Among the disadvantages of the requirement are the 'hesitations and delays' which result. Thus, the exhaustion of local remedies may be an obstacle to 'a more direct, quicker and more effective form of protection of human rights'.[121] Rigid insistence on exhaustion may even frustrate the resort to an international authority without producing full satisfaction for the breach within the internal legal system. In broader philosophical terms, one may also ask whether the establishment of a strong international legal order based on respect for human rights is well served by allowing states to sidestep international responsibility for even egregious violations of human rights by providing remedies under internal law.[122]

[118] [1977] 1 YB Int'l L. Comm'n 270, UN Doc. A/CN.4/SER.A/1977 (1978) (remarks of Mr Ushakov). See also ibid. at 271: 'In the case of human rights . . . exhaustion of local remedies was still a matter for domestic jurisdiction, and . . . it was a little too soon to require countries to accept compulsory international jurisdiction.' (remarks by Mr Jagota.)

[119] de Zayas, Möller, and Opsahl, *Application of the International Covenant on Civil and Political Rights under the Optional Protocol by the Human Rights Committee*, 28 Ger. YB Int'l L. 9, 24 (1985).

[120] Roberto Ago, Sixth Report on State Responsibility, [1977] 2 YB Int'l L. Comm'n (pt. 1) at 43, UN Doc. A/CN.4/SER.A/1977/Add.1 (Part 1) (1978).

[121] Ibid. at 42–3.

[122] In its *Commentary* on Art. 22 of its draft articles on state responsibility (part one), the ILC admitted that '[t]here are not exclusively advantages in the fact that a very large proportion of international obligations concerning the treatment to be accorded to private individuals ultimately allow the State to achieve the result required of it by stages. Nor are there exclusively advantages in the fact that such obligations allow conduct contrary to the internationally required result to be disregarded for the purposes of establishing international responsibility, provided that the result in question is eventually secured by subsequent conduct. It is precisely because of all the practical disadvantages inevitably attendant on these facts that various conventions expressly preclude the application of the principle of the exhaustion of local remedies to certain matters.' [1977] 2 YB Int'l L. Comm'n (pt.

In applying the rule of exhaustion of local remedies in the field of human rights, the interests of state sovereignty must of course be balanced with those of the effective protection of human dignity. The scope of the requirement and the conditions for its application must therefore be delineated in a manner that does not impair the effective protection of human rights.

This point leads to the second issue, the significance and impact of the characterization by human rights treaties of exhaustion as a general principle of international law. Because the requirement of exhaustion of local remedies is based in customary law,[123] international fora must apply this rule[124] in a manner consistent with customary law so these fora will not be prevented from considering human rights violations.

Which rules of customary international law demonstrate the limits of the requirement of exhaustion? The basic principle demands that remedies be both available and effective.[125] Thus, exhaustion may not be required when, because of strong animosity towards the nationals of a particular country[126] or a particular religious or ethnic group, redress through local remedies appears impossible. The ILC has delineated the general parameters of the exhaustion requirement,[127] beyond which exhaustion is not required, concluding:

(a) that a remedy should not be used unless it holds out real—even if uncertain—prospects of success. In other words, the individual concerned is under no obligation to waste his time attacking, before a domestic court,

2), above n. 108, at 49.

[123] 'The rule of exhaustion is a general rule of international law. . . .' de Zayas, Möller, and Opsahl, above n. 119, at 24.

[124] For the practice of the Human Rights Committee established under Art. 28 of the International Covenant on Civil and Political Rights, see ibid. at 24-5. See also below n. 131.

[125] [1977] 2 YB Int'l L. Comm'n (pt. 2), above n. 108, at 47.

In the *Velásquez Rodríguez Case*, the Inter-American Court of Human Rights stated that the 'generally recognized principles of international law' (Art. 46(1)(a) of the American Convention on Human Rights) refer not only to the formal existence, but also to the adequacy and effectiveness of such remedies. See also Art. 46(2). Judgment of 29 July 1988, Inter-American Court of Human Rights, Ser. C, Decisions and Judgments, No. 4, para. 63. The Court decided that a remedy which is not adequate in a specific case, need not be exhausted. Ibid. para. 64. It concluded that remedies available in Honduras during the relevant period were entirely ineffective. Ibid. para. 80.

[126] [1977] 2 YB Int'l L. Comm'n (pt. 2), above n. 108, at 43.

[127] Ibid. at 47.

a State measure which is, in fact, final. He cannot be required to use a remedy which would be a mere formality, as, for example, where it is clear from the outset that the law which the court will have to apply can lead only to rejection of the appeal (case of appeal against a measure in conformity with a law which cannot be set aside; of a court bound by a previous judgment rejecting a similar appeal or by a well-established body of unfavourable precedent; of proven partiality of the court, etc.); (b) that a remedy should not be used unless the success it may bring is not a merely formal success, but can actually produce either the result originally required by the international obligation or, if that is no longer possible, an alternative result which is really equivalent.[128]

The practice of the European Commission and Court of Human Rights, in applying the rule of exhaustion of local remedies stated in Article 26 of the European Convention, reveals that the general international law foundations of treaty requirements of exhaustion provided the rationale for conforming the application of the requirement of exhaustion to the principles of international customary law governing injuries to aliens. Because Article 26 characterizes this rule as confirming customary law, the significance of the Strasbourg jurisprudence under this Article[129] extends well beyond the application of the European Convention. The basic principle which the European Court of Human Rights enunciates is that of effectiveness; i.e. international law, to which Article 26 explicitly refers, only requires the exhaustion of remedies 'which are not only available to the persons concerned but are also sufficient, that is to say capable of redressing their complaints'.[130] The jurisprudence of the Human Rights Committee, established under Article 28 of the International Covenant on Civil and Political Rights, has similarly established that exhaustion of local remedies

---

[128] Ibid. at 48 (footnote omitted).

[129] In *De Wilde, Ooms and Versyp Cases*, the European Court of Human Rights stated: 'The rule of exhaustion of domestic remedies, which dispenses States from answering before an international body for their acts before they have had an opportunity to put matters right through their own legal system, is also one of the generally recognised principles of international law to which Article 26 makes specific reference.' 12 Eur. Ct. HR (Ser. A) 29 (1971).

[130] *Stögmüller Case*, 9 Eur. Ct. HR (Ser. A) 42 (1969). See also *De Wilde, Ooms and Versyp Cases*, above n. 129, at 33. The European Commission of Human Rights considered that the requirement of exhaustion of local remedies does not apply where the remedy is ineffective because of 'a well-established case-law of the Federal Constitutional Court'. Eur. Comm'n of Human Rts., Application No. 10282/83, *Joachim Englert* v. *Fed. Rep. Ger.*, Rep. Comm'n at 21 (9 Oct. 1985).

is required only to the extent that local remedies are both effective and available.[131]

Of equal importance is the question of whether Article 26 of the European Convention extends to interstate applications. The

[131] 39 UN GAOR Supp. (No. 40) at 117, UN Doc. A/39/40 (1984). The Committee held that an extraordinary remedy, such as seeking the annulment of a decision of the Ministry of Justice, does not constitute an effective remedy within the meaning of Art. 5(2)(*b*) of the Optional Protocol. Ibid. *Teti Izquierdo* v. *Uruguay*, Communication No. R.18/73, 37 UN GAOR Supp. (No. 40) at 179, 184, UN Doc. A/37/40 (1982).

The Committee also decided that Art. 5(2)(*b*) should be interpreted and applied in accordance with generally accepted principles of international law, as applied in the field of human rights. 'If the State party concerned disputes the contention of the author of a communication that all available domestic remedies have been exhausted, the State party is required to give details of the effective remedies available to the alleged victim. . . . [T]he Committee has deemed insufficient a general description of the rights available to accused persons under the law. . . .' 33 UN GAOR Supp. (No. 40) at 101, UN Doc. A/33/40 (1978). *Millán Sequeira* v. *Uruguay*, Communication No. R.1/6, 35 UN GAOR Supp. (No. 40) at 127, 129, UN Doc. A/35/40 (1980). See also *Pinkney* v. *Canada*, Communication No. R.7/27, 37 UN GAOR Supp. (No. 40) at 101, 108–9, UN Doc. A/37/40 (1982).

In *J.R.T. and the W.G. Party* v. *Canada*, Communication No. 104/1981, the Committee considered that domestic remedies have been exhausted when, 'in view of the ambiguity ensuing from the conflicting time-limits laid down in the laws in question . . . a reasonable effort was indeed made to exhaust domestic remedies in this respect . . .'. 38 UN GAOR Supp. (No. 40) at 231, 236, UN Doc. A/38/40 (1983).

In *A. and S.N.* v. *Norway*, Communication No. 224/1987, 43 UN GAOR Supp. (No. 40) at 246, UN Doc. A/43/40, the authors of the petition did not bring their complaint before Norwegian courts claiming that the practice which they challenged was not in conflict with Norwegian law but with the Political Covenant which, however, would not be applied by a Norwegian Court. Ibid. at 247, 249. The government of Norway argued that 'the Norwegian courts have given considerable weight to international treaties and conventions in the interpretation of domestic rules, even if these instruments have not been formally incorporated into domestic law. It points to several Supreme Court decisions concerning the relationship between international human rights instruments and domestic law and concerning possible conflicts between the International Covenant on Civil and Political Rights and domestic statutes. Although the Supreme Court has, in these cases, ruled that there was no conflict between domestic law and the relevant international instrument, it has expressed clearly that international rules are to be taken into consideration in the interpretation of domestic law. In this context, the State party reiterates that 'the possibility of setting aside a national statute altogether on the grounds of conflict with the Covenant cannot be disregarded' and emphasizes that, in every case in which international human rights instruments have become relevant, the Supreme Court has taken a decision on the issue of conflict between a domestic statute and the international instrument and not refused to test it.' Ibid. at 248. The Committee found, in accordance with Norway's arguments, that exhaustion could not be deemed *a priori* futile. Because local remedies had not been exhausted as required by Art. 5(2)(*b*) of the Optional Protocol, the communication was deemed inadmissible. Ibid. at 250.

meaning of those provisions in human rights treaties that subject applications by states to the requirement of exhaustion is not always clear.[132] However, Article 21(1)(*c*) of the Convention Against Torture and Other Cruel, Inhuman or Degrading Treatment or Punishment, which concerns interstate complaints, states that exhaustion of local remedies which is unlikely to bring effective relief to the victim is not required. This suggests that the requirement of exhaustion applies to state complaints involving individual victims of violations, but not to state complaints alleging widespread violations.

The limits on the application of the exhaustion requirement articulated by the European Court and Commission of Human Rights will have a significant impact on the development of customary human rights law. The European Court has clearly explained that, although exhaustion under Article 26 is required both with regard to individual (Article 25) and interstate (Article 24) applications, the relevance of Article 26 to the latter is limited to cases 'when the applicant State does no more than denounce a violation or violations allegedly suffered by "individuals" whose place, as it were, is taken by the State'.[133] In principle, however, the requirement of exhaustion does not apply

where the applicant State complains of a practice as such, with the aim of preventing its continuation or recurrence, but does not ask the Commission or the Court to give a decision on each of the cases put forward as proof or illustrations of that practice.[134]

Similarly, the European Commission held that exhaustion is not required in the case of the 'five [interrogation] techniques [which] constituted an administrative practice' challenged in *Ireland* v. *United Kingdom*.[135] More generally, exhaustion is not required when an application brought by a state concerns the compatibility with the Convention 'of legislative measures and administrative practices, regardless of any individual or specific injury . . .'.[136]

[132] On the scope of the exhaustion rule, see generally Meron, *The Incidence of the Rule of Exhaustion of Local Remedies*, 35 Brit. YB Int'l L. 83 (1959). On the inapplicability of the exhaustion requirement to 'direct injuries', see *Case Concerning the Air Services Agreement of 27 March 1946*, above n. 56, at 324–5.

[133] *Ireland* v. *United Kingdom*, 25 Eur. Ct. HR (Ser. A) 64 (1978).

[134] Ibid. reprinted in 17 ILM 680, 701 (1978).

[135] Application No. 5310/71, 1972 YB Eur. Conv. Hum. Rts. 92, 246 (Eur. Comm'n of Hum. Rts.)

[136] *Austria* v. *Italy*, Application No. 788/60, 1961 YB Eur. Conv. Hum. Rts.

The requirement of exhaustion as construed by the European Commission and Court thus has not been allowed to obstruct consideration of the most important complaints brought by states, which are those involving patterns of violations.

Finally, let us consider the applicability of exhaustion to human rights claims governed by customary law rather than by treaties. Exhaustion clearly applies to a claim by an alien that a host country has violated his or her international human rights. However, does the requirement of exhaustion apply 'also to determination[s] of the fulfilment or breach of international obligations concerning [citizens]'?[137] Viewed as a principle of customary law which extends to international human rights, exhaustion by an individual constitutes a condition precedent to permitting a state to bring a claim of a person not possessing its nationality before such international fora as the ICJ.[138] In his sixth report[139] Special Rapporteur Ago clearly suggests that customary law generally requires exhaustion even by nationals of the implicated state in observing that 'it would be injudicious to tamper with the existing general scope of the principle in the name of an alleged progressive development . . .'.[140] He argues forcefully that the draft Article on local remedies[141] should address the need for all individuals, not only aliens, to exhaust local remedies:

We see no reason whatsoever why the State should avoid incurring international responsibility by rectifying, necessarily on the initiative of the persons concerned, situations that are incompatible with the result required by international obligations in cases where that result concerns foreigners and not in cases where it concerns nationals. . . . States are already disinclined to allow frequent intervention by other States where the stated purpose of such intervention is the protection of nationals of those other States; they will be even less inclined to allow interventions of this kind where the stated purpose is the protection of their own nationals. It is hence unthinkable that they should consent to forgo, precisely with

116, 152. See also *Greece* v. *United Kingdom*, Application No. 176/56, 1958-9 YB Eur. Conv. Hum. Rts. 182, 184.

[137] [1977] 2 YB Int'l L. Comm'n (pt. 2), above n. 108, at 42.

[138] Assuming, of course, the existence of an adequate jurisdictional basis. See Art. 36(1)-(2) of the Statute of the International Court of Justice.

[139] Ago, above n. 120.

[140] Ago, above n. 120, at 43. The preparatory work of the International Covenant on Civil and Political Rights supports Professor Ago's position. See below n. 145.

[141] For the text of draft Art. 22 as proposed by Ago in his sixth report, see Ago, above n. 120, at 43.

regard to a possible breach of obligations concerning the treatment of their own nationals, the valuable 'screening' afforded by the requirement of prior exhaustion of local remedies. The very fact that the principal international conventions relating to the protection of human rights expressly impose the requirement of prior exhaustion of local remedies rules out the possibility that States might lay aside this shield in the case of obligations of customary nature.[142]

The majority of the Commission preferred, however, not to refer to individuals in general, but only to aliens.[143]

In its *Commentary* on Article 22, the Commission itself took a rather cautious view of the scope of the requirement:

There remains the question of possible extension of the application of the principle of the exhaustion of local remedies from the traditional sphere of the treatment to be accorded to foreign individuals to that of the treatment a State undertakes to accord to *national* individuals. The problem is relatively new because States have only recently recognized—and so far only to a limited degree—that international law lays duties upon them in this regard. The principal conventions relating to the protection of human rights always expressly impose the requirement of prior exhaustion of local remedies by the persons concerned. This is understandable[,] for States are already disinclined to allow frequent intervention by other States when the purpose is to protect nationals of those other States, and they will naturally be even more unwilling when the purpose of the intervention is to protect their own nationals. Without in any way disregarding the existence of a few customary international rules on the subject, and without ruling out the possibility—even the likelihood—that such rules will increase in number, we are bound to conclude that, today, the international obligations of the State in regard to the treatment of its own nationals are almost exclusively of a conventional nature and that, in the instruments imposing them, the requirement of the exhaustion of local remedies by the persons concerned is nearly always expressly stated. That having been said, and without in any way prejudging the possible future development of general international law, the Commission considered that it might be premature at the present stage to extend the requirement stated in article 22, as a general principle, to the determination of the breach of international obligations concerning the treatment to be accorded to nationals.[144]

[142] Ibid. at 40–1 (footnote omitted).

[143] [1977] 1 YB Int'l L. Comm'n at 278, 281, UN Doc. A/CN.4/SER.A/1977 (1978).

[144] [1977] 2 YB Int'l L. Comm'n (pt. 2), above n. 108, at 46 (emphasis in original) (footnote omitted).

Compare the Opinion of the Committee of Jurists presented to the Council of the League of Nations on 24 May 1933, which held that 'it would be mistaking

The articulation of the requirement of exhaustion for victims (regardless of their nationality) of human rights violations in every human rights treaty demonstrates that the framers considered this rule appropriate for the field of human rights, and may also offer some evidence that it was believed to embody customary law.[145] Although the ILC left open the question of the applicability under customary law of the requirement of exhaustion to human rights obligations,[146] this requirement has either already matured into a norm of customary human rights law or, at the very least, is rapidly crystallizing as such a norm. Because the ICJ is both responsive to concerns of state sovereignty and familiar with the rationale for and deep roots of the requirement of exhaustion in international law, it would probably decide that exhaustion reaches violations by a state of the customary human rights of its citizens.

Admittedly, exhaustion makes it easier for states to accept and support human rights obligations *vis-à-vis* their own nationals. Tempered by reasonable limits on the applicability of the rule and by the requirement that available remedies be effective, insistence on exhaustion will not provide those states intent on ignoring their human rights obligations with a simple means to avoid remedying human rights violations. Rather, the requirement will shield those states that genuinely attempt to meet their obligations from unnecessary international scrutiny.

IV. OBLIGATIONS OF MEANS AND OBLIGATIONS OF RESULT

Obligations of means, also known as obligations of conduct, and

[the] significance and purpose to extend [the exhaustion rule], as a general rule applicable in case of doubt, outside the sphere of international responsibility.' 14 LNOJ 813–14 (1933), reprinted in International Protection of Human Rights, above n. 1, at 276, 277. The Committee emphasized that the object of the minorities regime 'is to provide not occasional reparation for certain damage, but the normal and regular operation of a body of rules laying down the status of the minorities'. Ibid. See also above n. 112.

[145] In discussing Art. 2(3) of the International Covenant on Civil and Political Rights, Professor Capotorti observed that 'even if provision was made for recourse to an international authority, it was an established principle of general international law that domestic remedies must be exhausted first.' 18 UN GAOR C.3 (1257th mtg.) para. 14, UN Doc. A/C.3/SR.1257 (1963).

[146] The customary law requirement of exhaustion could apply also to the breach of human rights obligations contained in a treaty which is silent on the question of exhaustion.

obligations of result are described in Articles 20[147] and 21[148] of the ILC's draft articles on state responsibility (part one). The concepts underlying such obligations and the distinction between them derive from contemporary treaties; however, both older treaties and, perhaps to a lesser extent, customary law[149] also contain norms which fit the pattern of obligations of means and obligations of result. Customary law characteristically addresses the object to be achieved, often without specifying the means to be employed in order to achieve it.[150]

The concepts of obligations of means and of result are useful tools for interpreting human rights instruments, analysing the object and scope of specific norms, understanding what constitutes a breach of those norms, and determining the moment when the breach occurs. Characterizing a conventional obligation as one of means or of result naturally depends on the interpretation of the relevant instrument. Such characterization is more difficult with respect to customary law, where one must also ascertain both the existence of the customary norm and the definition of its content.[151]

Obligations of result leave the state with the discretion to choose the means necessary for achieving the desired goal, perhaps as a manifestation of respect for the 'internal freedom of the State'.[152] This latitude does not imply, however, that obligations of means

[147] Art. 20 of the ILC's draft articles on state responsibility (part one) reads as follows: 'There is a breach by a State of an international obligation requiring it to adopt a particular course of conduct when the conduct of that State is not in conformity with that required of it by that obligation.' [1977] 2 YB Int'l L. Comm'n (pt. 2), above n. 108, at 11. See Combacau, *Obligations de résultat et obligations de comportement: quelques questions et pas de réponse*, in Mélanges offerts à Paul Reuter, Le Droit international: Unité et diversité 181 (1981).

[148] Art. 21 of the ILC's draft articles on state responsibility (part one) reads as follows: '1. There is a breach by a State of an international obligation requiring it to achieve, by means of its own choice, a specified result if, by the conduct adopted, the State does not achieve the result required of it by that obligation.

2. When the conduct of the State has created a situation not in conformity with the result required of it by an international obligation, but the obligation allows that this or an equivalent result may nevertheless be achieved by subsequent conduct of the State, there is a breach of the obligation only if the State also fails by its subsequent conduct to achieve the result required of it by that obligation.' [1977] 2 YB Int'l L. Comm'n (pt. 2), above n. 108, at 11.

[149] Ibid. at 13.

[150] Ibid. at 20.

[151] Ibid. at 16.

[152] Ibid. at 19. The ILC points out that initial freedom of choice of means to be used to fulfil the obligation is characteristic of most human rights. Ibid. at 21.

are not guided by a particular goal or result. The ILC has aptly explained that

[w]hat distinguishes the first type of obligation from the second is not that obligations 'of conduct' or 'of means' do not have a particular object or result, but that their object or result must be achieved through action, conduct or means 'specifically determined' by the international obligation itself, which is not true of international obligations 'of result.'[153]

Historically, obligations of means have frequently been required in 'direct relations' between states.[154] To limit states' freedom to choose the measures through which national implementation of human rights is to be attained, and also to enhance the effective implementation of international standards, obligations of means are increasingly stated in contemporary human rights treaties for government–citizen relations. The goal of human rights instruments is not merely to ensure the adoption of stated legislative and administrative measures (*de jure* conformity), but also to ensure the *de facto* conformity of the internal legal system with international human rights. Obligations of means and obligations of result do not compete with, but complement, one another. Joining obligations of result, such as attainment of racial equality, with obligations of means, such as repeal of racist laws and the adoption of those legislative measures necessary to combat racial discrimination, constitutes the most effective method of implementing human rights in a state's internal legal system. Many human rights treaties reflect such an approach. While obligations of result are perhaps more common than obligations of means, international human rights instruments as well as humanitarian law instruments characteristically impose on states obligations both of means[155] and of result.[156]

---

[153] Ibid. at 13–14.   [154] Ibid. at 13.

[155] See e.g. Art. 2(*g*) of the Convention on the Elimination of All Forms of Discrimination against Women, which requires the repeal of all national penal provisions which constitute discrimination against women. See also Art. 10(3) of the International Covenant on Economic, Social and Cultural Rights. In the *Velásquez Rodríguez Case*, the Inter-American Court of Human Rights stated that the duty of the state to investigate acts that violate an individual's rights is an obligation of means or conduct which is not breached merely because the investigation does not produce a satisfactory result, provided that such an investigation is undertaken in a serious manner and not as a mere formality. Judgment of 29 July 1988, Inter-American Court of Human Rights, Ser. C, Decisions and Judgments, No. 4, para. 177. For examples derived from a humanitarian law instrument, see Geneva Convention No. III, Arts. 70–1, which concern 'capture cards' and correspondence of prisoners of war.

[156] See e.g. Art. 2(*e*) of the Convention on the Elimination of All Forms of Discrimination Against Women, which requires states to take all appropriate

A typical provision containing an obligation of means requires the state to enact or to repeal certain types of legislative provisions, or to perform or refrain from performing specified administrative acts. The ILC emphasized that such an obligation is directly breached by a state's failure to conform to the internationally required conduct. Thus, according to the ILC, a state's failure to enact the legislation required by Article 10(3) of the International Covenant on Economic, Social and Cultural Rights, which provides for the duty to make certain types of employment of minors 'prohibited and punishable by law', constitutes a breach of the Covenant, even if no instances of the employment prohibited by the Covenant have occurred and the omission to act has not resulted in harmful consequences.[157]

The breach of an obligation of result, where the state is given varying degrees of discretion to choose the means utilized to attain the required result, presents a different set of considerations. If that result is not achieved, the state may not seek exoneration in the fact that it has undertaken unsuccessful efforts at implementation through, for example, legislative enactments. The ILC suggests that, depending on the content of a norm, a state would not breach international law where, if the legislative and administrative measures first employed by the state to carry out an obligation of result fail, different measures subsequently taken achieve the required result (e.g. a new act of parliament or a decision of a higher administrative or judicial authority).[158] The ILC's *Commmentary* on Article 21 states that when

contrary to the requirements of the international conventions on human rights, the police authorities of a State deny certain persons freedom to

measures to eliminate discrimination against women by any person, organization or enterprise. Another example, Art. 2 of the International Covenant on Civil and Political Rights, contains obligations both of means and of result. Schachter, above n. 17, at 311. For an example derived from a humanitarian law instrument, *see* Geneva Convention No. IV, Art. 29, which provides that the party to the conflict in whose hands protected persons may be is responsible for the treatment accorded to them by its agents, and Art. 27, which states that women shall be protected against any attack on their honour.

[157] [1977] 2 YB Int'l L. Comm'n (pt. 2), above n. 108, at 16.

[158] For example, there is no breach of an international obligation where an administrative authority at first refuses to issue a passport to an individual, in conflict with the obligation of result to grant everyone the freedom to leave one's own country required by Art. 12(2) of the International Covenant on Civil and Political Rights, if the same or a different administrative authority eventually vindicates the right by issuing a passport or an equivalent travel document.

reside in the place of their choice, freedom of association, freedom to profess their religion, or the like . . . the State can still . . . create a situation compatible with the internationally required result, provided that the country has a higher administrative authority or an administrative or civil court, which is competent and materially able to revoke the prohibition of residence or association or to remove the obstacles to the practice of the chosen religion.[159]

Although the content of the norm in question and the factual context provide some guidance, it is still difficult to determine when the breach of an obligation of result becomes definitive.[160] In any event, human rights goals clearly will be frustrated if states delay the implementation of their human rights obligations over an unreasonably long period of time by invoking successive measures aimed at reaching the result required. States should not be permitted unduly to delay meeting required obligations of result. Identification of the moment when a breach occurs can perhaps be facilitated by reference to factors normally resorted to in evaluating whether the exhaustion of local remedies has been unreasonably prolonged. In addition, human rights provisions stating obligations of result must not be interpreted to permit solutions which could frustrate the principal goals of such provisions.[161]

The distinction between obligations of means and obligations of result is a useful interpretative tool but not an end in itself. The ILC has perhaps overburdened the distinction between obligations of means and obligations of result by using it to outline the parameters of the requirement of exhaustion of local remedies.

[159] [1977] 2 YB Int'l L. Comm'n (pt. 2), above n. 108, at 28-9.

[160] Would the enactment of a statute containing a provision which is in conflict with an international obligation of the state constitute a breach of an obligation of result requiring conformity of the national laws with the international norms even before the statute's implementation? Compare *Applicability of the Obligation to Arbitrate under Section 21 of the United Nations Headquarters Agreement of 26 June 1947*, 1988 ICJ 12, 32 (Advisory Opinion of 26 Apr. 1988; ibid. at 52-4 (Schwebel J. sep. op.).

[161] The ILC suggested that a state would not commit a final breach of international law if, having violated the main result called for by Art. 9(1) of the International Covenant on Civil and Political Rights, namely the prohibition of arbitrary deprivation of liberty, it satisfies the 'alternative result' provided for by the 'primary' obligation in question by making reparation under Arts. 9(4)-(5) for the injury suffered. [1977] 2 YB Int'l L. Comm'n (pt. 2), above n. 108, at 22, 29 and n. 104. If the goal of an international human rights instrument is to secure freedom from arbitrary deprivation of liberty, should a state that compensates victims of deprivation of liberty, as required by that instrument, be exonorated from any international responsibility for violating the agreement in the first place?

Article 22 of the ILC's articles on state responsibility (part one)[162] states that the requirement of exhaustion applies to obligations of result, which implicitly bars its applicability to obligations of means. The *Commentary* makes this point *expressis verbis*:

[C]ases . . . exist in which an international obligation concerning the treatment to be accorded to foreign individuals is breached 'immediately' as it were, and in which there can be no question of the exhaustion of local remedies by the individuals concerned before the breach can be established. These are mainly cases in which the international obligation concerning the treatment to be accorded to aliens is an obligation 'of conduct', not 'of result'. For example, if the international obligation specifically requires the State to enact a law on a matter affecting the status of certain aliens in its territory, the mere failure to enact that law is in itself a breach of the obligation. Likewise, if the obligation imposed on a State by a treaty is that the frontier police should take action in favour of a national of another contracting State, the mere failure to take such action constitutes a definitive breach of the obligation. The article is therefore worded so as to make it clear that the requirement of the exhaustion of local remedies applies only to obligations 'of result'.[163]

Although this principle gained support in an important international arbitration,[164] it appears overbroad as articulated by the ILC. Certainly, the requirement of exhaustion of local remedies does not normally apply to a complaint by state A against state B alleging that it suffered a direct injury caused by state B. Cases in which a state itself is the victim of a breach of international law and thus brings a claim in order to secure objectives principally its own should be distinguished from those in which a state, while complaining of such a breach, is merely espousing the cause of its subject.[165] Obviously, because of the principle *par in parem non habet jurisdictionem* the requirement of exhaustion of local remedies does not apply to cases of direct injury caused by one state to another. Exhaustion is not required where local remedies are unavailable or ineffective, or when the complaint challenges an entire pattern of conduct by the state accused of violating international law. Obligations of means typically involve treaty commitments to enact or to annul legislation. Domestic remedies are seldom available for

---

[162] Above n. 110.
[163] [1977] 2 YB Int'l L. Comm'n (pt. 2), above n. 108, at 49–50.
[164] *Case Concerning the Air Services Agreement*, above n. 56, at 324–5.
[165] Meron, above n. 132, at 84–7.

the breach of such commitments. However, their availability in some countries should not be entirely excluded.

In other cases, however, an obligation of means contemplates administrative or police action in favour of an individual. It is entirely possible that the conduct of such authorities, when in breach of the state's international obligations, can be appealed to a higher administrative authority or to a court of law competent to revoke the initial decision. The rationale for excluding such cases from the requirement of exhaustion is not clear. Whether exhaustion is required should not depend on the distinction between obligations of result and obligations of means, but primarily on the availability and effectiveness of remedies, and such considerations as the individual or massive character of acts impugned, and whether the case can be characterized as one of direct injury caused by one state to another. It would, therefore, appear that as regards the question of exhaustion of local remedies, ILC's distinction between obligations of means and obligations of result appears unnecessary and perhaps even misleading.

V. OBLIGATIONS *ERGA OMNES*

Although the concept of obligations *erga omnes* is commonly attributed to the important but ambiguous dictum by the International Court of Justice in its judgment in the *Barcelona Traction* case (to be discussed below in this Section) the antecedents of *Barcelona* must not be overlooked. The concept of customary obligations *erga omnes*, which dates back at least to the Hugo Grotius' discussion (1625) of humanitarian intervention,[166] became prominent in the nineteenth century in the context of protection of minorities. In an undated note (*circa* 1872) addressed to the French Minister of Foreign Affairs, the US Minister in France, referring to the persecution of Jews in Moldo-Walachian principalities, stated:

Although the United States government is not a party to the treaty and had abstained, according to the rule it follows, from intervening, directly or indirectly, in European affairs, the injury . . . is so flagrant and moreover, of such a universal and cosmopolitan nature, that all governments and

---

[166] H. Grotius, De jure belli et pacis, Bk. II, Chapter XXV, VIII, §§1, 2, Whewell's Translation, vol. II, at 438–40, reprinted in Sohn and Buergenthal, above n. 1, at 138–9.

all religious denominations have an interest in demanding that it be redressed.[167]

In its advisory opinion on *Reservations to the Convention on Genocide*, the ICJ laid the foundations for the concept of *erga omnes* by emphasizing that the principles underlying the Genocide Convention were both recognized by civilized nations as binding on states even in the absence of any conventional obligation, and intended 'to be definitely universal in scope'.[168] Eleven years later, the *South West Africa Cases* followed this advisory opinion. In that judgment, the Court rejected South Africa's objection that the dispute brought before the Court did not constitute a dispute under Article 7 of the Mandate because it did not 'affect any material interests of the Applicant States or their nationals'.[169] Instead, the Court interpreted the Mandate as supporting the concept of a 'legal right or interest' which belongs to every member of the League of Nations *ut singulus*. It declared that

the manifest scope and purport of the provisions of . . . Article [7] indicate that the Members of the League were understood to have a legal right or interest in the observance by the Mandatory of its obligations both toward the inhabitants of the Mandated Territory, and toward the League of Nations and its Members.[170]

In a significant separate opinion, Judge Jessup demonstrated that, already in the past, treaties both recognized the legal interests of states in general humanitarian causes and frequently provided procedural means by which states could secure respect for those interests.[171] Examples included protection of minorities, labour rights,[172] and mandates. Judge Jessup emphasized that in none of

---

[167] RGDIP 476 (1903), reprinted in 2 A. Kiss, Répertoire de la pratique française en matière de droit international public 629 (1966) (my translation).

[168] *Reservations to the Convention on Genocide*, 1951 ICJ Rep. 15, 23 (Advisory Opinion of 28 May 1951).

[169] *South West Africa Cases (Preliminary Objections) (Ethiopia* v. *South Africa; Liberia* v. *South Africa),* 1962 ICJ Rep. 319, 343 (Judgment of 21 Dec. 1962).

[170] Ibid.

[171] Ibid. at 425 (Jessup J. sep. op.).

[172] See e.g. Arts. 26–31 of the Constitution of the International Labour Organisation. Art. 26, which has produced considerable practice, permits any member to file a complaint with the ILO alleging that any other member is not observing any ILO Convention which both states have ratified. Under Arts. 26 and 29, such complaints may eventually be referred to a Commission of Inquiry and the ICJ. Constitution of the International Labour Organisation 18–19 (International Labour Office 1988). For the practice of the ILO under Art. 26, see Wolf, *Human*

these cases would it be necessary for a state invoking the jurisdiction of the Court to claim that it had a direct material interest for itself or for its nationals.[173]

In such treaties, and also in human rights treaties such as the International Covenant on Civil and Political Rights, a state's standing to bring an action for a breach is not limited to cases where its own nationals were injured. Common Article 1 of the Geneva Conventions (discussed in Chapter I, Section III, above, and Section IX, below) is clearly a precursor of the concept of obligations *erga omnes*. *Erga omnes* obligations thus clearly have firm foundations in human rights and humanitarian treaties.

In its judgment in the second phase of the *South West Africa Cases*, the Court dismissed the suit, holding that 'the equivalent of an "*actio popularis*", or right resident in any member of a community to take legal action in vindication of a public interest [was] not known to international law' as it then stood.[174] Instead, the Court maintained that the claimant states had to demonstrate a legal right or interest in the suit, i.e. that they were parties to whom the defendant state was 'answerable under the relevant instrument or rule of law'.[175] However, the Court did not completely retreat from its earlier position concerning non-material injury. Rather, it explained that the applicant states' lack of legal rights or interests in the matter was not based on the requirement that any such right or interest must have a material or tangible object, but on the rule that such rights or interests must be clearly vested in parties claiming them 'by some text or instrument, or rule of law . . .'.[176]

Four years later, perhaps in response to the negative reaction triggered by its second phase decision in the *South West Africa Cases*,[177] the Court in *Barcelona Traction* declared the right of any state to vindicate *erga omnes* obligations, asserting that

Rights and the International Labour Organisation, in 2 Human Rights in International Law, above n. 14, at 273, 288–90; Valticos, *Les commissions d'enquête de l'Organisation Internationale du Travail*, 91 Rev. gén. droit int'l pub. 847, 853–5 (1987).

[173] 1962 ICJ Rep. at 430.

[174] *South West Africa Cases* (*Second Phase*) (*Ethiopia* v. *South Africa; Liberia* v. *South Africa*), 1966 ICJ Rep. 6, 47 (Judgment of 18 July 1966).

[175] Ibid. at 34.

[176] Ibid. at 32. Professor Henkin observes that the majority of the ICJ implied that 'had the petitioners been parties to the mandate agreement they would have had a legal interest to enforce it . . .'. Henkin, *Human Rights and "Domestic Jurisdiction"*, in Human Rights, International Law and the Helsinki Accord 21, 33 (T. Buergenthal ed. 1977).

[177] Schachter, *International Law in Theory and Practice*, 178 Recueil des cours 341 (1982-V).

[w]hen a State admits into its territory foreign investments or foreign nationals, whether natural or juristic persons, it is bound to extend to them the protection of the law and assumes obligations concerning the treatment to be afforded them. These obligations, however, are neither absolute nor unqualified. In particular, an essential distinction should be drawn between the obligations of a State towards the international community as a whole, and those arising vis-à-vis another State in the field of diplomatic protection. By their very nature the former are the concern of all States. In view of the importance of the rights involved, all States can be held to have a legal interest in their protection; they are obligations *erga omnes*.

34. Such obligations derive, for example, in contemporary international law, from the outlawing of acts of aggression, and of genocide, as also from the principles and rules concerning the basic rights of the human person, including protection from slavery and racial discrimination. Some of the corresponding rights of protection have entered into the body of general international law . . . others are conferred by international instruments of a universal or quasi-universal character.[178]

Some international obligations are thus so basic that they run equally to all other states, and every state has the right to help protect the corresponding rights. When a state breaches an obligation *erga omnes*, it injures every state, including those not specially affected. As a victim of a violation of the international legal order, every state is therefore competent to bring actions against the breaching state.

The ILC subsequently attempted to clarify the Court's pronouncement. Although in international law a correlation between the obligation of one state and the 'subjective right' of another always exists, the ILC found that 'this relationship may extend in various forms to States other than the State directly injured if the international obligation breached is one of those linking the State, not to a particular State, but to a group of States or to all States members of the international community.'[179] When an obligation *erga omnes*, in whose fulfilment all states have a 'legal interest', is breached, the breaching state's responsibility is engaged *vis-à-vis* all of the other members of the international community. Therefore, 'every State must be considered justified in invoking—probably

---

[178] *Barcelona Traction, Light and Power Co., Ltd.* (*Belg.* v. *Spain*), 1970 ICJ Rep. 3, 32 (Judgment of 5 Feb.).

[179] [1976] 2 YB Int'l L. Comm'n (pt. 2) at 76, UN Doc. A/CN.4/ SER.A/1976/Add.1 (Part 2) (1977).

through judicial channels—the responsibility of the State committing the internationally wrongful act.'[180] Claims brought before the ICJ under Article 36(1) or 36(2) of the ICJ's Statute by states not directly affected by breaches are therefore based on the 'legal interest' or 'legal right' of all states in the observance of certain fundamental norms of international law.

Even with this clarification by the ILC, the Court's pronouncement leaves some questions unanswered. For example, are 'basic rights of the human person', which give rise to obligations *erga omnes*, synonymous with human rights *tout court*, or are the former limited to those rights which are intimately associated with the human person and human dignity and are generally accepted as legal norms, such as protection from slavery and racial discrimination? Moreover, the distinction between 'basic rights of the human person' and 'ordinary' human rights is not self-evident. *Erga omnes* status is a consequence, not a cause, of a right's fundamental character. The *erga omnes* criterion is therefore unhelpful to the conceptually difficult[181] and politically contentious[182] process of characterizing rights as fundamental. If the Court intended to set the basic rights of the human person apart from other human rights, categorizing certain human rights as basic rights of the human person would depend on their acceptance as general international law or on their incorporation into universal or quasi-universal instruments.

The opinion in *Barcelona Traction* contains an indication that the Court perhaps did not intend to bestow *erga omnes* character upon all human rights, but only on rights which have matured into customary or general law of nations. The Court emphasized that, in contrast to the European Convention, 'which entitles each State which is a party to the Convention to lodge a complaint against any other contracting State for violation of the Convention, irrespective of the nationality of the victim',[183] 'on the universal level, the instruments which embody human rights do not confer on States the capacity to protect the victims of infringements of

[180] Ibid. at 99.

[181] Difficulties arising in attempts to distinguish between fundamental human rights and ordinary human rights are discussed in T. Meron, above n. 33, at 173–89.

[182] [1983] 1 YB Int'l L. Comm'n 142, UN Doc. A/CN.4/SER.A/1983 (1984) (remarks of Mr McCaffrey).

[183] *Barcelona Traction*, 1970 ICJ Rep. at 47.

such rights irrespective of their nationality'.[184] The Court thus seemingly suggests that, while basic rights of the human person give rise to obligations *erga omnes* and can be protected by states regardless of the victim's nationality, other human rights or ordinary human rights under some of the agreements embodying such rights can be espoused only by the victim's state of nationality. Perhaps the Court also intended to intimate that 'general human rights agreements do not contemplate diplomatic protection by one state party on behalf of an individual victim of a violation by another state party', at least where the victim was not a national of the protecting state.[185]

The reference by the Court to protection by a state which depends upon the victim's nationality may cause some confusion. The concept of the diplomatic protection of citizens is largely foreign to international human rights agreements. Such agreements often recognize the entirely different right of states parties to bring interstate complaints against perpetrators of human rights violations irrespective of the nationality of the individual victims[186] and of whether the violation resulted in material injury.

The contrast drawn by the Court between a state's right to bring an action based on the breach of a non-national's human rights under universal systems of human rights protections and that right under regional systems is flawed. Thus, Article 41 of the International Covenant on Civil and Political Rights, which concerns interstate complaints by a state party alleging that another state party is not fulfilling its obligations under the Covenant, does not refer to the nationality of the victims.

This dictum in *Barcelona Traction* will obviously create confusion when the need arises to characterize human rights as either ordinary or basic. Most observers would probably agree that protecting such rights as the right to life from arbitrary deprivation and protecting the human person from torture, egregious racial discrimination, and prolonged arbitrary detention are fundamental rights. Most observers would also agree that the small, irreducible core of rights that are deemed non-derogable under the International Covenant

---

[184] Ibid.
[185] Restatement, above n. 1, § 703, Reporters' note 2.
[186] Ibid. See Section I, above. While most human rights equally protect nationals and aliens, some human rights protect either nationals or aliens, but not both. See discussion, above text accompanying and preceding n. 42.

on Civil and Political Rights and the European and American Conventions on Human Rights constitute fundamental, and perhaps even peremptory, norms of international law. But that irreducible core consists of only four rights: the right to life and the prohibitions of slavery, torture, and retroactive penal measures. Although a consensus on additional core rights will no doubt evolve, it has not yet clearly emerged. While some observers feel that due process rights are fundamental and indispensable for ensuring all other rights, others feel that the rights to food and other basic needs take precedence over due process. Superficially attractive formulae, such as designating those rights linked to the physical and mental well-being of the human person as fundamental, are not helpful because these concepts involve clusters of rights whose components each require scrutiny.

One point is clear, however. The Court's reference to general international law and to universal or quasi-universal agreements suggests that a fundamental right must be firmly established in general international law, and that mere moral claims or policy goals, important as these may be, do not qualify as *erga omnes* obligations.

The examples of basic human rights mentioned by the Court, protection from slavery and racial discrimination, may well reflect the Court's conception of *jus cogens* norms which it did not explicitly articulate. *Erga omnes* rights are not necessarily identical with *jus cogens* rights, however; despite a degree of overlap, the latter set of rights is narrower than the former. The examples given by the Court also appear to indicate that *erga omnes* obligations concern significant and gross violations, rather than individual or sporadic breaches.

The impact of the *erga omnes* principle is felt far beyond statements that refer to it in terms. The principle underlies the assertions by states of the right, rooted in the general interest of the international community, to demand the observance of human rights by other states. Following the judgment in *Barcelona Traction*, and perhaps under its influence, there has been a growing acceptance in contemporary international law of the principle that, in addition to the increasing number of human rights agreements granting each state party *locus standi* against the other states parties regardless of the nationality of the victims (conventional *erga omnes*), all states have a legitimate interest in, and the right to protest against, significant violations of customary human rights regardless of the nationality of the victims (customary *erga omnes*). It is now generally accepted that, on the basis of the human rights provisions of the Charter, states not directly affected by a breach of human rights have the right both to make representations directly to the state accused of such violations, and to complain before the organs of the United Nations or other international organizations. In a significant statement, the UN Assistant Secretary-General for Human Rights, Dr Kurt Herndl, emphasized that the United Nations has consolidated the principle that human rights are an international concern that the international community is entitled to discuss.[187] The general principle establishing international accountability and the right to censure can thus be regarded as settled law.[188]

This crystallization of the *erga omnes* character of human rights, grounded in Articles 55 and 56 of the UN Charter, is progressing despite the uncertainty voiced by some commentators concerning whether a state not directly involved in a matter by, for example, the need to protect its nationals may *ut singulus* bring an action for reparation against the violating state.[189] While questions persist concerning which remedies such a state can demand while acting only to vindicate the general international legal order, the *locus standi* of a state not specially affected is seldom questioned in principle, if the tribunal involved has the necessary jurisdiction *ratione personae* and *ratione materiae*.

The question of standing is sometimes intertwined with that of material injury or damage.[190] Sinclair, a critic of the concept of obligations *erga omnes*, observed:

[I]n the broadest of all possible senses, it could be said that every State had an interest in all rules of international law being observed. The real

---

[187] UN Press Release No. HR/1733 at 2 (Geneva, 6 Aug. 1985).

[188] See generally Schachter, *International Law Implications of U.S. Human Rights Policies*, 24 NYL Sch. L. Rev. 63, 66–74 (1978); Schachter, above n. 177, at 200. In 1987, the government of the United Kingdom, for example, stated that it deplored all human rights violations throughout the world and that '[i]n recent years we have made an increasing number of joint *démarches* [with our partners in the European Community] in third countries and have expressed our joint concern in common statements at the UN and in the CSCE.' Reprinted in 58 Brit. YB Int'l L. 534–5 (1987).

[189] I. Sinclair, The Vienna Convention on the Law of Treaties 213 (2nd edn. 1984); Schachter, above n. 177, at 196–9, 341–2.

[190] See Section VI, below.

question, however, was whether a State was qualified to present itself as an injured State in respect of damage not inflicted upon itself or any of its nationals. . . . He personally remained unconvinced that the materials at the Commission's disposal were sufficient to justify the confident assertion that the concept of the injured State could be dispensed with in the case of a breach of an obligation *erga omnes* and that every State without exception could be regarded as having an equal legal interest in the matter.[191]

However, Sinclair does not challenge the right of a state to pursue claims of persons other than its nationals under multilateral human rights treaties. Standing to pursue interstate complaints of human rights violations is explicitly confirmed in many human rights treaties without any requirement of proof of material damage. Standing to ensure respect for customary human rights (*erga omnes* in *lex generalis*) is conceptually different from standing under human rights treaties: *ratione personae*, the latter is limited to the parties, and *ratione materiae*, primarily to the norms stated in the treaty in question. However, the practical differences between the two decrease as the number of parties to widely accepted treaties covering a broad spectrum of human rights increases.

Significantly, the ILC has not included the requirement of material damage in the list of the elements of an internationally wrongful act stated in Article 3 of its draft articles on state responsibility (part one). Even some of the scholars who believe that claims can normally be pursued only when the claimant state's legal interests were materially damaged agree that human rights norms and obligations *erga omnes* constitute exceptions to the rule.[192]

The most interesting feature of the development of the law since *Barcelona Traction* is that the growing acceptance of the *erga omnes* character of human rights has not been restricted to the basic rights of the human person. The US Restatement played a crucial role in this development. Section 703(2) of the Restatement provides that '[a]ny state may pursue international remedies against any other state for a violation of the customary international law of human rights.'[193] The Reporters elaborated on this section as follows:

---

[191] [1983] 1 YB Int'l L. Comm'n, above n. 182, at 130.

[192] See e.g. Schachter, above n. 177, at 193.

[193] Restatement, above n. 1. Elsewhere (§ 901, Reporters' note 1), the Reporters observe that '[t]he obligation of a state to make reparation for a violation of international law . . . may run to a state otherwise entitled to present a claim based

The customary law of human rights . . . protects individuals subject to each state's jurisdiction, and the international obligation runs equally to all other states, with no state a victim of the violation more than any other. Any state, therefore, may make a claim against the violating state.[194]

It should, however, be noted that the Restatement (discussed in Chapter II, Section I, above) defines as breaches of customary human rights only breaches committed as state policy, thus including significant breaches and excluding sporadic violations.

The *erga omnes* character of human rights obligations contained in a treaty is also suggested by Article 5(d)(iv) of the draft articles on state responsibility (part two) proposed by the ILC's Special Rapporteur, Professor Riphagen, which states:

For the purposes of the present articles 'injured State' means . . .

(d) if the internationally wrongful act constitutes a breach of an obligation imposed by a multilateral treaty, a State party to that treaty, if it is established that . . .

(iv) the obligation was stipulated for the protection of individual persons, irrespective of their nationality.[195]

The ILC's report to the UN General Assembly furthered the consolidation of the concept of conventional *erga omnes* obligations by emphasizing that, in the situations mentioned in Article 5(d)(iv),

on the violation, either because the obligation is *erga omnes* . . . or because the obligation runs to all parties of a multilateral agreement, such as a human rights convention.'

[194] Ibid. at § 703(2), Reporters' note 3. 'Remedies available to states parties under international human rights agreements . . . and remedies available to all states for violation by any state of the customary law of human rights . . . do not depend on the nationality of the individual victim.' § 703, Reporters' note 4. Contra Graefrath, *Human Rights and International Cooperation: 10 Years of Experience in the Human Rights Committee*, 14 GDR Committee for Human Rights Bulletin No. 1 at 5, 16–17 (1988) (who asserts that less grave violations than those mentioned in *Barcelona Traction* have no *erga omnes* effects).

[195] [1985] 2 YB Int'l L. Comm'n (pt. 2) at 20 n. 66, UN Doc. A/CN.4/SER.A/1985/Add.1 (Part 2) (1986); [1984] 2 YB Int'l L. Comm'n (pt. 2) at 100 n. 322, UN Doc. A/CN.4/SER.A/1984/Add.1 (Part 2) (1985). Although Sinclair argued that the nationality of claims rule was highly relevant for the definition of the 'injured state' 'since the phrase "irrespective of their nationality" would seem to deny any such rule in the case of a breach of an obligation stipulated in a multilateral treaty for the protection of individual persons', [1984] 1 YB Int'l L. Comm'n 303–4, UN Doc. A/CN.4/SER.A/1984 (1985), Riphagen insisted that, with regard to fundamental human rights, 'the injured State could not be determined on the basis of nationality.' Ibid. at 318.

'no *particular* State party to the treaty could be considered to be the "injured" State.'[196]

While the 1984 text of the Riphagen draft of Article 5(d)(iv) concerned only obligations imposed by treaties, Riphagen did not deny the existence of customary obligations in the field of human rights whose violation injures all states. Riphagen perhaps believed that those human rights obligations overlap with obligations whose violation constitutes an international crime. Article 5(e) proposed by Riphagen stated that if the internationally wrongful act constitutes an international crime (such as 'serious breach on a widespread scale of an international obligation of essential importance for safeguarding the human being') (Article 19(2)(*c*) of the ILC's draft articles on state responsibility (part one)), all other states are injured. In any event, the ILC amended Riphagen's article in 1985 to clarify that the principle stated in it also applied to international customary law.[197] The amended Article 5(2)(*e*)(iii), as provisionally adopted by the ILC, defined 'injured State' as follows:

(e) if the right infringed by the act of a State arises from a multilateral treaty or from a rule of customary international law, any other State party to the multilateral treaty or bound by the relevant rule of customary international law, if it is established that . . .
(iii) the right has been created or is established for the protection of human rights and fundamental freedoms. . . .[198]

In its *Commentary* on this provision, the ILC explained that '[t]he interests protected by such provisions are not allocatable to a particular State. Hence the necessity to consider in the first instance every other State party to the multilateral convention, or bound by the relevant rule of customary law, as an injured State.'[199] Strikingly, the distinction between basic rights of the human person and ordinary human rights is addressed neither in the Restatement nor in the ILC's draft articles.[200]

[196] [1984] 2 YB Int'l L. Comm'n (pt. 2), above n. 195, at 102 (emphasis in original).
[197] UN Doc. A/CN.4/389 (1985), reprinted in [1985] 2 YB Int'l L. Comm'n (pt. 1) 3, 5, UN Doc. A/CN.4/SER.A/1985/Add.1 (Part 1) (1986).
[198] [1985] 2 YB Int'l L. Comm'n (pt. 2), above n. 195, at 25. The *Commentary* explained that '[t]he term "human rights and fundamental freedoms" is here used in the sense which is current in present-day international relations.' Ibid. at 27.
[199] Ibid. at 27.
[200] However, the ILC has entered a caveat, cautioning that the provision 'cannot and does not prejudge the question to what extent "primary" rules of international law, either customary or conventional, impose obligations on States and create or

Scholarly writings point in the same direction. In a thoughtful study of international accountability and the right to censure human rights violations, Professor Schachter does not distinguish between the basic rights of the human person and human rights *tout court*. He rightly notes that, in the absence of their own specific interests, states tend to focus on censuring violations of 'fundamental norm[s] of humanity'.[201] However, it is unclear whether this tendency appears to reflect foreign policy considerations and an assessment of the significance of the breach rather than a formal distinction between fundamental and ordinary rights, or between systematic and individual violations.

In sum, both international practice and scholarly opinion seem to have moved well beyond the *erga omnes* dictum of *Barcelona Traction*. The distinction between basic human rights and human rights *tout court*, as regards their *erga omnes* character, can no longer be regarded as settled law. The emerging desuetude of the confusing distinction in *Barcelona Traction* between basic rights and other human rights, and the growing recognition of the *erga omnes* character of all human rights, greatly enhance the prospects of acceptance of complaints brought by any state to protect such rights. In my opinion, contemporary international law permits states, whether or not directly affected, to bring at least some actions involving human rights violations before competent international judicial or quasi-judicial organs.

It is, however, less clear whether this right of states not directly affected is limited to gross and systematic violations. Because of scarcity of practice, the customary law on this point is not yet settled. Human rights treaties allow states not directly affected to bring claims even for sporadic violations of human rights. Sooner or later, this approach, increasingly supported by *opinio juris*, will be clearly recognized with regard to breaches of customary human

establish rights of States for the protection of human rights and fundamental freedoms'. Ibid.

[201] Schachter, *International Law Implications of U.S. Human Rights Policies*, above n. 188, at 70. Principle 2 of the Principles for the International Law of the Future, prepared by a private group of experts, emphasized the duty of each state to 'treat its own population in a way which will not violate the dictates of humanity and justice or shock the conscience of mankind'. 38 AJIL Supp. 72, 74 (1944). These terms can be traced to the preambular Martens clause to (Hague) Convention (No. IV) Respecting the Laws and Customs of War on Land, with Annex of Regulations, 18 Oct. 1907, 36 Stat. 2277, TS No. 539. See Meron, *On the Inadequate Reach of Humanitarian and Human Rights Law and the Need for a New Instrument*,

rights. It is significant that, as discussed in Chapter II, Section I, the Concluding Document of the Vienna Meeting 1986 of Representatives of the Participating States of the Conference on Security and Co-operation in Europe allows participating states to bring up in bilateral talks with other participating states both situations *and* specific cases concerning respect for human rights, with a view to resolving them. Although states not directly affected still hesitate to bring claims against those which violate human rights, the growing recognition of the competence of all states to bring such actions has a symbolic significance highlighting the deeply rooted community values attached to the universal protection of human rights.[202] It is hoped that this recognition will also help to deter states from committing egregious violations of human rights.

Fears have been expressed in some quarters that the concept of obligations *erga omnes* and the growing recognition in international law of a right akin to *actio popularis* will be abused by states to initiate politically motivated actions against other states, thereby prompting a greater reluctance by states to accept the compulsory jurisdiction of the ICJ and intensifying the tendency of states to enter reservations to such acceptance.[203] However, such fears have not been borne out by post-*Barcelona Traction* experience. In most cases, complaints of human rights violations have been raised with prudence through bilateral diplomatic channels, brought before the organs of the United Nations and other international organizations, and submitted by states parties to regional human rights treaties before regional courts and commissions. In some cases, states have complained of treatment of persons with whom they have a special ethnic or religious link. Such complaints are based on a special relationship of a state with a particular group in another state

77 AJIL 589, 593, and n. 24 (1983).

[202] For an example of invocation of the *erga omnes* principle in a recent UN report, see P. Kooijmans, Torture and other Cruel, Inhuman or Degrading Treatment or Punishment, UN Doc. E/CN.4/1987/13 at 14–15: '[A]ll States have a legal interest in compliance with the prohibition of torture . . . the transgressor . . . is responsible to the international community as a whole and, in principle, other States may bring a claim as representatives of that community.'

The emerging state practice involving obligations *erga omnes* in the judicial and extra-judicial arenas is discussed in Tanzi, *Is Damage a Distinct Condition for the Existence of an Internationally Wrongful Act?*, in United Nations Codification of State Responsibility 1, 33, and nn. 118–19 (M. Spinedi and B. Simma eds. 1987).

[203] See e.g. Schachter, above n. 177, at 201, 343.

rather than on the substance of a particular norm. In some cases
states not directly affected have responded to violations by taking
countermeasures (discussed in Section XI, below) against states
which egregiously violate the human rights of their own citizens.
For example, the United States has restricted bilateral economic
or military aid to, or suspended services under aviation agreements
with, states alleged to have committed such breaches (Section XI,
below).

VI. JUDICIAL REMEDIES: IS DAMAGE A CONDITION FOR STATE RESPONSIBILITY?

The question of whether damage is a constituent element of a
breach of an international human right (Section V, above) merits
a more detailed examination. Few tasks have posed greater difficulty
than that of identifying the appropriate judicial remedies which a
state may request in bringing an action to vindicate violations of
the human rights of persons who are not its nationals. Analogizing
human rights law to the international law governing injuries to
aliens exacerbates these difficulties. In most cases, under alien
injuries law, the Vattelian theory that '[w]hoever uses a citizen ill,
indirectly offends the state'[204] is augmented to encompass actual
material injuries suffered by the citizen of the claimant state and
sometimes elements of direct injury (e.g. the breach of a treaty)
caused by the defendant state to the claimant state.

Even in the absence of material damage, international law has
always recognized that states have standing to sue for non-material
or moral damage in cases involving, *inter alia*, offences to representatives, the flag, and the dignity, sovereignty, and territorial
integrity of the state. Such breaches have resulted in appropriate
reparation, such as 'satisfaction' in the form of apologies, punishment of responsible officials, declaratory judgments[205] (i.e. an
adjudication of the rights of the litigants even when no consequential

[204] E. de Vattel, The Law of Nations (1758), Bk. 2, sec. 71, at 161 (J. Chitty ed. 1852).
[205] The ICJ considered its declaration that the United Kingdom violated Albanian sovereignty to constitute appropriate satisfaction for Albania in the *Corfu Channel* case (*UK* v. *Alb.*), 1949 ICJ Rep. 4, 35-6 (Judgment of 9 Apr.). See also discussion of declaratory judgments in Section I, above.

relief is awarded) and sometimes injunctive relief, monetary compensation,[206] or a combination of several of these remedies.

The situation is relatively straightforward in cases where individuals who are victims of human rights violations have direct access to international tribunals such as the European Commission of Human Rights (Article 25 of the European Convention on Human Rights) and an indirect access to the Court through the Commission or through a state (Article 48 of the Convention). In a case originally introduced before the Commission by an individual, the Court can award monetary compensation and other appropriate remedies such as declaratory judgments where material or moral damage exists.[207] In a case where such damage has not been claimed or established, the Court can grant declaratory judgments (a finding that a breach of the European Convention has occurred).[208] The reparation granted by the Court is measured on the basis of the material or moral damage suffered by the individual. Where a case originally introduced by an individual is brought before the Court by the Commission, perhaps the Commission, as a collective organ of states parties to the European Convention, can be regarded as acting on behalf of all of them against the wrongdoing state. Should one still insist on the 'fiction' that the damage suffered by an individual is suffered by a state, the reparation which is awarded to the victim of the violation can perhaps be deemed satisfaction given to all the other states parties.

I now consider the question of damage in cases where reparation

---

[206] The arbitral tribunal in the 1933 '*I'm Alone*' case ordered the US government to acknowledge the illegality of its conduct, apologize to the government of Canada, and pay 'a material amend'. 3 UNRIAA 1609, 1618 (1949).

[207] See e.g. *Milasi Case*, 119 Eur. Ct. HR (Ser. A), 48 (1987) (a finding of a breach and award of monetary compensation for non-pecuniary damage); *De Cubber Case*, 124 Eur. Ct. HR (Ser. A), 19 (1987) (a finding of monetary compensation for non-pecuniary damage); *Bagetta Case*, 119 Eur. Ct. HR (Ser. A), 34–5 (1987) (a finding of a breach and award of monetary compensation for both material and non-material damage); *Capuano Case*, 119 Eur. Ct. HR (Ser. A), 15 (1987) (a finding of a breach and award of monetary compensation for both material and non-material damage); *Unterpertinger Case*, 110 Eur. Ct. HR (Ser. A), 15–16 (1986) (a finding of a breach and award of monetary compensation for both material and non-material damage). See also above n. 25 and accompanying text.

[208] See e.g. *Deumeland Case*, 100 Eur. Ct. HR (Ser. A), 30–1 (1986) (the Court considered its finding of a breach to constitute adequate just satisfaction). In the interstate case of *Ireland* v. *United Kingdom*, the claimant government made it clear that the claim's object was not to obtain compensation for any individual victim of a breach of the Convention. In what was in effect a declaratory judgment, the Court found the United Kingdom to be in breach of the Convention. 1978 YB

is awarded after a claim originally presented by one state party against another in accordance with Articles 24 and 48 of the European Convention, or even outside the framework of that Convention. Under the European Convention, interstate claims for reparation of human rights violations may be submitted either by the national state of the victim of the violation (in terms of damage, this case would present the simplest situation), or by another state party. Where a state seeks to vindicate the human rights of non-nationals through interstate claims, the state has suffered neither material nor moral damage to its protected interests or national sovereignty. The moral or material injury suffered by the individual involved must therefore serve as a yardstick for reparation, just as in the case originating with the claim submitted to the Commission by the victim himself. The reparation can be regarded as satisfying, at the same time, the interstate claim and the victim's grievance.

In *Barcelona Traction* the Court recognized that all states have 'a legal interest in [the] protection [of] obligations *erga omnes*',[209] which are the concern of all states, without straining to fit the fiction in the Vattelian theory that a breach of a person's basic human rights generates a claim *belonging* to the protecting state which is not directly affected. In interpreting *Barcelona Traction*'s *erga omnes* dictum, the ILC has emphasized, going perhaps further than the Court, that with regard to obligations *erga omnes* there exists a correlation between the obligation of one state and the 'subjective' right of another (discussed in Section V, above).

This interpretation, while consistent with the thesis that in the classical international law every obligation has a corresponding, 'subjective' right, appears strained with regard to international human rights or humanitarian norms. There is nothing unreasonable in a state's assertion that it is entitled to vindicate such basic community values as human rights and to demand remedies for their breaches,[210] without resorting to the concept of a 'subjective right', which is rather artificial in the human rights context.

The concept of conventional human rights as involving objective,

Eur. Conv. Hum. Rts. 606–10.

[209] *Barcelona Traction*, 1970 ICJ Rep. at 32.

[210] '[I]t is essential, in a dispute between states, to take into account not only the injuries suffered . . . but also the importance of the questions of principle arising from the alleged breach.' *Case Concerning the Air Services Agreement*, above n. 56, at 338.

rather than reciprocal obligations, whose breach constitutes a violation of international public order, is reflected in the established jurisprudence of the organs of the European Convention on Human Rights. The European Commission of Human Rights has departed from the theory that human rights obligations have corresponding 'subjective' rights. It explicitly declared that, when a state party to the European Convention brings an action claiming a violation of the Convention, it is not enforcing its own rights, or the rights of its nationals, but vindicating the 'public order of Europe':[211]

[I]n becoming a Party to the Convention, a State undertakes, vis-à-vis the other High Contracting Parties, to secure the rights and freedoms defined in Section I to every person within its jurisdiction, regardless of his or her nationality or status . . . it undertakes to secure these rights and freedoms not only to its own nationals and those of other High Contracting Parties but also to nationals of States not parties to the Convention and to stateless persons. . . .

The obligations undertaken by the High Contracting Parties in the Convention are essentially of an objective character, being designed rather to protect the fundamental rights of individual human beings from infringement by any of the High Contracting Parties than to create subjective and reciprocal rights for the High Contracting Parties themselves; . . .

the objective character of the engagements undertaken by the High Contracting Parties similarly appears in the machinery provided in the Convention to guarantee their observance; [and] . . .

Article 24 provides that 'any High Contracting Party may refer to the Commission, through the Secretary-General of the Council of Europe, any alleged breach of the provisions of the Convention by another High Contracting Party'; . . . therefore, the High Contracting Parties have empowered any one of their number to bring before the Commission any alleged breach of the Convention, regardless of whether the victims of the alleged breach are nationals of the applicant State or whether the alleged breach otherwise particularly effects the interests of the applicant State. . . .

It [thus] follows that a High Contracting Party, when it refers an alleged breach of the Convention to the Commission under Article 24, is not to be regarded as exercising a right of action for the purpose of enforcing

---

[211] *Austria* v. *Italy*, Application No. 788/60, [1961] YB Eur. Conv. on Hum. Rts. 116. See also *Denmark, Norway, Sweden, and Netherlands* v. *Greece*, Application Nos. 3321/67, 3322/67, 3323/67 and 3344/67, [1968] YB Eur. Conv. on Hum. Rts. 730, 762-4; *The Effect of Reservations on the Entry into Force of the American Convention* (*Arts. 74 and 75*), Advisory Opinion OC-2/82 of 24 Sept. 1982, Inter-American Court of Human Rights, Ser. A, Judgments and Opinions, No. 2, at paras. 27-9 (1982).

its own rights, but rather as bringing before the Commission an alleged violation of the public order of Europe. . . .[212]

There is no reason why the same principle should not govern customary human rights. Such an approach would be consistent with the language of *Barcelona Traction*.

The selection of judicial remedies is particularly difficult in interstate claims in which a state not directly concerned alleges a whole pattern of violations of human rights of persons who are not its citizens. Neither the damage suffered by the victims, nor the injury suffered by the claimant state as a victim of a violation of norms of the international legal order, are easily quantifiable. Monetary compensation, which is so important in cases involving sporadic or individual violations of human rights, thus is not the most appropriate remedy for systematic violations. Instead, the remedy should be selected from among the many alternatives recognized by international law.[213]

Because *Barcelona Traction* seeks to ensure respect for certain fundamental norms of the international legal order by conferring a protective capacity upon all states, the Court's opinion provides a strong rationale for the right to request a declaratory judgment, accompanied where appropriate by an injunction. Declaratory relief, preferably coupled with injunctive relief, flows naturally from the objective character of human rights obligations. In tandem these remedies are also the most appropriate response to patterns of human rights violations, where the principal goal is to halt existing violations and to ensure the future observance of human rights. This is demonstrated by the practice of the European

[212] *Austria* v. *Italy*, above n. 211, at 140.
[213] See Restatement, above n. 1, § 901, comments *c–d*.
Draft Art. 6 proposed by Special Rapporteur Riphagen in his fifth report is of interest here. It reads as follows:
'1. The injured State may require the State which has committed an internationally wrongful act to: (*a*) discontinue the act, release and return the persons and objects held through such act, and prevent continuing effects of such act; and (*b*) apply such remedies as are provided for in its internal law; and (*c*) subject to article 7, re-establish the situation as it existed before the act; and (*d*) provide appropriate guarantees against repetition of the act.
2. To the extent that it is materially impossible to act in conformity with paragraph 1(*c*), the injured State may require the State which has committed the internationally wrongful act to pay to it a sum of money corresponding to the value which a re-establishment of the situation as it existed before the breach would bear.'
[1984] 2 YB Int'l L. Comm'n (pt. 1) at 3, UN Doc. A/CN.4/SER.A/1984/Add.1 (Part 1) (1986).

Commission and Court of Human Rights which, in considering interstate applications, routinely find that breaches of the Convention have occurred.[214] Such interstate applications

will most likely be concerned with a general practice, specific laws, a system or pattern of treatment rather than with one individual case. That, however, is only the result of practical considerations whereby States will take up an issue under Art. 24 only if specific reasons of a more general nature exist. As the application Austria v. Italy shows these reasons may sometimes exist where only one individual case is in issue.[215]

A clear declaration that a government's conduct violates human rights sensitizes national and international public opinion, thus bringing pressure to bear on the government to conform its conduct to international standards.

A request for a declaratory judgment has the additional advantage of obviating the requirement of proof that the breach proximately caused the damage suffered. Requiring proof of causation may divert attention from the tasks of establishing and stopping gross violations of human rights to that of demonstrating the material damage suffered by one individual victim. Judge Fitzmaurice aptly described this aspect of declaratory awards:

By not claiming any compensation, the Applicant State placed itself in a position in which, had the Court proceeded to the merits, the Applicant could have obtained a judgment in its favour merely by establishing that breaches of the Trust Agreement had been committed, without having to establish, as it would otherwise have had to do (i.e. if reparation had been claimed) that these breaches were the actual and proximate cause of the damage alleged to have been suffered. . . . The result is that . . . the Court . . . would have found itself in the position of being obliged to give judgment against the Respondent State, *irrespective* of whether these irregularities had been the cause of the damage complained of.[216]

Judge Fitzmaurice believes that international tribunals should not apportion blame *in vacuo*. However, he agrees that the request for

---

[214] See e.g. *Ireland* v. *United Kingdom*, [1978] YB Eur. Conv. HR 602, 604-10 (Eur. Ct. HR). See also European Convention, Arts. 31(1), 32(1) and 50, concerning the power of the European Commission of Human Rights, the Committee of Ministers and the Court of Human Rights to determine whether a breach of the Convention has occurred.

[215] *Ireland* v. *United Kingdom*, [1976] YB Eur. Conv. on Hum. Rts. 512, 936-8 (Eur. Comm'n of Hum. Rts.) (footnote omitted).

[216] *Northern Cameroons* (*Camer.* v. *UK*) (*Preliminary Objections*), 1963 ICJ Rep. 15, 99-100 (Fitzmaurice J. sep. op.) (emphasis in original).

a declaratory judgment not accompanied by a claim for compensation is appropriate 'in relation to a still continuing legal situation in which a pronouncement that illegalities have occurred may be legally material and relevant'.[217] This comment is particularly fitting to requests for judgments declaring continuing patterns of conduct which are not in conformity with a state's human rights obligations to be illegal.

The ILC, the Restatement,[218] and commentators agree that damage caused by one state to another is not required to establish the internationally wrongful character of an act of state. In some areas of international law, such as that governing injuries to aliens, economic or moral damages are frequently essential elements of an act considered internationally wrongful; that is, objective elements which must be satisfied to establish a violation of a specific primary norm. However, this is not necessarily true of other international obligations, such as those governing human rights and humanitarian norms. In its *Commentary* on Article 3 of its draft articles on state responsibility (part one), the ILC states:

International law today lays more and more obligations on the State with regard to the treatment of its own subjects. For examples we need only turn to the conventions on human rights or the majority of the international labour conventions. If one of these international obligations is violated, the breach thus committed does not normally cause any economic injury to the other States parties to the convention, or even any slight to their honour or dignity. Yet it manifestly constitutes an internationally wrongful act, so that if we maintain at all costs that 'damage' is an element in any internationally wrongful act, we are forced to the conclusion that any breach of an international obligation towards another State involves some kind of 'injury' to that other State. But this is tantamount to saying that the 'damage' which is inherent in any internationally wrongful act is the damage which is at the same time inherent in any breach of an international obligation.[219]

Damage is thus an element inherent in the breach of an international

217 Ibid. at 100.
218 Restatement, above n. 1, § 901, comment *a*: 'Ordinarily, claims for damages require injury, but other forms of redress may be available even if there is no injury, or to prevent an injury.' Comment *d*: '[I]n some instances compensation may be required even though no monetary damage had occurred.'
219 [1973] 2 YB Int'l L. Comm'n 183, UN Doc. A/CN.4/SER.A/1973/Add.1 (1975) (footnote omitted).

norm;[220] indeed, any breach of an international obligation 'involves some kind of "injury" to [another] State'. On this point, Professor Graefrath aptly observes that 'it is the violation of the obligation and not the damage that entails the State's responsibility . . . '.[221] The ILC's approach to the question of damage supports both the concept of obligations *erga omnes* presented in *Barcelona Traction* and the feasibility of ensuring the observance of obligations *erga omnes* through actions brought by a state to vindicate the human rights of persons who are not its nationals. If by violating the human rights of its nationals a state offends the general international legal order, and thereby also equally offends every other state, then every state has the necessary standing to bring an action against those that perpetrate violations of norms of international human rights and humanitarian norms.[222]

VII. VIOLATIONS AS INTERNATIONAL CRIMES AND INTERNATIONAL DELICTS

For many years now, national courts have heard charges of war crimes involving egregious breaches of human rights and

---

[220] Tanzi, above note 202, at 3 (footnote omitted).

[221] Graefrath, *Responsibility and Damages Caused: Relationship between Responsibility and Damages*, 185 Recueil des cours 9, 37 (1984-II).

[222] See e.g. the following comments of ILC members: 'Treaties dealing with human rights laid an obligation on States to take certain legislative measures for the benefit of their own citizens; failure to do so could be invoked by any of the other States parties to the treaty since it was sufficient in itself to cause injury to them.' [1973] 1 YB Int'l L. Comm'n 26, UN Doc. A/CN.4/SER.A/1973 (1974) (remarks by Chairman Castañeda).

'[A]ny act or omission on [the] part [of a state] which was contrary to [an international] undertaking constituted an injury. The existence of material or moral damage in addition to that injury was not necessary to make [sic] an internationally wrongful act. In all cases there was infringement of the international legal order. . . . If a State party to [ILO] conventions . . . infringed the human rights of its citizens . . . it did not cause damage to any other State; but if the conventions were to have any meaning, the other States parties must be able to hold it responsible for an internationally wrongful act.' Ibid. at 27 (remarks by Mr Ago).

'[W]hen a State acted contrary to the European Convention on Human Rights, a complaint could be lodged against it by a State other than that to which the injured person belonged; that was none the less enough to set international reparation machinery in motion.' Ibid. at 23. (remarks by Mr. Reuter).

'[T]he breach of some international obligations [such as the International Convention on the Elimination of All Forms of Racial Discrimination] might give rise to responsibility without the existence of any prejudice.' [1981] 1 YB Int'l L. Comm'n 142, UN Doc. A/CN.4/SER.A/1981 (1982) (remarks by Mr Ushakov).

'Injury was not a constituent element of responsibility and account had been taken only of legal, abstract injury resulting from any breach of an international humanitarian norms whether under national or international law or under both. And, of course, a small number of extremely important international tribunals have heard charges of war crimes and crimes against humanity. A growing body of international agreements recognizes the international criminal responsibility of those who perpetrate certain crimes against human dignity. Provisions in some agreements, such as the grave breaches clauses of the Geneva Conventions (50/51/130/147), are based on the universality principle of jurisdiction.[223] This principle requires states either to bring before their own courts or to extradite persons charged with committing grave breaches or ordering their commission. Imposing criminal responsibility on the perpetrators of egregious breaches of human rights should assist in deterring further breaches and secure greater respect for human rights and humanitarian norms.

A recent example of a treaty criminalizing one particularly egregious violation of human rights is the Convention Against Torture and Other Cruel, Inhuman or Degrading Treatment or Punishment, which requires each state party to 'ensure that all acts of torture are offences under its criminal law'.[224] Article 7 of the Convention obliges states either to extradite the perpetrators or to 'submit the[ir] case[s] to [their] competent authorities for the purpose of prosecution' (*aut dedere aut punire*).

The criminal responsibility of individuals for egregious breaches of international human rights must be assessed in the context of state responsibility. A state which does not comply with its international obligations to prosecute or extradite perpetrators commits a wrong which entails its international responsibility. However, a state does not necessarily exonerate itself from its international responsibility by punishing a perpetrator of egregious human rights violations.[225]

---

obligation.' [1984] 1 YB Int'l L. Comm'n 278, UN Doc. A/CN.4/SER.A/1984 (1985) (remarks by Mr Reuter in support of draft Art. 5 proposed by Special Rapporteur Riphagen).

[223] See e.g. Dinstein, above n. 86, at 206; T. Meron, above n. 86, at 34–6. See generally Randall, *Universal Jurisdiction under International Law*, 66 Tex. L. Rev. 785 (1988); Clark, *Offenses of International Concern: Multilateral State Treaty Practice in the Forty Years Since Nuremberg*, 57 Nordic J. Int'l L. 49 (1988).

[224] Convention Against Torture and Other Cruel, Inhuman or Degrading Treatment or Punishment, Art. 4, above n. 39.

[225] The ILC has pointed out that '[t]he obligation to punish personally individuals

The well-settled concept of the individual responsibility of those who perpetrate certain egregious human rights or humanitarian norms violations, or 'crimes under international law', must be distinguished from the ILC's concept of 'international crimes'.[226]

In its famous dictum in *Barcelona Traction*, the ICJ gave currency to the idea of a hierarchy of norms by suggesting that 'basic rights of the human person' create obligations *erga omnes*. The ILC construed this dictum to mean that 'there are in fact, a number, albeit a small one, of international obligations which, by reason of the importance of their subject-matter for the international community as a whole, are—unlike the others—obligations in whose fulfilment all States have a legal interest.'[227] The ILC explained that 'the pre-eminence of these obligations over others is determined by their content [and] not by the process by which they were created [or] on the basis of their "origin" [e.g. in customary

who are organs of the State and are guilty of crimes against the peace, against humanity, and so on does not . . . constitute a form of international responsibility of the State, and such punishment certainly does not exhaust the prosecution of the international responsibility incumbent upon the State for internationally wrongful acts which are attributed to it in such cases by reason of the conduct of its organs.' [1976] 2 YB Int'l L. Comm'n (pt. 2) at 104, UN Doc. E/CN.4/SER.A/1976/Add.1 (Part 2) (1977).

[226] The ILC observed that 'in adopting the designation "international crime", the Commission intends only to refer to "crimes" of the State, to acts attributable to the State as such. Once again it wishes to sound a warning against any confusion between the expression "international crime" as used in . . . article [19 of the ILC's draft articles on state responsibility (part one)] and similar expressions, such as "crime under international law", "war crime", "crime against peace", "crime against humanity", etc., which are used in a number of conventions and international instruments to designate certain heinous individual crimes, for which those instruments require States to punish the guilty persons adequately. . . .' Ibid. at 119.

See generally M. Spinedi, *Les Crimes internationaux de L'Etat dans les travaux de codification de la responsabilité des Etats entrepris par les Nations Unies* (1984); Mohr, *The ILC's Distinction between "International Crimes" and "International Delicts" and its Implications*, in United Nations Codification of State Responsibility, above n. 202, at 115; P. M. Dupuy, *Observations sur le "crime international de l'Etat"*, 84 Rev. gén. droit int'l pub. 449 (1980); P. M. Dupuy, *Action publique et crime international de l'Etat: à propos de l'article 19 du projet de la Commission du Droit International sur la responsabilité des Etats*, 25 Annuaire français de droit international 539 (1979); Simma, *International Crimes: Injury and Countermeasures: Comments on Part Two of the ILC Work on State Responsibility*, in International Crimes of State 283 (J. Weiler, A. Cassese, and M. Spinedi eds. 1988). Concerning punishment of individuals for war crimes and crimes against humanity, see 1 L. Oppenheim, above n. 84, at 341-2; 2 ibid. 316-17, 406, 566-88 (7th edn. H. Lauterpacht 1952).

[227] [1976] 2 YB Int'l L. Comm'n (pt. 2), above n. 225, at 99.

or conventional norms] but rather by taking account of the undeniable fact that the international community has a greater interest in ensuring [observance] of [such] obligations. . . .'[228] The ILC acknowledged that there is no special source of law for creating fundamental principles in international law.

Extrapolating from *Barcelona Traction* into international criminal responsibility, the ILC adopted on first reading[229] the controversial Article 19(3)(*c*) of the draft articles on state responsibility proposed by Special Rapporteur Roberto Ago. Article 19(3)(*c*) provides that an international crime may result, *inter alia*, from 'a serious breach on a widespread scale of an international obligation of essential importance for safeguarding the human being, such as those prohibiting slavery, genocide and *apartheid*'.[230] The ILC thus introduced a twofold test for international crimes based on the seriousness of both the violation ('serious breach on a widespread scale') and the norm itself ('international obligation of essential importance').[231] Breaches of lesser or non-fundamental international human rights which are not international crimes still constitute, of course, international delicts or international wrongs.[232] While grave

[228] Ibid. at 85-6.

[229] Ibid. at 73.

[230] Art. 19 of the ILC's draft articles on state responsibility (part one), entitled 'International crimes and international delicts', reads as follows:

'1. An act of a State which constitutes a breach of an international obligation is an internationally wrongful act, regardless of the subject-matter of the obligation breached.

2. An internationally wrongful act which results from the breach by a State of an international obligation so essential for the protection of fundamental interests of the international community that its breach is recognized as a crime by that community as a whole, constitutes an international crime.

3. Subject to paragraph 2, and on the basis of the rules of international law in force, an international crime may result, *inter alia*, from: (*a*) a serious breach of an international obligation of essential importance for the maintenance of international peace and security, such as that prohibiting aggression; (*b*) a serious breach of an international obligation of essential importance for safeguarding the right of self-determination of peoples, such as that prohibiting the establishment or maintenance by force of colonial domination; (*c*) a serious breach on a widespread scale of an international obligation of essential importance for safeguarding the human being, such as those prohibiting slavery, genocide and *apartheid*; (*d*) a serious breach of an international obligation of essential importance for the safeguarding and preservation of the human environment, such as those prohibiting massive pollution of the atmosphere or of the seas.

4. Any internationally wrongful act which is not an international crime in accordance with paragraph 2, constitutes an international delict.' Ibid. at 95-6.

[231] Ibid. at 121.

[232] Ibid. at 97, 121.

breaches of the Geneva Conventions normally implicate only the individual criminal responsibility of persons committing or ordering such breaches to be committed, a systematic and massive resort to such breaches could certainly be considered an international crime in the meaning of Article 19(3)(*c*), for which the state concerned would bear responsibility.[233] The same could be true of breaches of the Additional Protocols. While grave breaches of Protocol I are described in Article 85(5) as war crimes, i.e., crimes involving only individual responsibility, grave breaches which are massive and systematic could be considered crimes of states.

Professor Kooijmans, the UN Special Rapporteur on torture, has pointed out that '[i]f the practice of torture takes on a "massive", "persistent" or "systematic" character, it may . . . fall within the concept of an "international crime".'[234] To be sure, by its very terms Article 19(3) is not exhaustive. Egregious violations of additional norms may mature into international crimes.

Significantly, the ILC considered the examples of international crimes mentioned in Article 19(3), including certain essential human rights, as *lex lata*. The Commission emphasized that it referred to 'international law now in force'[235] under multilateral treaties or custom. Commentators such as Professor Brownlie have, however, questioned both whether the evidence adduced by Special Rapporteur Ago 'gives more than very equivocal support for the existence of the category as positive law [and] the practical utility of the concept of the criminal responsibility of states'.[236] The ILC

---

[233] Condorelli and Boisson de Chazournes, *Quelques Remarques à propos de l'obligation des Etats de "respecter et faire respecter" le droit international humanitaire "en toutes circonstances"*, in Studies and Essays on International Humanitarian Law and Red Cross Principles in Honour of Jean Pictet 17, 34 (C. Swinarski ed. 1984).

[234] UN Doc. E/CN.4/1987/13 at 15 (1987).

[235] [1976] 2 YB Int'l L. Comm'n (pt. 2), above n. 225, at 120.

[236] I. Brownlie, above n. 62, at 33 (footnote omitted).

A writer generally supportive of the concept of crimes of states, Professor Cassese, acknowledges the 'paucity' of state practice which might be interpreted as reflecting an intention to 'punish' states guilty of gross violations of human rights. Cassese, *Remarks on the Present Legal Regulation of Crimes of States*, in 3 International Law at the Time of its Codification: Essays in Honour of Roberto Ago 49, 56 (1987). He concludes that the response of states to violations of human rights 'does not come within the purview of the legal régime of responsibility for crimes of States. . . . In the case of massive disregard for human rights the violation of obligations *erga omnes* only gives rise to the right of international subjects other than the one directly injured (if any), to claim cessation of the international delinquency.' Ibid. at 63.

itself could not discern 'any real consensus of opinion as to what kind of 'action' or 'measures' may legitimately be taken to deal with the acts referred to, or upon other delicate points of law . . .'.[237] In addition, the ILC held only a preliminary and inconclusive discussion on lawful measures which states not specially affected could, individually or collectively, take to compel a state which perpetrates international crimes to comply with its international obligations, leaving this question to a more thorough examination in the context of part two of its draft articles (forms of responsibility). Some members of the Commission argued that crimes of states justified collective intervention on behalf of the victims of apartheid;[238] in contrast, other members questioned the right of third states to vindicate international crimes even through 'non-military intervention'.[239]

Whether appropriate international institutions and processes exist which can vindicate international crimes is, of course, the critical question here. One member, acknowledging that international crimes 'called for something much more than reparation',[240] insisted nevertheless that

[w]hereas ordinary breaches would continue to be dealt with by the traditional remedy of reparation and would constitute a purely legal problem—to be decided by the International Court of Justice, or by arbitration if other means of settlement failed—international crimes would be dealt with by the Security Council, the only political body that could authorize collective action to maintain or restore international peace.[241]

Special Rapporteur Riphagen attempted to clarify this issue further. The text of Article 6 (part two of the ILC's draft articles) proposed in his third report envisages the possibility of collective, not individual, action which would be subject to the UN Charter,[242] while each individual state would have an obligation 'not to act in

---

[237] [1976] 2 YB Int'l L. Comm'n (pt. 2), above n. 225, at 108.
[238] [1976] 1 YB Int'l L. Comm'n at 80, UN Doc. A/CN.4/SER.A/1976 (1977) (remarks by Mr Bedjaoui).
[239] Ibid. at 77 (remarks by Mr Kearney).
[240] Ibid. at 67 (remarks by Mr Sette Câmara).
[241] Ibid. at 68.
[242] For the text of Art. 6, see UN Doc. A/CN.4/354 and Adds. 1-2, reprinted in [1982] 2 YB Int'l L. Comm'n (pt. 1) at 23, 48, UN Doc. A/CN.4/ Ser.A/1982/Add.1 (Part 1) (1984).

such a way as to condone such crime'.[243] Draft Article 14 proposed
by Professor Riphagen in his fifth report states that international
crimes entail all the legal consequences of internationally wrongful
acts and, in addition, such rights and obligations as are determined
by the applicable rules accepted by the international community as
a whole.[244] It may be noted that draft Article 14 incorporates draft
Article 6. Draft Article 15 (fifth report) states that the crime of
aggression entails all the consequences of an international crime
and, in addition, such rights and obligations as are provided for in
or by virtue of the UN Charter.

The answers to many questions remain unclear, even when
Riphagen's draft articles are considered. Such difficulties are both
conceptual and related to institutional structures and processes.
Conceptual difficulties include the characterizing of some rights
as fundamental,[245] the still inadequate doctrinal rationale for
distinguishing between the civil and criminal responsibility of states,
and the continuing need to clarify which remedies are appropriate
for criminal responsibility. Questions related to institutions and
processes include whether competent organs are available to
determine whether a state is guilty of an international crime, and
whether credible and objective implementation procedures exist for
vindicating international crimes by the organized international
community. A related problem is the danger that the concept of
international crimes will be abused for political reasons and thus
encourage individual states to assume prosecutorial roles. Such a
development might destabilize international peace and security.
These dangers inherent in international crimes are also inherent in
obligations *erga omnes*; however, these difficulties are obviously
intensified where the norms impose criminal rather than civil
responsibility on states.

While the concept of obligations *erga omnes* has had a very
considerable influence on the development of international human
rights law, the concept of crimes of states has yet firmly to take
root in contemporary international law. However, the concept of

[243] Ibid. (*Commentary* to Art. 6).
[244] UN Doc. A/CN.4/380, reprinted in [1984] 2 YB Int'l L. Comm'n (pt. 1) at
1, 4, UN Doc. A/CN.4/SER.A/1984/Add.1 (Part 1) (1986).
[245] For an analysis of this problem, see Meron, *On a Hierarchy of International
Human Rights*, 80 AJIL 1 (1986). See also Meron, *Lex Lata: Is there already a
Differentiated Regime of State Responsibility in the Geneva Conventions*, in International Crimes of State, above n. 226, at 225.

international crimes undeniably has significant ethical and moral underpinnings. As Professor Tammes cogently proposed, '[i]f humanitarian international law called for special sanctions, it was because of its moral quality, in other words, its source or 'status' above the law, as well as its content.'[246] The concept of state crimes suggests that the international community cannot be relied upon to tolerate endlessly certain egregious violations of human rights. This ethically important concept should be allowed to develop through international practice and a growing international consensus. General acceptance of this concept would go far towards deterring human rights violations in the future. More immediately, the inclusion of some basic human rights in Article 19(3) consolidates their status as an authentic and cardinal branch of positive international law.

VIII. STATE OF NECESSITY AND DEROGATIONS

Customary law rules providing exceptions to the normally applicable obligations of states, such as those based on *force majeure*, state of necessity, and self-defence, may preclude the wrongfulness of an act which does not conform to a state's international obligations.[247] The ILC explained that '[t]he term state of necessity . . . denote[s] the situation of a State whose sole means of safeguarding an essential interest threatened by a grave and imminent peril is to adopt conduct not in conformity with what is required of it by an international obligation to another State.'[248] Because states often invoke 'necessity' to justify deviations or derogations from the conduct required by human rights and humanitarian norms law, the applicability of this exception to these obligations requires close scrutiny.

It is now generally accepted that humanitarian instruments, having been adopted to govern situations of armed conflict,[249] are not subject to derogations on such grounds as public emergency except in the rather narrow context of such provisions as Article 5

---

[246] [1976] 1 YB Int'l L. Comm'n, above n. 238, at 15.
[247] Draft Arts. 31–4 of ILC's draft articles on state responsibility (part one), [1980] 2 YB Int'l L. Comm'n (pt. 2) at 33, UN Doc. A/CN.4/SER.4/1980/Add.1 (Part 2) (1981).
[248] Ibid. at 34.
[249] T. Meron, above n. 86, at 156 and n. 52.

of Geneva Convention No. IV[250] and Article 45(3) of Protocol
I.[251] These provisions parallel the limitation clauses of human rights
instruments. Imperative military concerns, military necessity or
security reasons mentioned, for example, in Articles 49(2), 64(1) or
78(1) of Geneva Convention No. IV, grant states certain additional
freedoms only when such freedoms are explicitly stated in the
treaties concerned.[252] Invoking other necessity-related exceptions
derived from customary law would clash with the purpose of
humanitarian instruments. The principles both of effectiveness
and of *expressio unius est exclusio alterius* preclude any other
interpretation.[253]

This conception of humanitarian instruments is strongly supported by the ILC's *Commentary* on draft Article 33 on the state
of necessity.[254] The ILC has adduced several reasons why a situation

[250] Convention Relative to the Protection of Civilian Persons in Time of War
(Geneva Convention No. IV), Aug. 12, 1949, 6 UST 3516, TIAS No. 3365, 75
UNTS 287.

[251] Protocol Additional to the Geneva Conventions of 12 August 1949, and
Relating to the Protection of Victims of International Armed Conflicts, opened for
signature 12 Dec. 1977, 16 ILM 1391 (1977).

[252] T. Meron, above n. 86, at 15 and n. 44.

[253] Special Rapporteur Roberto Ago argued that the international law of war
was not necessarily 'an absolutely closed area as regards any posssible application
of "state of necessity" as a circumstance precluding the wrongfulness of conduct . . .'. R. Ago, Addendum to the Eighth Report on State Responsibility, UN
Doc. A/CN.4/318/Adds. 5–7, reprinted in [1980] 2 YB Int'l L. Comm'n (pt. 1) at
37, UN Doc. A/CN.4/SER.A/1980/Add.1 (Part 1) (1981). The ILC's *Commentary*
did not follow Professor Ago's position on this question.

[254] Art. 33 of the ILC's draft articles on state responsibility (part one) reads as
follows:
'1. A state of necessity may not be invoked by a State as a ground for precluding
the wrongfulness of an act of that State not in conformity with an international
obligation of the State unless: (a) the act was the only means of safeguarding an
essential interest of the State against a grave and imminent peril; and (b) the act
did not seriously impair an essential interest of the State towards which the
obligation existed.
2. In any case, a state of necessity may not be invoked by a State as a ground
for precluding wrongfulness: (a) if the international obligation with which the act
of the State is not in conformity arises out of a peremptory norm of general
international law; or (b) if the international obligation with which the act of the
State is not in conformity is laid down by a treaty which, explicitly or implicitly,
excludes the possibility of invoking the state of necessity with respect to that
obligation; or (c) if the State in question has contributed to the occurrence of the
state of necessity.' [1980] 2 YB Int'l L. Comm'n (pt. 2), above n. 247, at 34.
For the ILC's discussion of humanitarian intervention, see ibid. at 44–5; R. Ago,
Addendum to the Eighth Report on State Responsibility, above n. 253, at 43. See
also N. Ronzitti, Rescuing Nationals Abroad through Military Coercion and
Intervention on Grounds of Humanity (1985). A paper prepared in 1984 by the

of necessity cannot excuse a state from compliance with rules of humanitarian law which, in order to attenuate the rigours of war, limit the belligerents' choice of means and methods for conducting hostilities.[255] First, some humanitarian law rules constitute norms of *jus cogens* and are thus non-derogable.[256] Second, even in regard to non-peremptory humanitarian law obligations, invoking a state of necessity to justify precluding the wrongfulness of state conduct conflicts directly with the purpose of humanitarian treaties, which seek to subordinate the immediate military objectives of belligerents to higher, humanitarian interests. Humanitarian law principles already reflect a certain equilibrium between military necessity and consideration of humanity. As such, they cannot yield to additional unilaterally perceived requirements of military necessity. Third, clauses which permit states to invoke such exceptions as urgent military necessity

apply only to the cases expressly provided for. Apart from these cases, it follows implicitly from the text of the conventions that they do not admit the possibility of invoking military necessity as a justification for State conduct not in conformity with the obligations they impose. . . . [T]he Commission took the view that a State cannot invoke a state of necessity if that is expressly or implicitly prohibited by a conventional instrument.[257]

Thus, in interpreting humanitarian instruments, it is appropriate to resort to the principle of non-derogability on grounds of necessity. The drafters of humanitarian agreements did not intend to permit states to invoke the customary law exception of state of necessity regarding the norms stated in those agreements. By contrast, human rights instruments, which are subject to derogations in most cases, do not share this rule of non-derogability with humanitarian law instruments. However, the ILC's position, set forth in Article 33(2)(*b*), that a state cannot invoke a state of necessity which is expressly or implicitly prohibited by a conventional instrument applies as well to human rights instruments. This principle is especially applicable to those instruments which contain provisions

staff of the British Foreign and Commonwealth Office doubts whether a state has the right to have recourse to a humanitarian intervention abroad on behalf of persons who are not that state's nationals. Foreign and Commonwealth Office, *Foreign Policy Document* No. 148, reprinted in 57 Brit. YB Int'l L. 614 (1986).

[255] [1980] 2 YB Int'l L. Comm'n (pt. 2), above n. 247, at 46–7.
[256] The relationship between *jus cogens* and derogability is discussed below.
[257] [1980] 2 YB Int'l L. Comm'n (pt. 2), above n. 247, at 46–7.

on derogations, such as the International Covenant on Civil and Political Rights. The language of the Covenant prohibits any derogation not explicitly permitted by Article 4, thus excluding invocation of the customary law exception of state of necessity. Therefore, the Article 4 exceptions from the Covenant's obligations are comprehensive. Anything not expressly included among the already very broad freedoms which Article 4 grants to states parties[258] is inherently incompatible with the primary goal of the Covenant, which is to ensure respect for human rights.[259]

The Reporters of the Restatement suggest that '[t]he derogations permissible in emergency under the [Political] Covenant are presumably permissible . . . in relation to nationals of other states as a matter of customary law.'[260] Perhaps there is considerable overlap in international law between derogations permitted by Article 4 and customary law rules of exception in the law governing state responsibility. It is not certain, however, that these customary rules correspond exactly to the concept of 'public emergency' under Article 4 or that the scope of the derogations allowed by Article 4 and by customary law is identical.

A more difficult question is whether, in the absence of a provision governing derogations on grounds of necessity, a state may invoke necessity to preclude the wrongfulness of its conduct which does not conform with norms stated in a human rights treaty. The answer differs with the treaty concerned. For example, did the drafters of the African Charter on Human and Peoples' Rights, which contains no provisions on derogations, intend to exclude the right of states under customary law to invoke justifications such as state of necessity? It is not clear that the Charter's *travaux préparatoires* would support such an interpretation, although it would undoubtedly serve the cause of the effective protection of human rights. Regrettably, there is a danger that the absence of a derogations clause in the Charter will be used to infer that the

[258] For a critique of derogation clauses, see T. Meron, above n. 33, at 86–100.

[259] This conclusion is supported by the *travaux préparatoires* of Art. 4, which confirm that '[t]he main concern was to provide for a qualification of the kind of public emergency in which a State would be entitled to make derogations from the rights contained in the covenant which would not be open to abuse. . . .' M. Bossuyt, above n. 12, at 85–6. It was essential 'to prevent States from derogating arbitrarily from their obligations where such an action was not warranted by events'. Ibid. at 87.

[260] Above n. 1, § 711, comment *h*.

Charter implicitly allows states to invoke the customary law exception of state of necessity to derogate from the rights enumerated in the Charter, without the safeguards routinely built into such clauses.[261] It is to be hoped, however, that, when it begins to function, the African Commission on Human and Peoples' Rights will balance the various interests implicated and not allow necessity and the 'preeminence of state interest'[262] to take precedence over the human rights which are stated in the Charter.

If a treaty interpretation that excludes the customary law

[261] See Umozurike, *The African Charter on Human and Peoples' Rights*, 77 AJIL 902, 909-10 (1983). It is noteworthy that the African Charter contains a number of limitation clauses, e.g. Arts. 6, 11, 12. See also Weston, Lukes, and Hnatt, *Regional Human Rights Regimes: a Comparison and Appraisal*, 20 Vand. J. Transnat'l L. 585, 627-8 (1987).

The practice of the ILO suggests that such customary international law exceptions as state of necessity, *force majeure*, and self-defence may be applied in order to assess the lawfulness of suspension of International Labour Conventions which do not contain provisions pertaining to derogations. See International Labour Office, 1 International Labour Code 1951 at XCVI-XCVII (1952); Report of the Commission Appointed under Article 26 of the Constitution of the International Labour Organisation to Examine Complaints concerning the Observance by Greece of the Freedom of Association and Protection of the Right to Organise Convention, 1948 (No. 87), and of the Right to Organise and Collective Bargaining Convention, 1949 (No. 98), ILO Official Bulletin, Vol. LIV, No. 2, Special Supp. at 26 (1971); Report of the Commission Instituted under Article 26 of the Constitution of the International Labour Organisation to Examine the Complaint on the Observance by Poland of the Freedom of Association and Protection of the Right to Organise Convention, 1948 (No. 87), and the Right to Organise and Collective Bargaining Convention, 1949 (No. 98), ILO Official Bulletin, Vol. LXVII, Special Supp., Ser. B at 126-7 (1984). ILO organs have emphasized that the invocation of such exceptions was subject to the principle of proportionality; measures affecting the application of the conventions must be limited in scope and in duration to what is strictly necessary to deal with the situation in question. Ibid.

[262] Okere, *The Protection of Human Rights in Africa and the African Charter on Human and Peoples' Rights: A Comparative Analysis with the European and American Systems*, 6 Hum. Rts. Q. 141, 143 (1984).

It may be noted that, prior to the entry into force of the American Convention on Human Rights, the Inter-American Commission on Human Rights in its discussion of derogations resorted to the norms stated in Art. 27 of the Convention as reflecting regional customary law: 'With respect to American international law—which is the normative system that the Commission must take primarily into account—it must be understood that, in the absence of conventional standards in force in this area, the 'most accepted doctrine' is that which is set forth in the American Convention on Human Rights . . . which has been signed by twelve American countries (among them Chile), and whose ratification has already begun.

The Convention contains an express provision in Article 27 . . .' Inter-American Commission on Human Rights, Report on the Status of Human Rights in Chile, OAS Doc. OEA/Ser.L/V/II.34 Doc. 21, Corr. 1 at 2-3 (1974), discussed in Buergenthal, *The Revised OAS Charter and the Protection of Human Rights*, 69 AJIL 828, 835 at n. 37 (1975).

exception of state of necessity is not credible, the state derogating
from a human rights obligation binding upon it in relation to either
its nationals or aliens must still discharge the burden of establishing
both the state of necessity and the justification for derogation from
a given norm. In some circumstances, the state may, perhaps, even
be required to demonstrate a particularized need to apply the
derogations to the individuals concerned. The ILC suggests that
even if a state proves that its breach of a legal obligation was
justified by the requirements of necessity, the state may still incur
the obligation to make reparation for damage caused by the act in
question on grounds other than responsibility for a wrongful act.[263]
The ILC's draft Article 35 leaves this question unresolved.[264]
Perhaps an award of compensation on equitable grounds would be
appropriate in such cases.

Initially, the state concerned must assess the extent to which
particular circumstances constitute a situation of emergency or
necessity that justifies derogations from a state's international
obligations. Because of the important community values implicated
in protecting human rights, a state which desires to be excused
from a breach of an international human right on grounds of
necessity which are not authorized by explicit treaty language
should carry a heavy burden of proof.[265]

Where a state cannot successfully discharge the burden of proof
to establish that the state of necessity excuses the deviation from
the norm, the principle applies (as pointed out by Professor Marek,
citing Professor Verdross[266]) that a single state is not permitted to
break any rule of international law, peremptory or not.[267] The
difference between *jus cogens* and *jus dispositivum* in this context is
that, in the case of *jus cogens*, the prohibition of deviation from
the norm, even when allowed by either an international agreement
or unilateral state action, is absolute. A treaty purporting to allow
derogations from a peremptory norm would itself be void, in

---

[263] [1980] 2 YB Int'l L. Comm'n (pt. 2), above n. 247, at 61.

[264] Art. 35 states that '[p]reclusion of the wrongfulness of an act of a State by
virtue of the provisions of articles 29, 31, 32 or 33 does not prejudice any question
that may arise in regard to compensation for damage caused by that act.' Ibid.

[265] On the latitude which states have in deciding when a situation of emergency
exists, see M. Bossuyt, above n. 12, at 87.

[226] Marek, *Sur la notion de progrès en droit international*, 38 Annuaire suisse de
droit international 28, 35 (1982).

[267] See Meron, *On a Hierarchy of International Human Rights*, above n. 245, at
20.

accordance with Article 53 of the Vienna Convention on the Law of Treaties. Although both the concept and the process of identifying *jus cogens* obligations have been discussed elsewhere,[268] their relationship to the unilateral invocation of necessity by a state merits comment.

The International Law Commission unequivocally applied the term 'peremptory norms' outside the law of treaties to unilateral state action when it adopted the draft articles on state responsibility.[269] Article 33(2)(*a*) provides that 'a state of necessity may not be invoked by a State as a ground for precluding wrongfulness . . . if the international obligation with which the act of the State is not in conformity arises out of a peremptory norm of general international law.'[270] Alluding to the frequent abusive invocations of necessity by states, the ILC stated that if the consent of the injured state cannot preclude the wrongfulness of an act in conflict with a peremptory norm under draft Article 29 (regarding consent) of the ILC's draft articles on state responsibility (part one),

[t]his obviously means that peremptory rules are so essential for the life of the international community as to make it all the more inconceivable that a State should be entitled to decide unilaterally, however acute the state of necessity which overtakes it, that it may commit a breach of the obligations which these rules impose on it.[271]

In this context, however, peremptory norms may refer to categorical rules of international law or of international public policy, rather than strictly speaking to *jus cogens*, an analogous concept that resides primarily in the law of treaties (this is in contrast to the

---

[268] Ibid. at 13–23. See also Christenson, *Jus Cogens: Guarding Interests Fundamental to International Society*, 28 Va. J. Int'l L. 585 (1988).

[269] [1980] 2 YB Int'l L. Comm'n (pt. 2), above n. 247, at 30. The ILC's *Commentary* to draft Art. 12(b) on state responsibility (part two of the draft articles) mentions the reluctance of some members to apply the concept of *jus cogens* outside of the framework of the Vienna Convention on the Law of Treaties. Other members, however, supported the retention of that Article. The view was expressed that 'a provision relating to *jus cogens* required . . . a procedural provision along the lines of that provided for in the . . . Vienna Convention.' [1985] 2 YB Int'l L. Comm'n (pt. 2) at 23, UN Doc. A/CN.4/SER.A/1985/Add.1 (Part 2) (1986). See also H. Mosler, The International Society as a Legal Community 19–20 (1980). *Contra* Stein, *The Approach of the Different Drummer: The Principle of the Persistent Objector in International Law*, 26 Harv. Int'l LJ 457, 481 (1985).

[270] [1980] 2 YB Int'l L. Comm'n (pt. 2), above n. 247, at 33. See generally Gaja, *Jus Cogens beyond the Vienna Convention*, 172 Recueil des cours 271, 296–7 (1981-III).

[271] [1980] 2 YB Int'l L. Comm'n (pt. 2), above n. 247, at 50.

majority of the rules of international law, the *jus dispositivum*, from which states are permitted, *inter partes*, to contract out).

Judge Mosler characterized 'public order of the international community' as

consist[ing] of principles and rules the enforcement of which is of such vital importance to the international community as a whole that any unilateral action or any agreement which contravenes these principles can have no legal force. The reason for this follows simply from logic: the law cannot recognise any act either of one member or of several members in concert, as being legally valid if it is directed against the very foundation of law.[272]

Obviously, the rationale underlying the concepts of *jus cogens* and public order of the international community is the same: because of the decisive importance of certain norms and values to the international community, these norms merit absolute protection and may not be breached by states, whether jointly by a derogation right claimed under a treaty, or severally by unilateral legislative or executive action. It is in this sense that the International Court of Justice, in *United States Diplomatic and Consular Staff in Tehran*,[273] treated the 'imperative character of the legal obligations incumbent upon the Iranian Government'.[274]

IX. RESPONSIBILITY FOR VIOLATIONS OF INTERNATIONAL HUMANITARIAN LAW: SPECIAL PROBLEMS

The foregoing discussion of state responsibility for human rights violations is also relevant to violations of humanitarian rights. The latter pose additional problems which merit further consideration. These problems are intensified by the fact that, with such exceptions as Article 3 of the Hague Convention No. IV and Article 91 of Protocol I, humanitarian instruments generally focus on rules applicable during hostilities, not on reparation for damage.[275]

[272] H. Mosler, above n. 269, at 18.
[273] *United States Diplomatic and Consular Staff in Tehran* (*United States of America* v. *Iran*), 1980 ICJ Rep. 3.
[274] Ibid. at 41.
[275] Sandoz, above n. 84, at 154. I gratefully acknowledge the useful suggestions offered by Professor Marina Spinedi from which I benefited in writing this section. See also her remarks on *Implementation of International Humanitarian Law and Rules of International Law on States' Responsibility for Illicit Acts*, Int'l Rev. Red Cross, No. 261, Nov.-Dec. 1987, at 668-70.

As discussed in Section VIII, above, one of the distinct characteristics of international humanitarian instruments is that the customary law exception of state of necessity does not apply to them. In addition, these agreements do not permit one state's consent to another state's unlawful act to preclude the act's wrongfulness.[276] The Geneva Conventions[277] contain two common provisions that challenge the consent of either states or individuals to acts that breach humanitarian norms. The rationale underlying such provisions may lie in the conviction that only an absolute prohibition of such agreements will decisively defeat any claims that consent to them was freely given,[278] and in the principle that states may not agree to renounce rights of which not they, but individuals, are the beneficiaries.[279]

Common Article 6/6/6/7 thus states that no special agreement concluded by the contracting parties may adversely affect the situation of persons protected by the Convention or restrict the rights which the Convention confers upon such persons. Common Article 7/7/7/8 states that protected persons 'may in no circumstances renounce in part or in entirety the rights secured to them by the present Convention, and by the special agreements referred to in the foregoing Article, if such there be'.

The special rule of responsibility contained in Article 3 of the Hague Convention No. IV[280] was discussed in Section II, above. Article 3, which enunciates the principle that states are responsible for all acts committed by members of their armed forces irrespective of whether they acted as state organs or as private persons,[281] warrants further examination.

[276] See Art. 29 of the ILC's draft articles on state responsibility (part one), [1979] 2 YB Int'l L. Comm'n (pt. 2) at 93, UN Doc. A/CN.4/SER.A/1979/Add.1 (Part 2) (1980).

[277] Convention for the Amelioration of the Condition of the Wounded and Sick in Armed Forces in the Field (Geneva Convention No. I), Aug. 12, 1949, 6 UST 3114, TIAS No. 3362, 75 UNTS 31; Convention for the Amelioration of the Condition of Wounded, Sick and Shipwrecked Members of Armed Forces at Sea (Geneva Convention No. II), Aug. 12, 1949, 6 UST 3217, TIAS No. 3363, 75 UNTS 85; Convention Relative to the Treatment of Prisoners of War (Geneva Convention No. III), Aug. 12, 1949, 6 UST 3316, TIAS No. 3364, 75 UNTS 135; Convention Relative to the Protection of Civilian Persons in Time of War (Geneva Convention No. IV), Aug. 12, 1949, 6 UST 3516, TIAS No. 3365, 75 UNTS 287.

[278] *Commentary* on Geneva Convention No. IV, above n. 84, at 74-5.

[279] See ibid. at 70-1.

[280] Above n. 82.

[281] Above n. 84 and accompanying text. See also Sassòli, *Mise en œuvre du droit international humanitaire et du droit international des droits de l'homme: une*

Article 3 provides that a belligerent which violates the provisions of the Regulations annexed to the Convention shall, 'if the case demands, be liable to pay compensation'. Although *travaux préparatoires* of this Article indicate that the liability to pay compensation was meant to benefit individual victims of violations,[282] the language also applies to interstate claims, whether brought by a state on its own behalf or on behalf of individual victims. Concerning compensation for individuals, Article 3 appears to restrict the remedies to be awarded against the wrongdoing state to monetary compensation. The liability for breaches of the Regulations must be distinguished from the duty, stated in a number of the Regulations, to pay compensation for the lawful taking or use of property and to return such property when peace is made.[283] However, with regard to interstate claims, Article 3 should not be interpreted as excluding additional remedies recognized by general international law, such as apology and punishment of the offenders.[284] The *travaux préparatoires* of Article 3 further suggest that Article 3 establishes strict, objective international responsibility for violations of the Hague Regulations committed by members of a state's armed forces, regardless of whether that state failed to exercise due diligence and could be blamed for 'subjective fault'.[285] Many commentators share this interpretation of Article 3.[286]

What is the scope of applicability *ratione materiae* of Article 3? Commentators have noted that, while the letter of Article 3 requires payment of compensation only for violations of the Hague Regulations, 'there is no reason to doubt that the principle of Article 3 must find application to any rule of the law of war by the violation of which subjects of the enemy, or of neutral States, suffer damage.'[287] The duty to pay compensation for violations of

comparaison, 43 Annuaire Suisse de droit international 24, 41 (1987).

[282] Kalshoven, *State Responsibility for Acts of Armed Forces*, lecture delivered at the 12th Round Table of the International Institute of Humanitarian Law (San Remo, Sept. 1987). See also Sandoz, above n. 84, at 137.

[283] States are also obligated to pay compensation for the destruction, on grounds of absolute necessity, of submarine cables. Hague Regulations 53-4, above n. 82.

[284] 1 L. Oppenheim, above n. 84, at 363. Some cases of responsibility for the acts of armed forces are discussed at ibid. nn. 1-3.

[285] UN Doc. A/CN.4/315 (1977), reprinted in [1978] 2 YB Int'l L. Comm'n (pt. 1) 61, 92-3, UN Doc. A/CN.4/SER.A/1978/Add.1 (Part 1) (1980). See also Sandoz, above n. 84.

[286] [1978] 2 YB Int'l L. Comm'n, above n. 285, at 221-2, UN Doc. A/CN.4/315 (1977).

[287] 2 L. Oppenheim, above n. 226, at 594. Regarding the responsibility of a state

the law of war through, for example, war reparations is inherent in the very notion of a breach of international law. Because the Hague Convention No. IV governs only international armed conflicts, it is unclear whether the special rule of responsibility which it articulates applies to the conduct of members of armed forces either in peacetime or in non-international armed conflicts. In the case of *Affaire des Biens Britanniques au Maroc Espagnol* (*Spain* v. *United Kingdom*), Arbitrator Max Huber declared that the principle stated in Article 3, although not directly applicable, merits application also outside of war as such ('en dehors de la guerre proprement dite').[288] Strictly speaking, however, as with acts or omissions of other organs of state, conduct outside international armed conflicts is governed by customary law.[289]

Both the ICRC's *Commentaries* on common Article 51/ 52/131/148 of the Geneva Conventions and Article 91 of Protocol I further support the notion that the principle stated in Article 3 applies generally to humanitarian instruments such as the Geneva Conventions. Article 148 of Geneva Convention No. IV thus states that no party 'shall be allowed to absolve itself or any other High Contracting Party of any liability incurred by itself or by another High Contracting Party in respect of [Article 147 grave] breaches . . .'. States cannot evade responsibility for breaches of the Convention[290] or of Article 91 of Protocol I[291] on the grounds that the individual perpetrators have already been punished.[292] Referring explicitly to Article 3 of the Hague Convention No. IV, the ICRC *Commentary* on Article 148 of Geneva Convention No. IV observes that

Article 148 is intended to prevent the vanquished from being compelled in an armistice agreement or a peace treaty to renounce all compensation due for breaches committed by persons in the service of the victor. As

for acts of its armed forces abroad, see T. Meron, above n. 33, at 106–7 n. 73 and especially Application No. 8007/77, *Cyprus* v. *Turkey*, Eur. Comm. of Human Rights, [1978] YB Eur. Conv. on Hum. Rts. 100, 230–4.

[288] Report III, above n. 82.

[289] See M. Bothe, K. Partsch, and W. Solf, New Rules for Victims of Armed Conflicts 547 (1982).

[290] See also Section VII, above.

[291] See also Protocol I, Arts. 85–6.

[292] Art. 29 of Geneva Convention IV provides that '[t]he Party to the conflict in whose hands protected persons may be, is responsible for the treatment accorded to them by its agents, irrespective of any individual responsibility which may be incurred.'

regards material compensation for breaches of the Convention, it is inconceivable, at least as the law stands today, that claimants should be able to bring a direct action for damages against the State in whose service the person committing the breach was working. Only a State can make such claims on another State, and they form part, in general, of what is called 'war reparations'. It would seem unjust for individuals to be punished while the State . . . was released from all liability.[293]

Article 91 of Protocol I tracks the language of Article 3 of Hague Convention No. IV and reaffirms its principle of law, except that it provides that states are liable to pay compensation for their breaches of the Geneva Conventions or of Protocol I rather than of the Hague Regulations. Unlike common Article 51/52/131/148, Article 91 is not limited to responsibility for grave breaches. The ICRC's *Commentary* also mentions that Article 91 'literally reproduces' Article 3 of the Hague Convention, which embodies customary law.[294] As discussed in Chapter I, Section VI(B), because only a limited number of rules of international law applicable to non-international armed conflicts have evolved thus far, it is not surprising that Protocol II contains no similar provisions.

The question of which states, besides those directly injured by breaches, have standing to bring actions for violations of international humanitarian instruments is difficult to answer. Because the Hague Convention No. IV was adopted well before the principle of obligations *erga omnes* matured as a part of international law, only an injured party to the conflict or another injured state (e.g. a neutral state that was a victim of a violation of the Convention) was considered to have the necessary standing to vindicate breaches of the Convention. Although only 43 states are parties to Hague Convention No. IV,[295] the customary law status of the Regulations annexed to the Convention is universally recognized. Theoretically, after *Barcelona Traction* there is no reason why these Regulations should not be considered obligations *erga omnes*, in whose protection 'all states can be held to have a legal interest', at least with regard to systematic violations.

[293] Above n. 84, at 603.

[294] Commentary on the Additional Protocols of 8 June 1977 to the Geneva Conventions of 12 August 1949 at 1053 (Y. Sandoz, C. Swinarski, and B. Zimmermann eds. 1987).

[295] United States Department of State, Treaties in Force: A List of Treaties and Other International Agreements of the United States in Force on January 1, 1987, at 301–2.

The question of who has standing to bring actions for violations also arises under the Geneva Conventions which do not contain provisions (except for common Article 51/52/131/148) governing interstate claims for breaches. To vindicate such claims, states may utilize either diplomatic channels or an international tribunal such as the ICJ, provided it has the necessary jurisdiction under Articles 36(1) or 36(2) of its Statute. Common Article 1 of the Geneva Conventions is an important conceptual precursor of the principle of obligations *erga omnes*.[296] Although Article 1 clearly provides every state party with the authority to make representations before a wrongdoing state to bring it back into a position of compliance with the Conventions, it is not clear whether this authority in itself confers standing on all states parties to bring formal claims before international tribunals.[297] Common Article 51/52/131/148 appears to contemplate claims only by the injured state,[298] as indicated by common Article 52/53/132/149, which permits only a party to the conflict to request the institution of an inquiry into an alleged violation of the Convention.

However, the language of the Convention is not dispositive of the issue. The subsequent evolution of the general international law of state responsibility, and especially the recognition of the principle of obligations *erga omnes*, necessarily affect the Conventions' contemporary interpretation and application. The Geneva Conventions clearly epitomize those universal instruments that protect the basic rights of the human person which *Barcelona Traction* considered to be a source of obligations *erga omnes*. Under *Barcelona Traction*, a state party not directly affected by a breach of any one of the Conventions' numerous provisions which protect the human or humanitarian rights of individuals may perhaps bring an action against the wrongdoing state before a competent international tribunal, at least with regard to systematic violations. The ICJ's emphatic characterization of common Articles 1 and 3

---

[296] See above Chapter I, Section III.
[297] *Commentary*, above n. 84, at 16. Sassòli, above n. 281, at 40 appears to suggest that common Art. 1 confers such a standing on each party to the Conventions.
[298] See also Sandoz, above n. 84, at 142. *Commentary* on Geneva Convention No. IV states that '[t]he Convention does not give individual men and women the right to claim compensation. The State is answerable to another contracting State and not to the individual.' Above n. 84, at 211.

as customary law in the *Nicaragua* case[299] strengthens this conception of the Geneva Conventions.

Article 91 of Protocol I also raises the question of standing. Article 91 appears to contemplate claims under Protocol I only by states directly affected by a dispute, i.e., states parties to the conflict or neutral states which claim that they or their nationals are victims of a breach of Protocol I.[300] However, with regard to the international fact-finding commission to be established under Article 90 of the Protocol, the state party requesting an inquiry into allegations that another state party committed a grave or serious breach of the conventions or Protocol I need not be itself the victim of the violation. Rather, the only requirement is that both the complaining state and the 'defendant' state have accepted the Commission's competence under Article 90(2)(a).[301]

Like the Geneva Conventions, the Protocol should not be interpreted as excluding customary international law, which encompasses the principle of obligations *erga omnes*. Identifying such obligations in order to establish the standing of third parties to bring actions for violations creates difficulties which are exacerbated in the case of Protocol II,[302] because it does not contain any provisions on either implementation[303] or responsibility. The possibility of permitting a state not directly involved in a dispute to invoke obligations *erga omnes* would greatly aid the vindication of the important norms stated in Protocol II. However, the small number both of states parties to Protocol II and of clearly recognized rules of customary international law governing internal armed conflicts (i.e. the limited customary law content of Protocol II) creates major obstacles to asserting such claims.

---

[299] See above Chapter I, Section III.

[300] Commentary on the Additional Protocols, above n. 294, at 1054, 1056-7.

[301] M. Bothe, K. Partsch, and W. Solf, above n. 289, at 543. Art. 90(2)(*d*) provides that, in situations in which the Commission's competence has not been recognized in advance, the Commission may institute an inquiry at the request of a party to the conflict only with the consent of the other party. According to Art. 90(1)(*b*), such a commission can be established only after 'not less than twenty [parties] have agreed to accept [its] competence . . .'.

[302] See above Chapter I, Section VI(B).

[303] For a discussion of implementation provisions in the Geneva Conventions and Protocol I, see Dinstein, *Human Rights in Armed Conflict: International Humanitarian Law*, in 2 Human Rights in International Law, above n. 14, at 345, 356-62.

X. THE RELATIONSHIP BETWEEN REMEDIES IN HUMAN RIGHTS TREATIES AND OTHER REMEDIES

Representatives of East European states[304] and some commentators have suggested that the procedures for settlement of disputes and the remedies established under human rights treaties constitute a comprehensive system for redressing human rights violations which excludes *inter partes* resort to systems of settlement and remedies available under other treaties or under customary law. One commentator critical of this suggestion has explained that its rationale is derived from the reluctance of states to have human rights agreements enforced between the parties to the agreements, and the fear that states may resort to reprisals and forcible remedies to enforce human rights agreements to which they are parties.[305] The ICJ's assertion that rules of diplomatic law constitute 'a self-contained regime which [is] entirely efficacious',[306] a not entirely

[304] See e.g. Mohr, cited in Simma, *Self-Contained Regimes*, 16 Neth. YB Int'l L. 111, 130 n. 75 (1985).
Representatives of East European states on the UN Commission on Human Rights have argued that the mandate of the Special Rapporteur on torture and other cruel, inhuman, or degrading treatment or punishment extended only to states that have not become parties to the Convention against Torture and Other Cruel, Inhuman or Degrading Treatment or Punishment. See e.g. remarks by the USSR, UN Doc. E/CN.4/1988/SR.31 at 4; remarks by the Byelorussian Soviet Socialist Republic, UN Doc. E/CN.4/1988/SR.30/Add.1 at 8. The representative of Bulgaria thus argued that 'his delegation did not find very convincing the argument contained in paragraphs 4 to 13 of the report [of Special Rapporteur P. Kooijmans] that the mandates of the Committee and the Special Rapporteur were complementary rather than competitive.' Ibid. For the arguments adduced by the Special Rapporteur in favour of the complementarity of his functions and those of the Committee Against Torture, see UN Doc. E/CN.4/1988/17 at 2-4. The USSR has recently expressed readiness to accept ICJ's jurisdiction over disputes concerning the interpretation and application of several human rights treaties. *Soviets Accept World Court Rulings*, Int'l Herald Tribune, 10 Mar. 1989, at 2, col. 1.

[305] Henkin, above n. 176, at 30, 33. The principal protagonist of the view that the remedies established under human rights treaties exclude resort to other means of settlement is Professor Frowein. See Frowein, *The Interrelationship between the Helsinki Final Act, the International Covenants on Human Rights, and the European Convention on Human Rights*, in Human Rights, International Law and the Helsinki Accord, above n. 176, at 71, 79. See also Frowein, *Collective Enforcement of International Obligations*, 47 Zeitschrift für ausländisches öffentliches Recht und Völkerrecht 67, 76-7 (1987).

[306] *United States Diplomatic and Consular Staff in Tehran* (*United States of America* v. *Iran*), 1980 ICJ Rep. at 3, 40. In the *Nicaragua* case, the ICJ stated that 'where human rights are protected by international conventions, that protection takes the form of such arrangements for monitoring or ensuring respect for human rights as are provided for in the conventions themselves [and that in any event] the use of force could not be the appropriate method to monitor or ensure such respect.'

realistic statement, has intensified the interest in this question.[307] Because procedures for the settlement of disputes and remedies recognized by human rights treaties are often weak and based on optional acts of acceptance, which are not commonly resorted to, to endorse the exclusivity of treaty remedies would intensify the fragility and ineffectiveness of such treaties' norms. Such an endorsement would also accord human rights treaties 'a quality lower than that of other treaties'.[308] The latter can also be enforced through diplomatic channels, other procedures of dispute settlement, and lawful self-help, as well as by means of procedures for settlement of disputes which they provide. Therefore, the question of whether the remedies provided under human rights treaties, customary law, and other treaties applicable to the states concerned are cumulative or exclusive of each other is very important.

The ILC has aptly observed that, subject to peremptory norms, 'some States may at any time, in a treaty concluded between them, provide for a special régime of responsibility for the breach of obligations for which the treaty makes specific provision.'[309] To the extent that treaty language does not exclude recourse to remedies dehors the treaty, the rules of customary international law, of course, continue to apply as residual rules.[310] When a human rights treaty provides procedures for the settlement of disputes, it is necessary to determine whether those treaty provisions displace the

1986 ICJ Rep. 134. The ICJ did not assert generally, however, that treaty remedies are exclusive.

[307] See e.g. Simma, above n. 304, at 111.

[308] Simma, *Consent: Strains in the Treaty System*, in The Structure and Process of International Law: Essays in Legal Philosophy, Doctrine and Theory 485, 501 (R. Macdonald and D. Johnston eds. 1983).

[309] [1976] 2 YB Int'l L. Comm'n (pt. 2) at 80, UN Doc. A/CN.4/SER.A/1976/Add.1 (Part 2) (1977). Draft Art. 2 of the ILC's draft articles on state responsibility (part two), proposed by Special Rapporteur Riphagen in his second report, stated that '[a] rule of international law, whether of customary, conventional or other origin, imposing an obligation on a State, may explicitly or implicitly determine also the legal consequences of the breach of such obligation.' UN Doc. A/CN.4/344 (1981), reprinted in [1981] 2 YB Int'l L. Comm'n (pt. 1) 79, 100, UN Doc. A/CN.4/SER.A/1981/Add.1 (Part 1)(1983).

For an example of a treaty which, subject to a different stipulation by the parties, explicitly excludes remedies dehors the treaty, see Convention on the Settlement of Investment Disputes between States and Nationals of other States, Art. 26, signed 18 March 1965, 17 UST 1270, TIAS No. 6090, 575 UNTS 159.

[310] Compare Art. 3 of the ILC's draft articles on state responsibility (part two), [1985] 2 YB Int'l L. Comm'n (pt. 2) at 20, UN Doc. A/CN.4/SER.A/1985/Add.1 (Part 2) (1986).

general rules of state responsibility. Whether a particular human rights treaty excludes remedies dehors the treaty depends, of course, not on abstract legal theory but on a good faith interpretation of the terms of the treaty in light of their context and the object and purpose of the treaty.[311] Professor Henkin effectively answered the argument that there is a presumption in favour of interpreting human rights treaties as contemplating only treaty remedies when he demonstrated that nothing in the character of human rights agreements suggests any intention 'to eliminate the ordinary legal consequences of international undertakings and the ordinary remedies for their violation'.[312] Section 703(1) of the Restatement advances the thesis of the cumulative character of treaty remedies and remedies dehors the treaty. This section states that

[a] state party to an international human rights agreement has, as against any other state party violating the agreement, the remedies generally available for violation of an international agreement, as well as any special remedies provided by the particular agreement.[313]

§ 703(1) comment *a*, stating that '[u]nless the human rights agreement provides or clearly implies otherwise, the ordinary remedies are available to any state party against a state party violating the agreement, even if the violation did not affect nationals of the claimant state or any other particular interest of that state', dispels any doubt generated by the language of § 703(1).

The principle of effectiveness as well as the integrity of the treaty must be considered in the process of interpretation. For example, the comprehensiveness and effectiveness of the settlement of disputes procedures established by the EEC Treaty,[314] as further developed by the organs of the European Community, support the generally accepted view that the EEC's legal system constitutes a self-contained regime, and that resort to remedies dehors that system

[311] Vienna Convention on the Law of Treaties, opened for signature 23 May 1969, Art. 31(1), 1155 UNTS 331, reprinted in 63 AJIL 3875 (1969), 8 ILM 679 (1969).
[312] Henkin, above n. 176, at 31.
[313] Above n. 1. See also Chapter II n. 4 and accompanying text.
[314] Above n. 33.

is excluded.[315] Perhaps this conclusion may also apply to the ILO's international labour conventions.[316]

In view of the rather limited nature of the settlement of disputes procedures contained in the Political Covenant,[317] it is not surprising that Article 44 of the Covenant liberally allows states parties that have recognized the competence of the Human Rights Committee with regard to interstate complaints under Article 41 to resort to other means of settling disputes concerning the Covenant's interpretation and application, including the ICJ.[318] Article 44 provides that the Covenant's implementation provisions 'shall not prevent the States Parties . . . from having recourse to other procedures for settling a dispute in accordance with general or special international agreements in force between them'. The *travaux préparatoires* of Article 44 indicate that the Covenant's implementation procedures 'should not normally come into play where another procedure, available to the States Parties concerned under a general or special agreement . . . was more specifically adapted to provide a solution of the matter in issue . . .'.[319]

Regarding interstate disputes, the European Convention on Human Rights, which establishes a very effective settlement of disputes system, explicitly excludes resort to means of settlement dehors the Convention, such as the International Court of Justice or UN human rights organs.[320] Article 62 of the Convention provides that states parties, 'except by special agreement', may submit disputes concerning the interpretation or application of

[315] Compare Simma, above n. 304, at 123-9.

[316] Henkin, above n. 176, at 39 n. 20. The International Labour Organisation's Conventions do not contain provisions concerning non-ILO settlement of disputes procedures. T. Meron, above n. 33, at 218-19 and n. 16. Arts. 29, 31 and 32 of the ILO's Constitution, above n. 172, are viewed as an integral part of the ILO's settlement of disputes procedures. ILO's system of supervision of implementation is particularly comprehensive and effective.

[317] For settlement of disputes clauses in human rights treaties, see above Section I.

[318] T. Meron, above n. 33, at 217-18.

[319] M. Bossuyt, above n. 12, at 724. See also Sohn, above n. 40, at 393; Robertson, *The Implementation System: International Measures*, in The International Bill of Rights, above n. 17, at 332, 356. Professor Schachter notes that UN practice demonstrates that states have brought many complaints of human rights violations before UN organs, acting dehors settlement of disputes procedures stated in human rights treaties. Schachter, *International Law Implications of U.S. Human Rights Policies, above n. 188, at 73.*

[320] See T. Meron, above n. 33, at 235-6. On considering individual communications under Art. 5(2)(a) of the Optional Protocol to the International Covenant on Civil and Political Rights, see ibid. at 218, 222-9.

the Convention only to a means of settlement provided in the Convention.[321] The inclusion of Article 62 in the Convention indicates the drafters' understanding that, in absence of this provision, states parties would be permitted to use settlement of disputes procedures dehors the Convention. In 1970, the Committee of Ministers of the Council of Europe adopted Resolution (70) 17 concerning states that are parties to both the European Convention and the Political Covenant, and that have made a declaration under Article 41 of the Political Covenant. The resolution stated that such countries should normally use only the European Convention's procedure for interstate complaints relating to an alleged violation of a right covered in substance by both the Convention (or its Protocols) and the Covenant. At the same time, the Committee of Ministers indicated that the procedure under the Covenant may be utilized for rights not guaranteed by the Convention or in relation to states that are not parties to the Convention.

Regarding individual applications, the resolution suggested that the Council of Europe's member states make a declaration of interpretation or a reservation to the Political Covenant's Optional Protocol to the effect that the competence of the Human Rights Committee would not extend to receiving and considering individual complaints relating to cases that are, or have been, examined under the European Convention on Human Rights.[322] Such a declaration would apply to complaints of violations of rights protected in substance by both the European Convention and the Political Covenant.[323]

XI. COUNTERMEASURES, NON-JUDICIAL REMEDIES

Although the preceding discussion has emphasized the role of judicial remedies in vindicating human rights by states, in practice

---

[321] Compare the less restrictive approach followed by Art. 46(1)(*c*) of the American Convention on Human Rights.

[322] See T. Meron, above n. 33, at 236-7. On the interrelationship between the American and UN systems for protecting human rights, see ibid. at 229-34. Concerning the practice of the Human Rights Committee in relation to such reservations, see Ghandhi, *The Human Rights Committee and the Right of Individual Communication*, 57 Brit. YB Int'l L. 201, 229-37 (1986).

[323] Such declarations or reservations were made by Austria, Denmark, France, Iceland, Italy, Luxembourg, Norway, Spain and Sweden. Multilateral Treaties Deposited with the Secretary-General: Status as at 31 December 1987, at 152-3, UN Doc. ST/LEG/SER.E/6 (1988).

states rely much more frequently on non-judicial remedies or countermeasures. 'Non-judicial' does not, however, mean illegal or extralegal. International law does provide guidelines, albeit imprecise and general in nature, for the lawful use of countermeasures.

Countermeasures comprise a broad subject to which important studies by the special rapporteurs of the ILC and considerable literature[324] have been devoted. This discussion of the topic will be brief and limited to central aspects of human rights and humanitarian norms protection as relevant to the purposes of this study. Because states are reluctant to bring actions for human rights breaches, countermeasures are an extremely important mechanism for enforcing human rights.

In the context of this study, countermeasures not involving the use of armed force[325] fall into two principal categories. The first, reprisals, involves an act of state which would be internationally wrongful were it not committed as a lawful response to another state's internationally wrongful act; for example, a suspension by state X of a binding aviation treaty with state Y as a countermeasure to state Y's breach of its international obligations to respect human rights. The second, retorsions, involves an unfriendly but not unlawful act by one state in response to a breach of human rights by another state; for example, severing diplomatic relations or terminating discretionary aid. Unlike reprisals, states may undertake retorsions irrespective of prior violations by another state of its legal duties. As Professor Schachter points out, retorsions as practical and political matters are often more effective than reprisals.[326] Nevertheless, because retorsion falls within the sovereign discretion of states and, in principle, is not regulated by international law, it is beyond the scope of this discussion, which

[324] See e.g. Restatement, above n. 1, §905; Schachter, above n. 177, at 167–87; O. Elagab, The Legality of Non-Forcible Counter-Measures in International Law (1988); E. Zoller, Peacetime Unilateral Remedies: An Analysis of Countermeasures (1984); E. Zoller, Enforcing International Law through U.S. Legislation (1985); Regarding US practice concerning countermeasures in response to breach of human rights, see ibid. at 125–34. See also Zemanek, *Responsibility of States: General Principles*, [Instalment] 10 Encyclopedia of Public International Law 362, 370–2 (R. Bernhardt ed. 1987). See also below n. 329. For other cases of resort to countermeasures, see P. M. Dupuy, *Observations sur la pratique récente des "sanctions" de l'illicite*, 87 Rev. gén. droit int'l pub. 505, 526–47 (1983).

[325] Regarding reprisals under the Additional Protocols, see below text preceding and accompanying n. 353. Forceful countermeasures may only be carried out subject to the UN Charter.

[326] Schachter, above n. 177, at 169.

will focus on reprisals. It should be pointed out, however, that the ILC's draft Article 30 (to be discussed below) does not include retorsion in its concept of countermeasures. Conversely, the *Commentary* to draft Article 30 makes it clear that the Article was intended to encompass

measures [taken under the UN Charter in] 'legitimate' application of sanctions against a State which is found guilty within that system of certain specific wrongful acts. This view would, moreover, seem to be valid not only in cases where the duly adopted decision of the Organization authorizing the application of a sanction is mandatory for the Member States but also where the taking of such measures is merely recommended.[327]

Because the concept of obligations *erga omnes* has matured into general international law,[328] in principle every state, and not only the state directly affected, should be allowed to take lawful countermeasures in response to another state's breaches of such obligations. The United States has thus suspended the US–Polish Air Transport Agreement of 1972 in reaction to the repression by the Polish government of the Solidarity movement, although such a suspension may not have been provided for under the specific terms of that Agreement.[329] However, despite such emergent practice, at least with regard to countermeasures adopted outside the framework of the United Nations, it is still unclear whether such a rule has already crystallized as customary law. Ideally, an

[327] [1979] 2 YB Int'l L. Comm'n (pt. 2) at 119, UN Doc. A/CN.4/ SER.A/1979/Add.1 (Part 2) (1980).

[328] For discussion of the meaning and scope of obligations *erga omnes*, see above Section V.

[329] For the discussion of this case, see 76 AJIL 379–81 (1982). For the related suspension of US–USSR agreements, see ibid. at 382–4.

With regard to customary human rights, Professor Frowein agrees that in contrast to treaty human rights, 'a right to use reprisals against a State neglecting its obligations on a large scale and in an open and undisputable manner may well be accepted . . .'. Frowein, *Collective Enforcement of International Obligations*, above n. 305, at 76. Compare P. M. Dupuy, *Le Fait générateur de la responsabilité internationale des Etats*, 188 Recueil des cours 9, 58–9 (1984-V).

Professor Graefrath argues that '[f]rom being faced with an international crime or another violation of *erga omnes* obligation, it does not, however, follow, that every State not directly affected . . . [by an international crime or another breach of an *erga omnes* obligation] would have the right to apply individually sanctions exceeding what is called "unfriendly measures"'. Graefrath, above n. 221, at 67–8. Appropriate measures can be taken only 'within the framework of the United Nations.' Ibid. at 74. Riphagen holds a similar view. UN Doc. E/CN.4/366/Add.1 at paras. 25, 27 (1983).

effective UN institutional machinery would regulate recourse by states not specially affected to countermeasures. Where a binding Security Council resolution so requires, states are, of course, obligated to take appropriate countermeasures (which in this context are different from traditional reprisals). Thus, in the ICJ's advisory opinion on *Namibia*,[330] the Court declared that all UN member states were required to recognize the illegality of South Africa's presence in Namibia and the invalidity of its acts concerning Namibia, and to refrain from any acts and dealings implying recognition of the legality of, or lending support or assistance to, South Africa's presence and administration.[331]

Draft Article 30 of the ILC's draft articles on state responsibility (part one) sets forth the basic principle of international law governing countermeasures:

The wrongfulness of an act of a State not in conformity with an obligation of that State towards another State is precluded if the act constitutes a measure legitimate under international law against that other State, in consequence of an internationally wrongful act of that other State.[332]

Perhaps because the ILC believed that this task should be undertaken by the drafters of part two of the draft articles, Article 30 does not articulate rules for determining when a countermeasure constitutes 'a measure legitimate under international law'. Special Rapporteur Riphagen proposed some useful guidelines for assessing the legality of countermeasures. Riphagen's draft Article 9 provides that, although the injured state[333] is entitled, by way of reprisal, to suspend the performance of its other obligations toward the

---

[330] *Legal Consequences for States of the Continued Presence of South Africa in Namibia (South West Africa) Notwithstanding Security Council Resolution 276 (1970)*, 1971 ICJ Rep. 16.

[331] Ibid. at 58. These duties included 'abst[ention] from entering into treaty relations with South Africa in all cases in which the Government of South Africa purports to act on behalf of or concerning Namibia. With respect to existing bilateral treaties, member States must abstain from invoking or applying those treaties or provisions of treaties concluded by South Africa on behalf of or concerning Namibia which involve active intergovernmental co-operation.' Ibid. at 55. Multilateral treaties are discussed further below.

[332] The ILC's *Commentary* explains that 'an act of the State, although not in conformity with what would be required of it by a binding international obligation towards another State, is not internationally wrongful if it constitutes the application with respect to that other State of a measure permissible in international law as a reaction to an international offence which the latter State has committed previously.' Above n. 327, at 115.

[333] For discussion of this term, see above Sections V–VI.

state which has committed an internationally wrongful act, the exercise of this right 'shall not, in its effects, be manifestly disproportional to the seriousness of the internationally wrongful act committed'.[334] In the field of human rights, assessing whether a countermeasure conforms to the principle of proportionality[335] inevitably poses difficulties. Draft Article 10 requires that the injured state exhaust the international procedures available to it for peaceful settlement before taking countermeasures to apply Article 9.[336] This requirement seemingly encompasses the duty to give a warning or prior notice of a reprisal.[337] Draft Article 12(b), which prohibits suspending obligations constituting peremptory norms of international law by taking countermeasures,[338] is of particular significance to human rights and humanitarian norms. These draft articles do not include a provision generally prohibiting the suspension of norms protecting such rights through countermeasures. Although Professor Riphagen acknowledged that reprisals which breach 'objective regimes which impose on States the respect of human rights, whatever the nationality of the person affected, and whatever the circumstances [are] obviously inadmissible',[339] perhaps he believed that draft Article 4 on peremptory norms, proposed in his third report, already covered this prohibition.[340] Because not all human rights are peremptory norms, draft

---

[334] W. Riphagen, Fifth Report on the Content, Forms and Degrees of International Responsibility (part 2 of the draft articles), UN Doc. A/CN.4/380 (1984), reprinted in [1984] 2 YB Int'l L. Comm'n (pt. 1) 1, 3, UN Doc. A/CN.4/SER.A/1984/Add.1 (Part 1) (1986).

[335] Special Rapporteur Riphagen considered that the rule of proportionality was, 'in a broad sense, an existing rule of international law . . .'. [1981] 1 YB Int'l L. Comm'n 130, UN Doc. A/CN.4/SER.A/1981 (1982).

[336] [1984] 1 YB Int'l L. Comm'n 260, UN Doc. A/CN.4/SER.A/1984 (1985). See Professor Schachter's discussion of the question of whether recourse to peaceful settlement is required before resort to reprisals. Schachter, above n. 177, at 172-5. See also Damrosch, *Retaliation or Arbitration—or Both? The 1978 United States—France Aviation Dispute*, 74 AJIL 785, 802-7 (1980).

[337] On the question of the duty to give such notice, see Schachter, above n. 177, at 170. See also draft Art. 2 (part three of ILC's draft articles on state responsibility) proposed by Riphagen in his sixth report, UN Doc. A/CN.4/389, reprinted in [1985] 2 YB Int'l L. Comm'n (pt. 1) at 4, UN Doc. A/CN.4/SER.A/1985/Add.1 (Part 1) (1987).

[338] [1984] 2 YB Int'l L. Comm'n (pt. 1) 4, UN Doc. A/CN.4/SER.A/1984/Add.1 (Part 1) (1986).

[339] W. Riphagen, Fourth Report on the Content, Forms and Degrees of International Responsibility (part 2 of the draft articles), UN Doc. A/CN.4/366 and Add. 1 (1983), reprinted in [1983] 2 YB Int'l L. Comm'n (pt. 1) 3, 17, UN Doc. A/CN.4/SER.A/1983/Add.1 (Part 1) (1985).

[340] Ibid. at 6-7.

238   *Responsibility for Violation of Rights*

Article 4 did not comprehensively address the prohibition of reprisals involving the suspension of human rights.[341] Article 11(1)(c) of Professor Riphagen's fifth report corrected this deficiency with regard to human rights obligations stated in multilateral treaties, but not those contained in bilateral treaties or enshrined in customary law.[342] That provision stated that

[t]he injured State is not entitled to suspend the performance of its obligations towards the State which has committed the internationally wrongful act to the extent that such obligations are stipulated in a multilateral treaty to which both States are parties and it is established that . . . such obligations are stipulated for the protection of individual persons irrespective of their nationality.[343]

Article 11(1)(c) clearly builds on the ICJ's *Namibia* advisory opinion,[344] in which the Court stated that the obligation to abstain from invoking or applying bilateral treaties concluded by South Africa on behalf of or concerning Namibia does not apply to such multilateral, general conventions 'as those of a humanitarian character, the non-performance of which may adversely affect the people of Namibia'.[345] The Court stressed that 'non-recognition of South Africa's administration of the Territory should not result in depriving the people of Namibia [("the injured entity")] of any advantages derived from international cooperation.'[346]

There are obviously compelling reasons for excluding human rights and humanitarian norms from obligations, whether conventional or customary, that may be suspended, in response to a state's breach of international law. Conceptually, countermeasures are based on the principle of interstate reciprocity,[347] which,

---

[341] See the remarks by Mr McCaffrey, [1983] 1 YB Int'l L. Comm'n 144, UN Doc. A/CN.4/SER.A/1983 (1984).

[342] Perhaps Professor Riphagen's omission of a reference to customary law can be explained by his apparent belief that customary law contains no human rights obligations except those embodying norms of *jus cogens*, which were already addressed in his draft Art. 12(b).

[343] [1984] 1 YB Int'l L. Comm'n, above n. 336, at 260.

[344] W. Riphagen, Second Report on the Content, Forms and Degrees of International Responsibility (part 2 of the draft articles), UN Doc. A/CN.4/344 (1981), reprinted in [1981] 2 YB Int'l L. Comm'n (pt. 1) 79, 86–7, UN Doc. A/CN.4/SER.A/1981/Add. 1 (Part 1) (1983).

[345] 1971 ICJ Rep. 55.

[346] Ibid. at 56.

[347] Art. 8 proposed by Professor Riphagen in his fifth report provides that 'the injured State is entitled, by way of reciprocity, to suspend the performance of its obligations towards the State which has committed an internationally wrongful act,

generally speaking, is foreign to human rights.[348] Thus, in explaining why a violation of internationally protected human rights in one state cannot justify a violation of those rights in another state, Professor Riphagen aptly observed that 'the international obligations involved are not primarily inter-State obligations but rather parallel obligations of States for the protection of "extra-State" interests.'[349] In a later report, Professor Riphagen elaborated on this notion of 'extra-state interests' as follows:

[There are] tendencies in modern international law to recognize and protect interests which are 'extra-State' interests in the sense that their ultimate beneficiaries are entities which are not States, but individual human beings, peoples or even humanity as a whole. Since those entities are not normally—at least in general international law—given a status separate from but similar to that of a State, the rules of international law protecting their interests are still rules creating rights for and imposing obligations on States. Consequently, such rights and obligations must generally 'survive' a breach of an international obligation by a State to which those rights and obligations are given, so to speak, 'in trust', for the benefit of these extra-State entities.[350]

Commentators have observed that the prohibition of reprisals in humanitarian law results from the substance of the primary rules themselves, which, in contrast to other rules, have extra-state, objective, and normative characters.[351] Indeed, it must always be remembered that the beneficiaries of human rights are individuals, not states, and that many human rights entail obligations *erga omnes* which run to all states. Therefore, if a state were to resort to countermeasures involving the suspension of its human rights obligations, it would violate its obligations both to other states not involved in the breach which triggered the countermeasure, and to

if such obligations correspond to, or are directly connected with, the obligation breached.' Above n.334, at 3.

[348] T. Meron, above n. 33, at 146–7; Simma, above n. 304, at 131; W. Riphagen, Fourth Report, above n. 339, at 17.

[349] W. Riphagen, Preliminary Report on the Content, Forms and Degrees of International Responsibility (Part 2 of the draft articles on State responsibility), UN Doc. A/CN.4/330 (1980), reprinted in [1980] 2 YB Int'l L. Comm'n (pt. 1) 107, 127, UN Doc. A/CN.4/SER.A/1980/Add.1 (Part 1) (1982).

[350] W. Riphagen, Second Report, above n. 344, at 86.

[351] Combacau and Alland, *"Primary" and "Secondary" Rules in the Law of State Responsibility: Categorizing International Obligations*, 16 Neth. YB Int'l L. 81, 92 (1985).

innocent individuals within the state.[352] This result is obviously unacceptable.

Humanitarian law instruments address this proposition by explicitly prohibiting reprisals against civilians. While Geneva Convention Articles 46/47/13(3)/33(3) prohibit reprisals against persons whom they protect, Protocol I, Articles 51(6), 52(1), 53(c), 54(4), 55(2), and 56(4) significantly broaden the prohibition of reprisals against civilians and civilian objects. In effect, under Protocol I only armed forces and military objects remain as permissible targets for reprisals.[353]

Some additional consideration is necessary concerning the question of whether human rights or humanitarian treaties may be suspended by a state in response to a material breach of their provisions by another state. This question involves interlocking issues of the law of treaties, the law of state responsibility, and human rights law.[354] Article 60 of the Vienna Convention on the Law of Treaties,[355] viewed by the ICJ as a codification of existing customary law in many respects,[356] provides significant guidance in analysing this issue.

First, some prefatory comments about responses to breaches of treaties which do not concern human rights are necessary. Article 42 of the Vienna Convention on the Law of Treaties (to be discussed further below) provides that termination or suspension of a treaty may take place only as a result of the application of the provisions of the Vienna Convention. Regarding bilateral treaties, Article 60(1) provides that a material breach by one party entitles the other party to invoke the breach as a ground for terminating the treaty or suspending its operation in whole or in part. Concerning multilateral treaties, Article 60(2)(b) only allows the party specially

---

[352] Professor Schachter believes that the prohibition of reprisals involving human rights is less sweeping. He proposes a distinction between actions that relate to the basic rights of individuals, or grave violations of fundamental human rights, with regard to which countermeasures may not be taken, and privileges allowed to foreign nationals on the basis of treaty or comity, which are subject to suspension as part of countermeasures. Schachter, above n. 177, at 179-80.

[353] See Condorelli and Boisson de Chazournes, above n. 233, at 20-1.

[354] In its 1971 advisory opinion on *Namibia*, above n. 330, the ICJ noted that the right to terminate a treaty on account of breach 'has its source outside of the treaty, in general international law . . .'. 1971 ICJ Rep. 47.

[355] Above n. 311. The principal writings on Art. 60 are listed in I. Sinclair, above n. 189 at 201 n. 128.

[356] 1971 ICJ Rep. 47.

affected by the breach to invoke it as a ground for suspending the operation of the treaty in whole, or in part, in the relations between itself and the defaulting state. Except in cases covered by Article 60(2)(c),[357] the other parties may suspend the operation of a multilateral treaty or terminate it by unanimous agreement in response to a material breach by one party. On its face, Article 60(2)(b) appears to preclude states not specially affected by a breach from unilaterally suspending a treaty in response to that breach. Some commentators believe, however, that Article 60 does not displace general international law, which encompasses both the rules governing countermeasures and the principle of obligations *erga omnes*. Instead, it establishes a number of 'residuary rules'.[358] According to this view, which is seemingly contrary to Article 60(2)(b) of the Vienna Convention, even a state not directly affected by a breach of obligations *erga omnes* may unilaterally respond to that breach[359] by suspending the operation of a multilateral treaty in the relations between itself and the breaching state. Concerning humanitarian treaties, Article 60(5) articulates a special rule. It provides that paragraphs 1–3 of that Article 'do not apply to provisions relating to the protection of the human person contained in treaties of a humanitarian character, in particular to provisions prohibiting any form of reprisals against persons protected by such treaties'.

Although the Swiss delegation introduced the amendment leading to Article 60(5) at the Vienna Conference on the Law of Treaties primarily with the Geneva Conventions in mind, the delegation's broader intent was 'to put a curb on the harmful effects which the provisions of Article 57 [now Article 60] could have on individuals [and to create] a saving clause to protect human beings'.[360] Therefore, the principle of customary law embodied in Article 60(5) clearly applies to both humanitarian and human rights treaties. In theory, Article 60(5) leaves intact the right of a state to suspend those provisions which do not relate to the protection of the human person and do not constitute *jus cogens* norms in response to a

---

[357] Art. 60(2)(c) concerns a treaty 'of such a character that a material breach of its provisions by one party radically changes the position of every party with respect to the further performance of its obligations under the treaty'.

[358] I. Sinclair, above n. 189, at 188.

[359] Compare Schachter, above n. 177, at 183–4.

[360] United Nations Conference on the Law of Treaties, Official Records, 2nd Sess., 21st plenary mtg., 13 May 1969, UN Doc. A/CONF.39/11/Add.1 at 112

material breach of a humanitarian or human rights treaty.[361] Nevertheless, such provisions are often neither separable from the remainder of the treaty, nor of any significant weight in the balance of reciprocity between the states concerned. Article 60(5) does not affect the invocation of other lawful grounds for claiming the right to withdraw from a treaty, to denounce it, or to argue that it should be terminated or suspended.

The goal of increasing the effectiveness of international human rights and humanitarian norms could be advanced if the victim state could, in response to a breach of a human rights treaty or a humanitarian treaty, suspend the operation of a treaty which does not concern the protection of the human person. This goal must be balanced against that of securing the stability of international agreements and the principle of *pacta sunt servanda*.

The question is whether resort to countermeasures involving the non-performance of treaty A in response to a breach of human rights treaty B can be reconciled with Article 42(2) of the Vienna Convention on the Law of Treaties. This Article provides that the termination of a treaty, its denunciation or the withdrawal of a party, or the suspension of the operation of a treaty 'may take place only as a result of the application of the provisions of the treaty or of the present Convention'.

Did Article 42(2) intend to create a comprehensive system, excluding resort to customary law countermeasures involving treaties? This question is answered neither in the ILC's *Commentary* on draft Article 39(2),[362] which later became Article 42(2), nor in the following exchange between the British and Czechoslovak delegates that took place during the Vienna Conference on the Law of Treaties. Expressing doubts whether the grounds of invalidity, termination, denunciation, withdrawal and suspension mentioned in Article 39(2) were exhaustive, Sinclair (United Kingdom) pointed

(1970).

[361] Compare Henkin, above n. 176, at 39–40 n. 24. Plender correctly observes that 'a breach of a peremptory norm of general international law, embodied in a treaty, cannot be invoked by an innocent party as a ground for terminating or suspending the operation of the provision embodying that norm. . . . [B]y definition the obligation arises not under the treaty but *aliunde*; and if two parties cannot set aside that principle consensually, in their mutual relations, it must follow *a fortiori* that one party cannot set it aside unilaterally in its relations with another State that has failed to observe it.' Plender, *The Role of Consent in the Termination of Treaties*, 57 Brit. YB Int'l L. 133, 164 (1986).

[362] [1966] 2 YB Int'l L. Comm'n at 237, UN Doc. A/CN.4/SER.A/1966/Add.1

out that 'the articles did not seek to regulate the effect of the outbreak of hostilities on treaties, yet it was well known that that could constitute a sufficient ground for terminating or suspending the operation of a treaty obligation.'[363] He suggested that the ILC had 'intended to convey . . . that the grounds were exhaustive to the extent that the draft articles and the commentary read as a whole did not specifically exclude them'.[364] Myslil (Czechoslovakia) argued, however, that the enumeration contained in Article 39 was exhaustive and that '[t]he intention had been to replace the rules of customary law by rules of treaty law and thereby prevent a recourse to customary law in the future, except perhaps with regard to the effect of hostilities on treaties. . . .'[365]

Other provisions of the Vienna Convention are of course pertinent to our discussion. The Preamble to the Vienna Convention affirms the residuary role of customary law with regard to questions not regulated by the provisions of the Convention. Article 73 of the Convention states that the Convention's provisions shall not prejudge any question that may arise in regard to a treaty from a succession of states or from the international responsibility of a state or from the outbreak of hostilities between states, suggesting perhaps that suspension of a treaty's operation for reasons extraneous to the law governing the treaty and justifiable *aliter et aliunde*, i.e. by the general international law, as in the case of countermeasures, is not precluded.[366] The conflict between Article 30 of ILC's draft articles on state responsibility (part one) and Articles 42 and 60 of the Vienna Convention on the Law of Treaties is perhaps more apparent than real. Draft Article 30 does not suggest that the breach of an international obligation (in this case an international conventional obligation) is always lawful if it constitutes a countermeasure taken in response to an earlier breach of an international obligation. The determination of a

---

(1967).

[363] United Nations Conference on the Law of Treaties, Official Records, 1st Sess., 39th mtg. of the Committee of the Whole, 26 Apr. 1968, UN Doc. A/CONF.39/11/Add.1 at 218 (1969).

[364] Ibid.

[365] Ibid. at 220.

[366] See O. Elagab, above n. 324, at 157–8; E. Zoller, Peacetime Unilateral Remedies, above n. 324, at 17–18, 89, 92–3; Capotorti, *L'Extinction et la suspension des traités*, 134 Recueil des cours 417, 446–7 (1971-III). See generally Simma, *Reflections on Article 60 of the Vienna Convention on the Law of Treaties and its Background in General International Law*, 20 Österreichische Zeitschrift für öffen-

countermeasure's lawfulness is implicitly left to part two of the draft articles. Although the ILC has not yet adopted such articles, draft Articles 9 and 11 presented by Riphagen in his fifth report (1984) suggest that states may lawfully breach a treaty obligation not only in response to a breach of the same treaty, but also in response to an earlier violation of other treaties or of customary law, provided that the requirement of proportionality and other conditions are met. It would appear that the object of Article 60 was not exhaustively to enumerate all the cases in which suspension or termination of a treaty is lawful, but only to consider the effect of the breach of a treaty on the existence and operation of that treaty, as a matter of treaty law. That Article 60 did not intend to preclude the suspension or termination of a treaty as a form of state responsibility for the violation of obligations not contained in that treaty is supported also by Article 73 of the Vienna Convention on the Law of Treaties.

Eventually, the question will be clarified by the practice of states. Emerging practice indicates some support for the position advocated by Sinclair. Although the language of Article 60(1) of the Vienna Convention would suggest that a state may not terminate or suspend treaty A on the ground that a material breach of treaty B was committed, the arbitrators in the *Case Concerning the Air Services Agreement of 27 March 1946*, in the context of countermeasures cautiously noted the question 'whether or not all the obligations under consideration pertain to the same convention'.[367] The ICJ's allusion to countermeasures in the *Nicaragua* judgment is also indicative of their importance and broad applicability in customary law. While emphasizing that it was confining its decision to the points of law which were essential to the settlement of the dispute before it, the ICJ left open the question of the

direct reactions [which] are lawfully open to a State which considers itself the victim of another State's acts of intervention, possibly involving the use of force. Hence it has not to determine whether, in the event of Nicaragua's having committed any such acts against El Salvador, the latter was lawfully entitled to take any particular counter-measure.[368]

tliches Recht 5 (1970).
[367] Above n. 56, at 338.
[368] 1986 ICJ Rep. 14, 110.

Article 42(2) of the Vienna Convention notwithstanding, it is difficult to agree that international law allows countermeasures implicating customary law, but not those implicating treaties.

A number of humanitarian and human rights conventions reserve the right of states to denounce such conventions, whether or not in response to a breach.[369] Under the Geneva Conventions (common Article 63/62/142/158) the denunciation, which does not become effective until one year after it is announced, does not affect the customary law obligations of the state concerned.

[369] See e.g. Convention on the Prevention and Punishment of the Crime of Genocide, opened for signature 9 Dec. 1948, Art. 14, 78 UNTS 277. See also Chapter I, Section I, above and the denunciation clause of the Geneva Conventions, above n. 277, common Art. 63/62/142/158. Although these articles allow denunciation, they also provide that 'a denunciation of which notification has been made at a time when the denouncing Power is involved in a conflict shall not take effect until peace has been concluded, and until after operations connected with the release and repatriation of the persons protected by the present Convention[s] have been terminated.' De Preux thus correctly concludes that, under the Conventions, '[t]he legal obligations . . . remain unchanged, no matter what breaches are committed by the adverse party. The rule of reciprocity is not operative [here].' De Preux, *The Geneva Conventions and Reciprocity*, Int'l Rev. Red Cross, No. 244, Jan.-Feb. 1985, 25, 27. See also Vienna Convention on the Law of Treaties, Art. 56.

Concluding Remarks

It is not my goal here to set out in detail the conclusions of this study, which examines a wide range of related yet discrete questions. We have seen that a great many human rights and humanitarian norms have already crystallized into customary law, and we have examined the process by which human rights and humanitarian norms mature into customary law, including the relationship between custom and treaty. Many other norms will soon be recognized as customary law, and thus acquire universality, binding even those states that are not parties to the treaties setting forth those norms. Efforts to promote the universality of human rights through attempts to assure concordant behaviour both by non-parties to the pertinent instruments and by those states that have dissented from their adoption will and must continue, despite the tension which these efforts generate between the important values embodied in the relevant norms and the sovereignty of non-parties. The credibility of the norms requires that attempts to extend their universality and further to reduce the already contracting domain of domestic jurisdiction utilize irreproachable methods. The fabric of international law need not be torn to establish the legitimate place of human rights and humanitarian norms in general international law. To be sure, human rights and humanitarian norms have certain special characteristics, such as the greater focus on the role of the individual and, especially in human rights, the relatively minor significance of the principle of reciprocity. Unlike most other fields of international law, the observance of human rights is not based on reciprocal interests of states, but on the broader goal of states to establish orderly and enlightened international and national legal orders.

In the process of the formation of customary human rights, different types of evidence and of practice are important and *opinio juris* plays a dominant role. But this study of the creation of customary norms and of the evolving related norms of state responsibility demonstrates that such evidence and practice can be accommodated within the doctrine and methodology of international law.

However, the uniqueness of human rights and of humanitarian norms should not be exaggerated. Rules of sovereign immunity of states, for example, have been developed largely by national courts and national laws rather than by a state-to-state dialectic. Through the creative adaptation of the traditional and classical concepts and methods, it is possible to build the customary law of human rights and humanitarian norms in a process that will enhance their credibility and effectiveness. As human rights norms come to be reflected in national laws, the general principles of law (Article 38(1)(c) of the Statute of the ICJ) will and should increasingly become one of the principal methods for the maturation of human rights and humanitarian norms standards into the mainstream of international law. This process will demand greater analytical rigour on the part of human rights lawyers. As human rights and humanitarian norms evolve and expand, it is no longer adequate rhetorically to invoke human rights instruments; what is needed is the proper grounding of their binding nature as norms of international law.

We have seen that there has been an extensive interpenetration between the law of human rights and that of state responsibility. Each of these bodies of law has deeply affected the other. This trend will, of course, continue. States can and should take advantage of the already existing institutions and of the emerging principles of state responsibility to take up complaints for breaches of human rights and humanitarian norms through diplomatic channels or before international judicial and quasi-judicial bodies. As this study has shown, the principles are already in place or are in an advanced stage of crystallization. Both the norms and such institutions as have already been created have suffered from underutilization. What has largely been missing is the willingness of states to recognize that compliance with the norms serves their own interests as well as the common good and to be ready, therefore, to pay the political price consequent on raising such claims. Informed public opinion, including that generated by students of international law, may yet move states in this direction. It is only when rights are not only rhetorically asserted but are pressed seriously as legal

Concluding Remarks

entitlements, that human rights and humanitarian norms will become truly effective protections of human dignity.

On their part, generalist international lawyers should not regard human rights and humanitarian norms as merely theoretical principles or moral desiderata, but as norms of international law the breach of which has objective consequences which can and should be analysed by reference to the general law of state responsibility. By clarifying the relationship of human rights and humanitarian norms to state responsibility we can contribute to their effectiveness, create remedies for their violations, more effectively protect human dignity, and generally enhance their import and standing in the international community. If this study has made even a small contribution to these ends, I shall be gratified.

Index